Prize Money in Nelson's Navy

Prize Money in Nelson's Navy

Grahame Aldous

THE BOYDELL PRESS

First published 2026
The Boydell Press, Woodbridge

ISBN 978 1 83765 371 3

The Boydell Press is an imprint of Boydell & Brewer Ltd
and of Boydell & Brewer Inc.
website: www.boydellandbrewer.com

Our Authorised Representative for product safety in the EU is
Easy Access System Europe – Mustamäe tee 50, 10621 Tallinn, Estonia,
gpsr.requests@easproject.com

A CIP catalogue record for this book is available
from the British Library

To Vanessa

Contents

Preface

'The ancient custom of giving prize-money'

On 19 December 1945, during a quiet Wednesday afternoon, the First Lord of the Admiralty rose to address the House of Commons. They were sitting in the Lords' chamber after their own had been bombed in the blitz. Churchill had been defeated in the July general election despite his wartime leadership, and the Labour government of Clement Attlee had won office. With the end of war, food shipments from America under the Lend-Lease Act had come to an end and Britain was hungry. Housing, clothes and much else were rationed. It was hard to realise that London was the capital of a victorious country.[1] Outside, the British winter weather, unsettled and stormy, did nothing to relieve the misery. Amidst this gloom the First Lord's message was warmly welcomed. Albert Victor ('AV') Alexander was a Labour politician who had never seen active service. He served as a diligent wartime coalition administrator at the Admiralty, but one whose main function was to leave Churchill free to dictate naval strategy. His reward would come later, when he became the 1st Earl Alexander of Hillsborough. For now, he was First Lord of the Admiralty in Attlee's Labour government and had been asked by Vice-Admiral Sir Ernest Taylor, the member for Paddington South, whether a decision had been made about payment of prize money for vessels captured by the Royal Navy during the Second World War. Alexander was pleased to inform the House that rather than being paid as a bounty to those specifically involved in each capture, the prize fund would be divided between all those who had served in the Royal Navy or the RAF. The Vice-Admiral congratulated Alexander on his success 'in being able to maintain this ancient custom of giving prize-money'.[2]

The following day a headline in *The Times* thundered 'From Plunder and Pillage to Common Fund' over a celebration of 'the ancient custom

1 Lynne Olson, *Citizens of London: The Americans Who Stood with Britain in Its Darkest, Finest Hour* (London, 2015), p. 366.

2 Hansard, HC Debate 19 December 1945, vol. 417, cc 1312–14.

of giving prize-money'.[3] The report evoked the spirit of Drake and cited the Georgian age as 'the second golden period of prize-money'. *The Times* estimated that the total value of prize money for the Second World War would amount to £20 million, compared with the previous war of 1914–18 when the common fund had reached some £14 million, in which the then Captain Taylor would have shared.

Of less immediate apparent concern to his audience was the quiet post-script that Alexander added to his announcement: 'it is the government's intention that this shall be the last occasion on which prize-money will be paid.' And so it was. Thus did the 'ancient custom of giving prize-money' slip quietly away into history. How was it that this 'ancient custom', seemingly rooted in 'plunder and pillage', evolved to meet the needs of Nelson's navy and the nation in an era of total war, governed by the rule of law so as to continue into the twentieth century? To answer that, we need to strip away the myths that have surrounded prize money to reveal a dynamic system that adapted to the economic and social pressures of a war for national survival and was enhanced, rather than threatened, by the application of the rule of law. It is the story of real people at war.

3 *The Times*, 20 Dec. 1945, p. 5.

Acknowledgements

I am grateful to a large number of people for their help during my research for this book.

I have benefited from the help of the staff of the National Archives in Kew, the British Library, the Caird Library at the National Maritime Museum, Greenwich, Mulgrave Castle, Yorkshire, All Souls' Library, Oxford and the Maugham Library and Foyle Special Collections Library at King's College London. The staff at the Massachusetts Historical Society helped me to navigate the enormous archive of John Adams material that is available online and the archivists and law librarians at the Library of Congress and the US National Archives have patiently and promptly responded to my enquiries by email and in person. I have mined resources from the shelves of the Inner Temple Library with the help of the librarians, and as the Inner Temple parliamentary papers were destroyed in the blitz, I have benefited from the help of the Lincoln's Inn library staff to access their parliamentary records.

Dr Anna Brinkman, Dr Alan Anderson and Prof. Daniel Benjamin kindly shared their unpublished work with me. The Digby family welcomed me at Minterne House in Dorset to plunder their archive material about Sir Henry Digby, and Sim Comfort shared items such as Tucker's account book from his amazing collection in Wimbledon.

I am grateful for the time and wisdom that I have received from Prof. Andrew Lambert, Prof. Lord Guglielmo Verdirame KC, Dr Alan James, Dr James Davey, Prof. Stephen Neff and Dr Roger Knight. The contents of this book remain my responsibility for better or worse, but their input has been of great benefit to the development of both my thoughts and the means of their expression.

Many family members, friends and colleagues have supported me during the preparation of this book, but I should record my great debt to the late Dr Nick Slope, who first encouraged me to channel my research efforts after I had published articles in *The Mariner's Mirror* and *The Nelson Dispatch*. It is a great shame that he did not live to read this book, but I take comfort in the thought that he would have approved.

This book would not have made it into print without the help of the staff at Boydell and Brewer, who I first met while attending as a speaker at a new research conference run by the British Commission for Military History. I am grateful for the enthusiastic support of Peter Sowden since that first meeting, and to Alana Pulsford-Brooks, Abi Hood and Paul Pearson.

Note on English Legal Referencing and Abbreviations

Statutes

English statutes are referred to by the year of the reign of the sovereign in which they were passed, and then by the chapter number in that year, i.e. what numbered statute it was in that regnal year. The names of the sovereigns are latinised. Today all statutes are given short titles that include the year they were passed, e.g. Housing Act 1996, but that was not done in the eighteenth century. Even so, some Acts acquired short titles by usage, e.g. the Cruizers and Convoys Act 1708. The regnal reference to that Act is expressed as 6 Annae c. 13, i.e. it is the 13th Act of the 6th year of the reign of Queen Anne, 1708.

Between 1762 and 1807 a series of historical statutes was published in volumes called Statutes at Large. These volumes remain the most accessible form of early statutes. They are organised and referred to by their regnal years as described above.

The Acts and Ordinances of the Interregnum have been collected together and were published in 1911.[1]

Case Reports

English cases before 2001 are referenced by the volume of the reports they were published in. The date of the decision might appear in square brackets, e.g. [1800], as part of the reference, or in round brackets, e.g. (1800), simply as an indication of the date of the report. In the long eighteenth century, the round bracket format was the norm. The format of case references is normally as follows, e.g.: Lindo v Rodney (1781) 2 Doug. 614, 624.

This is a reference to the decision in the claim brought by Lindo versus (i.e. against) Lord Rodney. The judgment was reported in 1781 in the 2nd volume of the Douglas Reports at page 614. The particular passage being referred to is at page 624.

1 C. H. Firth and R. S. Rait (eds), *Acts and Ordinances of the Interregnum, 1642–1660* (London: HMSO, 1911).

Square bracket references are used where the reports were published in volumes covering a calendar year, thus: U. 61 [1921] 7 LLR 229 refers to the report of a judgment in a dispute about U-boat 61 that is reported in the 7th volume of the Lloyds Law Reports for 1921 at page 229.

Admiralty Court prize cases are normally referred to by the name of the prize ship and may also have the name of the master of the captured prize. Thus: The Flad Oyen, (Martenson) (1799) 1 Rob. 135 is the report of the case concerning the prize ship The Flad Oyen, whose master was named Martenson, heard by the Admiralty Court in 1799 and reported at page 135 in the 1st volume of Christopher Robinson's Admiralty Reports.

Some cases may be referred to in more than one report and therefore have more than one reference.

Between 1900 and 1932 many of the older reports up until 1866 were reproduced in 178 volumes known as the English Reports. In addition to their original reference in their original report, they have an ER reference to their place in the English Reports.

One exception to this method of referencing is the judgment in a case referred to as: In The Matter of Banda and Kirwee Booty (1866). It was a decision of the Admiralty judge, Dr Stephen Lushington, that was published separately under its own title.

It should be noted that court judgments are referred to without the 'e' that would normally appear in the word judgements.

In 2001 the English courts introduced a system of neutral citation as follows, e.g.: R (Miller and Dos Santos) v Sec. of State for Exiting the EU [2017] UKSC 5.

This relates to Gina Miller's action over serving Article 50 notice to trigger Brexit. It shows the names of the parties as 'R', short for Regina, i.e. the Queen, against the Brexit Secretary. The names in brackets are the parties at whose instigation the judicial review proceedings were brought in the name of the Queen against the Brexit Secretary. The reference is to the decision of the UK Supreme Court numbered 5 in 2017, hence [2017] UKSC 5.

The law report abbreviations referred to in this work are:

A. C.	Appeal Cases Reports
B. & C.	Barnewall & Cresswell's Reports
B. R.	Beavan's Reports
Br. & L.	Browning & Lushington Admiralty Reports
Bing.	Bingham's Reports
Bos. & Pull.	Bosenquet & Puller's Reports

Burrell	Burrell's Admiralty Cases
Campb.	Campbell's Reports
De G. F. and J.	De Gex, Fisher and Jones's Reports
Dods.	Dodson's Admiralty Reports
Dow. & Ry. K.B.	Dowling & Ryland's Reports
East	East's Reports
Edw. or Edw. Adm. Rep.	Edwards' Admiralty Reports
ER	English Reports
Ex. Div.	Exchequer Division Reports
F & F	Foster & Finlayson's Reports
H. Bl.	Henry Blackstone's Reports
Hag. Adm.	Haggard's Admiralty Reports
KB	King's Bench Reports
L. J. Ch. (N. S.)	Law Journal Chancery Reports (New Series)
Ld Raym.	Raymond's Reports
L. J. (O. S.) KB	Law Journal (Old Series) King's Bench Reports
LLR	Lloyds Law Reports
LR QB	Law Reports Queen's Bench Division
M&S	Maule & Selwyn's Reports
P	Probate Reports
QB	Queen's Bench Reports
Rob. or C. Rob.	Christopher Robinson's Admiralty Reports
Taunt.	Taunton's Reports
TR	Term Reports
UKSC	UK Supreme Court
Ves.	Vesey's Reports

Other abbreviations used in this work are:

ADM	The Admiralty Papers, the National Archives, Kew, England
BL	The British Library, London
Ex P.	Ex Parte, meaning on behalf of
HC	House of Commons Papers
HCA	The Papers of the High Court of Admiralty, the National Archives, Kew, England

HMSO	His Majesty's Stationery Office
J.	Mr Justice
KC	King's Counsel
MM	*The Mariner's Mirror*
NC	*The Naval Chronicle*
NDAR	Naval Documents of the American Revolution
NDQW	Naval Documents Relating to the Quasi War
NMM	The Caird Library, The National Maritime Museum, Greenwich, London
NRS	Navy Records Society
ONDB	Oxford National Dictionary of Biography
QC	Queen's Counsel
TNA	The National Archives, Kew, England

Introduction

The Lottery of War

When the Royal Navy captured enemy ships, including merchant ships, the proceeds were paid out to the officers and crew involved as a form of bounty providing private profit for public service. Although the role of such warfare is appreciated by students of naval warfare, it is still easy to dismiss commerce raiding incentivised by prize money as a rogue distraction from the proper business of sinking enemy fleets in battle. Our use of language has not helped. As N. A. M. Rodger has pointed out, linguistic pliability has caused considerable confusion in the writings of historians.[1] The war of the chase, referring to the capture of private merchant ships, has tended to be dressed in Mediterranean clothing. Italian, Spanish and Catalan writers adopted variants of *guerra di corso* to describe war at sea by chasing and capturing merchant ships. French scholars borrowed *guerre de course* to describe naval operations by king's ships and officers funded by private finance, before it took on a more general usage. English writers can slip into using this French phrase as referring to a form of war by attacking the merchant wealth and logistics of an enemy as a resort of the weak, forced into it by their inability to mount 'proper' fleet warfare. Those who engaged in such activities are thought of as being roguish, with the instincts and behaviours of pirates. Not quite gentlemanly. French naval squadrons intended to attack British commercial shipping in the Channel in the nineteenth century were dubbed 'corsair' squadrons.[2] In English the word 'corsair' has become entangled with 'pirates' and 'buccaneers', along with a large dose of what N. A. M. Rodger calls 'Byronic romanticism'.[3] The Cambridge Dictionary, for example, defines a corsair as 'a pirate', compounding the confusion by combining that with a 'person who sails in a ship and attacks other ships in

1 N. A. M. Rodger, 'The Law and Language of Private Naval Warfare', *MM* (2014), 5–13.

2 By Capt. Charles Hotham, see Andrew Lambert, *No More Napoleons* (London, 2025), p. 274.

3 Rodger, 'Law and Language', p. 12.

order to steal from them, especially one given permission by a government to attack enemy ships in the late 16th–18th centuries.'[4]

The prejudice runs deep into our language and assumptions.[5] The reputation of privateers, private ships authorised by the state to seize enemy ships, has polluted the reputation of all captures at sea, including those by the Royal Navy. As Corbett put it in 1907, when supporting the continued use of capture at sea by the Royal Navy as an instrument of war: 'The real reason why capture at sea got a bad name was due to privateers.'[6] The whiff of 'plunder and pillage' has hung over prize captures, and the money that was paid to the captors, in the public imagination, where it is seen as a form of state-approved piracy involving profiteering characteristics akin to privateering.[7] As Kert has put it in relation to privateering, 'many of the early practitioners under Queen Elizabeth I operated on their own account rather than the crown's. Their unsavoury reputation for piratical captures and the political problems they created prejudiced history's subsequent view of privateering.'[8]

The prejudice has persisted even though, as Kert notes, 'by the end of the eighteenth century, there was almost universal recognition that privateering was not only a legitimate pursuit in time of war, but a perfectly respectable one for members of mercantile society.'

Looking behind the prejudice, the full picture is quite different. By the eighteenth century, wars between nations were economic affairs, and were fought and determined ultimately by economic means. Wars were fought over the ability to trade, and states needed trade to fund their wars, involving applying pressure not only to enemy fleets, but to the whole enemy nation, its trade and peoples. The great naval battle became a means of enabling states to exert pressure through exercise of command of the sea and the control of maritime trade. Commerce raiding was not a distraction from fleet battles. Successful battles, won or threatened, provided the freedom to undertake commerce raiding, protect one's own coasts and shipping, and launch amphibious strikes on coastal targets, naval bases and economic centres. Enabling crippling economic warfare was the key

4 https://dictionary.cambridge.org/dictionary/english/corsair (accessed 27 Jan. 2025).

5 Including those of historians, as identified by N. A. M. Rodger, *The Price of Victory: A Naval History of Britain 1815–1945* (London, 2025) p. 256, n. 38.

6 Julian Corbett and Andrew Lambert, *21st Century Corbett: Maritime Strategy and Naval Policy for the Modern Era*, 21st Century Foundations (Annapolis, 2017), p. 77.

7 Casey Baker, *Britain's War for the Mediterranean: The Fight against Revolutionary France* (Annapolis, 2024), p. 30.

8 Faye Kert, *Prize and Prejudice: Privateering and Naval Prize in Atlantic Canada in the War of 1812* (St John's, 1997), p. 3.

element of British national strategy.[9] The seizure of enemy shipping was not a secondary form of warfare, but a primary aim of naval warfare.

For an island nation the exercise of naval power was a strategic means to establish security. As the former Liberal Solicitor General, Sir William Harcourt, put it in a House of Commons debate on the right of capture at sea in 1878:

> There is only one security for a great naval Power – as far as you could and as soon as you could – to sweep the enemy from the seas. Not only must we preserve our right to fight against our enemy, but to capture all the ships it possessed and all the means it possessed by which we might be attacked.[10]

The theme was picked up by Sir Julian Corbett in 1907:

> The sea cannot be the subject of ownership. You cannot do more, however complete your ascendancy, than deprive your enemy of his use of the sea; you can do no more than deny him that part of his national life which moves and has its being on the sea. This is what we mean when we speak of 'command of the sea' and not 'conquest of the sea.'[11]

Prize money was a significant incentive for officers and men of the Royal Navy, encouraging them in active service for the public good. That, after all, was the stated aim in the preamble to successive Prize Acts. As the renowned Admiralty judge from 1798 to 1828, Sir William Scott (later Lord Stowell), put it: 'The great intent of prize is to stimulate the present contest, and to encourage men to encounter present fatigue and present danger.'[12] Recruiting posters for sailors and marines proclaimed the opportunities for prize money in both Britain and the US. Michael Lewis in 1960 ranked prize money first in a list of financial inducements for service in the Royal Navy of this period, followed by freight money and only then by pay and allowances.[13] N. A. M. Rodger places prize money first among the attractive prospects for a career at sea in this period, describing it as 'the traditional

9 Peter Padfield, *Maritime Power and the Struggle for Freedom: Naval Campaigns That Shaped the Modern World 1788–1851* (London, 2003) p. 265; Roger Knight, *Convoys* (London, 2022), pp. 6–7; Lambert, *No More Napoleons*, pp. 402 and 456.

10 Hansard, HC Debate 22 March 1878, vol. 238, cc 1842–909.

11 Corbett and Lambert, *21st Century Corbett*, p. 78.

12 The Vryheid (1799) 2 Rob. 16, 28.

13 Michael Lewis, *A Social History of the Navy 1793–1815* (London, 1960), p. 340; for freight money, head money and booty see Chapter 8 below.

balm to the wounded naval spirit.'[14] Evan Wilson describes it as 'the navy's great equaliser', but as an equality of opportunity rather than delivery.[15] Brian Lavery has described it as giving seamen 'residual hope, like winning the lottery'.[16] The lottery pay-out could on occasion be enormous, and it was those payments that became legendary and filled sailors' dreams. Prizes taken by the Royal Navy during the wars of 1793–1815 had an estimated gross value of £30.8 million, of which £26.6 million was available for distribution to the captors.[17] That represents an average supplement to the income of the Royal Navy of £1.2 million per annum, which tallies with the estimate of George Rose as Treasurer to the Navy that the proceeds of prizes distributed in 1810 were over £1.3 million.[18] To put these figures in context, Nelson bought his country estate in Merton for £9,000.[19]

There is no comprehensive study of the law relating to the distribution of prize money in the existing literature. Some historians have considered prize money in the context of naval, legal, social, economic and international history, but none have provided a comprehensive review of the law or the way that it operated. The only modern history dedicated to the topic of the British system of prize money is Richard Hill's *Prizes of War*.[20] It is the work of a retired rear-admiral and distinguished naval historian who became Under-Treasurer, the equivalent of Chief Executive, of Lord Stowell's old Inn of Court, the Middle Temple. Making use of the inn's library of law reports, he researched a series of aspects of prize law and how it operated. The result is a useful introduction to the subject of prize law and its operation, but it treats prize law as an essentially static system, rather than a fluid one changing with political and social changes going on around it.

Hill did not attempt to set out what prize law was at different times or why it changed. He mentions four of the Prize Acts during the period,

14 N. A. M. Rodger, *The Wooden World* (London, 1988), p. 256; Cheryl Fury (ed.), *The Social History of English Seamen, 1650–1815* (Woodbridge, 2017), p. 69.

15 Evan Wilson, *A Social History of British Naval Officers, 1775–1815* (Woodbridge, 2017), pp. 145–53.

16 Brian Lavery, *Nelson's Navy* (London, 1992), p. 131.

17 Daniel K. Benjamin, 'Golden Harvest: The British Naval Prize System, 1793–1815' (unpubl. article), pp. 6–7.

18 Letter, from Rose at the Navy Pay Office to the Admiralty Board, 11 January 1811, Papers Relating to Proceedings of The Treasurer to the Navy on Prize Matters, 13 June 1811, HC (234), xi, 1811, p. 2.

19 Conveyance of Merton Place, Wimbledon Museum Archive LDWIM000426. Merton Place had been purchased in 1801 for £9,000 against the advice of his solicitor, William Haslewood, who considered the property over-priced and inappropriate, BL Add MS 34918/194.

20 Richard Hill, *The Prizes of War* (Stroud, 1998).

though he does not consider them as a series of interlinked changes. Whilst some historians such as Morriss and Knight[21] have recognised that there were changes in prize law throughout the period, most treat prize law as a fixed set of rules. There is occasional reference to isolated reforms, but they are scarcely investigated or set in context. Most published historians do not consider the way the rules changed during the period at all. There were at least 21 prize or prize-related Acts of Parliament between 1780 and 1817. Fourteen of them were passed between 1793 and 1815. There were a number of prize-related Orders-in-Council, the secondary legislation that implemented the Prize Act distribution system and laid down the entitlements to shares of prize money. By working out the pattern behind the Orders-in-Council it has been possible, like the periodic table of elements, to spot the gaps and search to fill them in. Fortunately, the Orders-in-Council were published in *The London Gazette*, which is now searchable online. Significant orders (or 'Royal Proclamations') were made in 1793, 1797, 1800, 1803, 1805, 1807, 1808, 1812 and 1815. Rarely, however, do published historians distinguish between them or consider in any detail how they compared with those such as in 1744 or 1756 during earlier conflicts. The research presented here attempts to fill this void by considering how and why prize law changed and what that tells us about the system and the way it operated.

The resulting research behind this work makes use of the wealth of historical material that can be found in the volumes of law libraries, as well as the corresponding documentation in naval archives, to reveal how and why the law developed, and what it tells us about the Royal Navy and naval warfare.

Winning the Lottery

In 1742, during the war against Spain that became known as the War of Jenkins' Ear and part of the War of Austrian Succession, the Admiralty sent eight ships to the Pacific to attack Spanish interests and encourage rebellion against Spain. A particular target was the annual treasure galleon that sailed between Mexico and the Philippines. Command of the squadron was given to Captain George Anson, but a series of disasters had reduced his squadron to one ship when he reached the Pacific the following April. *HMS Centurion*, with under half her normal complement gathered from the scurvy-hit squadron, was the lone survivor. Finally, Anson's luck changed,

[21] E.g. 1803, Roger Morriss, *The Royal Dockyards during the Revolutionary and Napoleonic Wars* (Leicester, 1983) p. 198; Roger Knight, *Britain against Napoleon* (London, 2013), p. 323.

and he captured the Manilla galleon *Nuestra Senora de Covadonga* with her cargo of 1,313,843 pieces of eight and 35,682 ounces of silver. Anson arrived back in England in June 1744, with just 145 men, some 10 per cent of those who had set out. Even they, however, managed to litigate over their entitlement to share in the treasure, as we will see in Chapter 4. The expedition is remembered as a feat of endurance, leadership and ingenuity, but above all for the magic of captured Spanish silver.[22] The capture made Anson a wealthy man and he became a reforming First Lord of the Admiralty, his success an inspiration to risk a life at sea in pursuit of wealth.

Anson's was not the only treasure offering inspiration to serve at sea in the lottery of prize money. Admiral James Dacres died in 1810 having been commander-in-chief of the lucrative Jamaica station and reported to have 'realized more money by prizes, than any Officer during the present war'.[23] As will be seen in Chapter 8, he left a legacy of litigation, but his experience of prize money began long before his time as an admiral. He joined the navy aged 13 in 1762, on board the frigate *HMS Active* under the command of Captain Herbert Sawyer just as Britain declared war on Spain towards the end of the Seven Years' War against France. On 21 May 1762, *Active* was cruising in company with the sloop *HMS Favourite* off the Portuguese coast when they captured the Spanish ship *Hermione*, which had sailed from the Caribbean before Britain's declaration of war and was unaware of the hostilities. The *Hermione* became another legendary prize capture. She carried a cargo of dollars, gold coin, gold and silver ingots, cocoa and tin worth over £500,000. Sawyer's share of the proceeds was over £65,000 and set him up as a very wealthy man able to marry the daughter of a Lisbon merchant.[24] Even Dacres' share ranking as an ordinary sailor amounted to 35 years' pay in a single capture.[25]

The capture of the *Hermione*, however, reveals a darker side of prize captures. *Hermione* and her cargo were insured by Isaac Fernandez Nunez, a neighbour of the writer Horace Walpole in Strawberry Hill, near Twickenham. Ordinarily shipowners and merchants managed to finance the loss of their ships to capture through an effective insurance market, with insurance rates fluctuating according to the perceived risks. Both insuring against the risk of capture and engaging in successful trade at heightened prices offered opportunities for profit in wartime, and there was considerable overlap between merchants and insurers as they shared the risks and

[22] N. A. M. Rodger, 'George, Lord Anson 1684–1757', in Le Fevre and Harding (eds), *Precursors of Nelson* (London, 2000), pp. 177–200.

[23] *The Morning Chronicle*, 18 November 1807, issue 12015.

[24] ONDB, Herbert Sawyer, J. K. Laughton, revised Julian Gwyn, 23 September 2004.

[25] ONDB, James Richard Dacres, Tom Wareham, 23 September 2004.

rewards among themselves.[26] The Royal Navy's task was to protect British shipping to keep their insurance rates low, but capture enemy shipping to push their rates up. Nunez had received an insurance premium for the *Hermione*'s cargo, but the size of the loss after war was declared was such that he was unable to meet the claim. A month after news of the capture hit the press Nunez shot himself through the head in his garden. His house and furniture were sold at auction to pay his debts.[27]

The notion of a profession being something of a lottery was not unique to the navy in the eighteenth century. As Adam Smith pointed out in *The Wealth of Nations* in 1776, the lottery applied to the 'liberal and honourable professions':

> Put your son apprentice to a shoemaker, there is little doubt of his learning to make a pair of shoes; but send him to study the law, it is at least twenty to one if ever he makes such proficiency as will enable him to live by the business. In a perfectly fair lottery, those who draw the prizes ought to gain all that is lost by those who draw the blanks. In a profession where twenty fail for one that succeeds, that one ought to gain all that should have been gained by the unsuccessful twenty.

Smith concluded that for those professions to which the nation entrusted its future health and lives, enhanced reward was justifiable for the risk: 'Such confidence could not safely be reposed in people of a very low or mean condition. Their reward must be such, therefore, as may give them that rank in society which such an important trust requires.'[28]

Indeed, his view was that both admirals and common sailors were under-rewarded by comparison with the army, despite the dexterity and skill required and the continual hardship and danger faced.[29]

Commanders of frigate squadrons made fortunes from their captures. Money was important to them, none more so than Thomas Cochrane, the voracious prize-taker Napoleon called the 'Sea-Wolf'. What they craved most though was professional success; the money came with success in particular areas of operation but was only one measure of success. Those who commanded in the east, such as Rainier and Pellew, made money from

26 Guy Chet, 'Britain and America 1650–1850: Harmonising Government and Commerce', in A. B. Leonard (ed.), *Marine Insurance Origins and Institutions 1300–1850* (Basingstoke, 2016), pp. 249–68.

27 Hilda Finberg, 'Jewish Residents in Eighteenth-Century Twickenham', *Transactions of the Jewish Historical Society of England* 16, 129–35, at p. 134.

28 Adam Smith, *The Wealth of Nations*, Book 1, Ch. X, Pt 1, Andrew Skinner (ed.) (London, 1999), p. 207.

29 Ibid., p. 212.

prizes captured by the ships under their command on the Royal Navy station in the Indian Ocean, and did their best to maximise their incomes. Each is said to have made over £200,000 in prize money in command of the East Indies station, Rainier over his 11 years in command there between 1794 and 1805, and Pellew in just five years between 1804 and 1809. Nelson's frequent complaints about his lack of prizes have given rise to a myth that he was hard done by on that score. In fact, he earned a considerable amount in prize money and was assiduous in collecting, and spending, it. As we will see in Chapter 5, one of his claims for prize money of over £13,000 was alone worth the price of a country estate, and he was prepared to litigate against his commander-in-chief to get it.

Recognising the concern of naval officers to maximise their incomes where they could is not to suggest, however, that it was prize money alone that motivated them. Success and respect is what they sought, and prize money was one measure of success.[30] Disputes about prize money could, however, be an unwelcome distraction from conflict with the enemy, and the anticipated benefits too large for the good of the service.[31] At times they turned military campaigns into counter-productive plunder.[32] The risk that captains ran of being condemned in damages for an unlawful seizure had the potential to do damage as well as good to motivation and efficiency in the navy, and as Sir John Knox Laughton identified, 'the bitterness which frequently arose out of considerations of prize-money was undoubtedly increased by the disproportionate share of the senior officers.'[33]

As in the case of Anson's voyage, prize money could be hard-earned. Nor was it always the balm that was dreamed of. In early 1810 Admiral Collingwood finally relinquished his command of the Mediterranean fleet and sailed from Minorca for home. He had been Nelson's second-in-command at Trafalgar, leading the starboard column on board *Royal Sovereign*. It was his dispatch that brought the news of victory and death to London, but he remained behind in command of the fleet in Nelson's place. Despite ill-health and longing for home he ensured British control of the Mediterranean for four more years after being begged to do so by the Admiralty.[34] Eventually his health declined to such an extent that the Admiralty had to give permission for him to return. Reporting his intended departure for home in a poor state of health, *The Morning Chronicle* said that

[30] The men sought respect as much as officers: N. A. M. Rodger, *The Command of the Ocean* (London, 2004), p. 489.

[31] Lewis, *A Social History of the Navy 1793–1815*, p. 332.

[32] Michael Duffy, *Soldiers, Sugar, and Seapower* (Oxford, 1987), pp. 106–14.

[33] John Knox Laughton, *Studies in Naval History* (London, 1887), p. 197.

[34] NMM LBK/40, Mulgrave to Collingwood, 25 September 1808.

Collingwood had 'accumulated an immense fortune – we believe, upwards of £200,000, in prize-money'.[35] He had even managed, from afar, to prevent his wife spending all his money, despite her best efforts, so as to secure his daughters' future.[36] But for all his wealth, Collingwood never set foot in Britain after Trafalgar. Nor did he see his wife and daughters ever again. He died at sea on 7 March 1810. When he returned to Britain his reward was not enjoyment of his prize money, but a tomb next to Nelson's in the crypt of St Paul's cathedral.

[35] *The Morning Chronicle*, 14 September 1809, issue 12588.

[36] Max Adams, *Admiral Collingwood* (London, 2005), p. 270.

1. The Origins of Prize Money

Prize capture is as old as war at sea, and its formalisation was part of the process of crafting and empowering state sovereignty. A right to take or authorise reprisals against the subjects of other sovereigns was an expression of sovereignty, both internally and internationally, becoming part of the administration of relations between states.

'Reprisal' comes from the French 'reprendre', meaning to resume or take in recompense for what has been lost.[1] Reprisals could take two forms, individual or general. Where a king's subject was wronged by the subject of another state whose sovereign refused any means of redress, then the king could grant them the right to seize the other state's ships and goods by way of redress. In contrast to these individual reprisals, a proclamation of general reprisals allowed all the king's ships to take reprisals against any ships or goods of an enemy state with whom the king was at war. In either case the ships and goods seized could be condemned by the Prize Court as valid prizes. Conditions on the exercise of individual reprisals introduced by the treaties of Ryswick in 1697 and Utrecht in 1713 led to their decline. General reprisals persisted and were enforced either by the national ships of the Royal Navy or by private ships authorised by the king to do so by Letters of Marque. These were either armed merchant ships that made captures opportunistically in addition to their trading activities, including the extensive fleet of the East India Company, or privateers, fitted out and crewed at private expense for the purpose of capturing prizes. The origin of the phrase 'Letters of Marque' reveals the nature of the disputes that gave rise to it. From the French 'lettre de merk', it refers to the so-called 'marcher law', or the 'law' of the lawless frontier areas separating nations known on land as 'the marches'.[2] It was thus something born out of areas of dispute, but also an attempt to provide a remedy for wrongs in order to restrain both wrongdoers and their sovereigns.

1 Thomas Bever, *A Course of Lectures on the Civil Law* (1763), All Souls Library, Oxford, MS 109c, Lecture 31, p. 108.

2 N. A. M. Rodger, 'The Law and Language of Private Naval Warfare', *MM* (2014), 5–7.

Vessels and goods taken as lawful prizes belonged in law to the Crown ('jure coronae'). The captors' right to prizes derived from the Crown, and the Crown determined what was, and was not, a valid prize.[3] The Crown also decided who took the benefit of prizes: 'As the sovereign only is invested with the power of waging war, and as this is usually carried on at the expense of the public, it is reasonable that he should be intitled to all captures, towards the support of fleets and armies.'[4]

Reprisals by capture of merchant ships and their cargoes may seem a brutal means of conducting international relations, and writers have not ignored that fact: 'Tho' it may have an odious appearance at first sight, to encourage the Robbery of innocent merchants by public Authority, yet as the trade that is carried on, and the money and materials that are imported by them, serve to supply the Hostile country with the means of protracting and increasing the miseries of war, it is certainly very necessary to cut off these resources as soon as possible.'[5]

For an island nation the exercise of such naval power was a strategic means to establish security. The general understanding of early prize law owes much to the research undertaken as part of a movement in the build-up to the First World War to found Britain's right to interfere with trade at sea in historical precedent, and to convince those in power of the need to keep that right in time of war. With each major naval war British writers sought to refresh this understanding of the rights of naval powers at sea. The Admiralty lawyer Reginald Marsden was amongst those who bent to the task. In 1909 he published his seminal article on 'Early Prize Jurisdiction and Prize Law in England' in *The English Historical Review*.[6]

Nor was the argument one that only needed to be won in war. It also needed to be won in the peace. In 1918 the American branch of the Oxford University Press published an anthology of extracts from works by jurists of many nations on international law dealing with the freedom of the seas in the context of the Armed Neutralities of 1780 and 1800.[7] Assembled by the American James Brown Scott, Director of the International Law Division of the Carnegie Endowment for International Peace, this was no mere historical curiosity, but an attempt to place the freedom of the seas on the agenda of the belligerent nations. The British Foreign Office, anticipating a

3 R. G. Marsden, 'Early Prize Jurisdiction and Prize Law in England', *The English Historical Review* 24:96 (1909), 675–97, at p. 677.

4 Per Bever, *A Course of Lectures on the Civil Law*, p. 110.

5 Ibid., p. 115.

6 Marsden, 'Early Prize Jurisdiction and Prize Law in England', *The English Historical Review* 24:96 (1909), 675–97.

7 James Brown Scott, *The Armed Neutralities of 1780 and 1800* (New York, 1918).

fresh assault on Britain's historical claims to interfere with trade at sea, had sought an historical briefing paper from the former Chief Justice of Hong Kong, Sir Francis Piggott.[8] They also recruited Corbett to write his persuasive paper on the League of Nations and the Freedom of the Seas.[9] The outcome of this propaganda effort was that the right to take prizes at sea survived the 1919 Versailles peace treaty, as it had the 1783 version after the war with France over American independence and the Congress of Vienna after the war against Napoleonic France.

Originally intended as a reward for valour, prize money developed into a method of regulating the conduct of war, as noted in 1866 by the Admiralty judge Dr Stephen Lushington:

> captures are made under all circumstances, and by the nature of the case are as often the result of careful vigilance or even fortuitous finding as of actual combat; and accordingly the system of ceding Prize to the takers is not limited, either in purpose or effect, to this primary object, the rewarding of successful valour. It may now, I think, be regarded as providing a stimulus to the performance of every kind of duty, by furnishing certain gratuities as incidental to certain services. Another result of the cession of Prize, and that by no means unimportant, is that it restrains pillage. That property captured at sea should be preserved intact is in the interest of all parties; of neutral and friendly powers, that, if not Prize, it may be restored; and of the Captors, that, if Prize, it may be legally distributed.[10]

The Early Years

From the thirteenth century the king decided what could be taken as prize, and who was to benefit, and settled disputes, either in person or in council. The meaning of 'prize' gradually became more clearly defined, and disputes as to the validity of prizes were determined by a specialist Admiralty Court. By the sixteenth century, lawyers practising in the court had their own professional body, referred to as Doctors' Commons. The Admiralty Court remained a distinct court until the second half of the nineteenth century and was only finally brought together with the other courts to form the

8 Sir Francis Piggott, *The Freedom of the Seas Historically Treated* (London, 1919); Sir Francis Piggott, *The Free Seas in War: A Talk to the Men and Women of Great Britain on the Freedom of the Seas* (London, 1918).

9 Corbett and Lambert, *21st Century Corbett*, p. 118.

10 In the Matter of the Banda and Kirwee Booty, 30 June 1866, p. 6.

High Court of Judicature by the Supreme Court of Judicature Act 1873. Still a court with its own procedures, the Admiralty Court now forms part of the King's Bench Division of the High Court.

Before Henry VIII there was no fixed and constant Royal Navy. Maritime towns fitted out their quota of ships of war when summoned to do so by the king. The customary disposition of the spoils of naval war was recorded in a collection of ancient Admiralty statutes 'to be observed both upon the ports and havens, the high seas and beyond the seas' known as the Black Book of the Admiralty. With almost mythical qualities, the Black Book of the Admiralty was said to have been engrossed upon vellum and written in an ancient hand, in 'the ancient French language'.[11] The ancient statutes included the so-called Rolls of Oleron, one of the earliest codes governing trade by sea with England that continued to influence the development of English maritime law. Although sounding like a creation of J. R. R. Tolkien, the Rolls of Oleron were the laws applied in the fourteenth century by the mercantile court on the island of Oleron, off the coast of France near La Rochelle. Oleron was handy for the wine trade between Gascony and England, then in common ownership by virtue of Eleanor of Aquitaine. With a wealth of disputes from the wine trade to resolve, the court codified the accepted practices of merchants relating to carriage by sea in terms that are still in use, such as 'demurrage' for the payments due where loading is delayed.[12]

The Black Book itself apparently dated from the fifteenth century and resided in the archives of the Admiralty Registry to be consulted by judges of the Admiralty Court. The original volume appears to have gone missing at the beginning of the nineteenth century, although the prize provisions were quoted by Dr Christopher Robinson in 1801 in his work on prize law and its historical justification.[13] Fortunately a number of copies existed, and in 1857 Sir John Romilly, the Master of the Rolls with responsibility for the Public Records Office before the Public Records Act 1958, suggested that key historical documents from the Roman invasion to Henry VIII be edited and published for the public record. The editing of the Black Book was entrusted to Sir Travers Twiss QC, who consulted the extant copies to produce an authoritative version, with translation into English, in 1871.

11 Per Dr Exton in *The Maritime Dicaeologie* (London, 1664) quoted in the introduction to Sir Travers Twiss (ed.), *The Black Book of the Admiralty* (London, 1871), vol. 1, p. ix.

12 Kert, *Prize and Prejudice*, p. 37; Timothy J. Runyan, 'The Rolls of Oleron and the Admiralty Court in Fourteenth Century England', *The American Journal of Legal History* 19:2 (1975), 95–111.

13 Christopher Robinson, *Collectanea Maritima, Being a Collection of Public Instruments etc ... Tending to Illustrate the History and Practice of Prize Law* (London, 1801).

Twiss was a barrister, the Queen's Advocate General and Regius Professor of Civil Law at Oxford, but editing the Black Book was the last task he would undertake before retiring from British public life. In 1862 Twiss had married, and presented his wife at court as Marie Van Lynseele, the daughter of a Polish aristocrat. Alexander Chaffers, an unscrupulous solicitor in London who had drafted a will for the future Lady Twiss, claimed, however, that Lady Twiss had in fact been a prostitute he had slept with and who had also been Twiss's mistress for three years before their marriage.[14] In an effort to blackmail Lady Twiss and her husband, Chaffers submitted inflated bills for legal work allegedly undertaken for her servant some years earlier. The bills were negotiated downwards and a reduced sum of £50 was paid over in purported full and final settlement of the demands. Chaffers had, however, made a statutory declaration at Bow Street Police Court of his allegations about Lady Twiss's past, which he began to distribute. To try and put an end to Chaffers' activities, Twiss brought a private prosecution against him for the criminal offence of libel with intent to extort money. Lady Twiss gave evidence and vehemently denied the allegations of impropriety during a torrid cross-examination by Chaffers, who represented himself. The evidence and the allegations were reported in the papers and devoured by the public, and Lady Twiss fled London. Faced with her refusal to return to give evidence, the court dismissed the case but expressed contempt for Chaffers' conduct.

The outcome was a disaster for Twiss. Lady Twiss's right to appear at Queen Victoria's court was revoked by the Lord Chamberlain and Twiss resigned from all his public positions. He never again appeared in, or at, court, nor did he see his wife again. Twiss carried on writing, including further editions of his works on the Law of Nations, and working on committees of the Institut de Droit International, and became 'a prolific, if somewhat pedestrian, authority on international law'.[15] The 'pedestrian' skills were suited, however, to piecing together the evidence of the contents of the Black Book and his work remains the best evidence that we have of its contents.

Article 19 of Book A of the Black Book provided that the king was to have a quarter share of all prizes taken by the king's ships. Where the king was paying to use a ship owned by someone else, then the owner also took a quarter share. If the ship was not in the king's pay, then the king took no

[14] Michael Taggart, 'Alexander Chaffers and the Genesis of the Vexatious Actions Act 1896', *Cambridge Law Journal* 63:3 (2004), 656–84.

[15] Ibid, p. 661; Gabriela Frei, *Great Britain, International Law, Evolution of Maritime Thought* (Oxford, 2020), p. 95.

share at all. In each case, however, each ship had to account to the admiral for part of their share. The Black Book suggests that the admiral was entitled out of the half that went to the mariners of ships paid for by the king to the same equal share as a mariner, or to two such shares if he was actually present at the time the prize was taken. In the case of prizes taken by privateers or others out of the king's pay then the admiral took two shares whether he was present or not. Twiss notes, however, that the admiral's share was actually traditionally regarded as one tenth, as it had been in France by the ordinance of Charles V of France in 1373.[16] It noted expressly that ships of the fleet out of sight of a capture were not entitled to share in the proceeds, but that those 'sailing towards the prize and within sight, soe that they are likely by sailing to helpe the takers of the prize if need be' at the time of capture were entitled.[17]

Similar divisions were adopted elsewhere. In the Iberian Peninsula one fifth of the spoils of war went to the Crown, known as the Royal Fifth.[18] As with England, the arrangement was rooted in the feudal power of the Crown, but it was infused with the Islamic influence of the Moorish occupation of the peninsula, when the Caliphal administration had co-opted the provision in the Qur'an that:

> out of all the spoils of war that ye may acquire, a fifth share is assigned to Allah,– and to the Messenger, and to near relatives, orphans, the needy, and the wayfarer.[19]

Henry VIII put the English navy on a more permanent footing, building ships of war and erecting yards and magazines. In return for his paying the costs of wages and victualling of the fleet the admiral had to account to the king for one half of any proceeds, together with any artillery or ordinance and apparel captured in ships taken by the fleet.[20]

Prize-taking continued under Elizabeth I; indeed, her reign is regarded as the first golden age of prize-taking because of Drake and his contemporaries.[21] Sir William Monson in his *Naval Tracts* suggested, however, that despite the destruction they wrought on Spanish commerce, most Elizabethan adventurers made losses rather than fortunes. Writing in his final

16 Twiss (ed.), *The Black Book of the Admiralty*, vol. 1, p. 23, n. 5.

17 See further, Chapter 4.

18 C. H. Haring, 'Ledgers of the Royal Treasurers in Spanish America in the Sixteenth Century', *The Hispanic American Historical Review* 2 (1919), 173–87.

19 Qur'an, verse 8:41.

20 Robinson, *Collectanea Maritima*, p. 190.

21 See e.g. *The Times*, 20 December 1945, p. 5.

years before his death in 1643, Monson was recalling an adventure-filled life. He matriculated from Balliol College, Oxford at 14 and ran away to sea at 16, participating in fighting the Armada and the capture of the rich spice ship *Madre de Dios*. After studying for the Bar at Gray's Inn, he went back to sea and became an admiral. Oppenheim, who edited the *Naval Tracts* for the Naval Records Society,[22] adopted Monson's assessment in his own *History of the Administration of the Royal Navy*.[23] Oppenheim also confirms that the admiral's one-tenth share remained the rule, at least in theory. In practice, Oppenheim suggests, the distribution was somewhat more pragmatic: 'Officer and men pillaged first, the captains took what they could from them, and when the admiral came up ... he plundered the captains.'[24] The queen then demanded the lion's share as she saw fit.[25] Unlike the second, Georgian, golden age, the rule of law had little part to play, either internationally or in sharing the spoils during the Elizabethan golden age.

As Sir William Holdsworth put it in his *History of English Law*, 'It is clear that in the sixteenth and seventeenth centuries the judges of the court of Admiralty, exercising [prize] jurisdiction, were very much under the thumb of the Crown, which was accustomed to issue its Orders to them.'[26] Some of the evidence for this might not be as clear cut as is sometimes presented, however. For example Marsden recites a letter of 1593 from the Lord High Admiral, Howard of Effingham, to the Admiralty judge, Sir Julius Caesar, under the title 'Letter from Howard to Caesar directing him to condemn a Spanish prize to the captor, although she was not captured under letters of marque'.[27] The text in fact reveals a rather more nuanced message:

> Mr Caesar,
>
> One captaine Berie, having order from Sir Francis Drake to goe on the coaste of Spaine for discoverie of the enemye's enterprises and forces prepared there, which was don with my privity and allowance, happened to take a brasill prize at sea, and to bring her into Plymouthe. And

22 *The Naval Tracts of Sir William Monson*, ed. Michael Oppenheim, NRS (London, 1902).

23 Michael Oppenheim, *A History of the Administration of the Royal Navy 1509–1660* (London, 1896), p. 165.

24 Ibid., pp. 166–7.

25 Ibid., p. 165.

26 William S. Holdsworth, *History of English Law* (London, 1903), vol. 1, p. 566.

27 R. G. Marsden, *Documents Relating to Law and Custom of the Sea*, NRS (London, 1915), vol. I, p. 281.

having sent [her] up for adjudication in the Admiralty Courte, I have thought good to let you knowe the premises, and to require you that the want of a commissione may be noe let unto the same. And soe fare you hartelye well. From the courte at Windsor the 27th November 1593.

Your loving freind,

Howard

Thus, the letter in fact reveals a rather touching appreciation of the niceties of Admiralty Court procedure and the need for proper adjudication by the court. Howard is conveying his evidence that, far from acting as an unauthorised pirate, Berie was acting under Admiralty orders at the time of the capture and accordingly the captured ship could properly be condemned by the court as a prize.

The Stuarts, Interregnum and Restoration

In 1628, after the assassination of Buckingham, the functions of the Lord High Admiral were placed in the hands of Commissioners for the Admiralty, where they remained apart from brief periods after the Stuart restoration. But the Admiralty still had to be paid for. Raising funds to pay for the navy was a contributing factor to the English Civil War. By 1634 Charles I was faced with a naval build-up by the French and the Dutch across the Channel, threatening Spanish control of Flanders. Fear of having two powerful navies to contend with, operating from bases with ready access to the Thames, led Charles to enter secret negotiations to support the Spanish, but meeting the threat of the French and Dutch required an increase in his navy. Unwilling to seek authorisation from Parliament to raise the funds, he tried using the supposed royal prerogative of raising ship money from the counties to pay for a navy. Controversial enough in time of war, the medieval practice of requiring the payment of funds from the shires by royal command to pay for a navy in time of peace created considerable opposition, so he appointed a committee under the Attorney General, William Noy, to explore a justification for raising ship money. It concluded that the danger to England was 'both imminent and eminent', and that the king must use his powers to call for ship money to meet it. The committee considered allowing the counties to share in the profits from prizes and fleet convoy duties, but they were not implemented, and the committee lost impetus with the death of Noy in August 1634.[28] Resistance to ship money contributed to civil strife and the downfall of the established regime, replaced by a Cromwell who, whilst adopting the language of the levellers, appointed himself Lord Protector. Both leveller instincts and ideas of sharing prize profits with the counties reappeared a century later in the rebel colonies in America, as will be seen in Chapter 9.

Parliament embraced the idea of prize seizure during the interregnum, with its own twist.[29] During the commonwealth, captors were granted half the value of a captured warship, the other half going for the relief of sick and wounded sailors, widows and dependants. Enemy warships sunk in action were deemed prizes and valued by the number of guns they had. Payments to ships' officers and crews were calculated at £10 per gun above a minion in size, or more for guns of a flagship. Proceeds from captured merchantmen and their cargoes were shared equally between the captors, the state and the relief fund, while the tenth traditionally paid to the Lord Admiral was assigned for medals and gratuities rewarding outstanding service.[30]

The combination of a cash-strapped king following the restoration and the need to incentivise a navy for war with the Dutch led to a number of attempts to revise prize provision. Various adjustments to the division of shares enjoyed by the state, the officers and crew and a relief fund for sailors were attempted but proved in practice to be little more than wishful thinking, with payments so long delayed as to remove them as an effective incentive.[31] Nevertheless, the principle of prize payments remained intact. Regulation of behaviour towards the goods and crew of captured ships, which had been a matter of concern down the years, was, however, addressed with lasting effect. Charles II's Navy Act of 1661 expressly provided that nothing should be taken out of a prize ship until it was condemned by the Admiralty Court. An account then had to be given of everything seized 'of the whole without fraud' on pain of court-martial or such other punishment as the Admiralty Court might decree. Personal items 'above the gun deck' were, however, excluded from the injunction and remained subject to a right of plunder by the captors. The right was claimed by custom and usage, even though the word 'plunder' had only

[28] Patricia Haskell, 'Ship Money in Hampshire', in Webb, Yates and Peacock (eds), *Hampshire Studies* (Portsmouth, 1981), pp. 73–107, at p. 77.

[29] See head money in Chapter 8.

[30] Bernard Capp, *Cromwell's Navy: The Fleet and the English Revolution 1648–1660* (Oxford, 1992); Firth and Rait (eds), *Acts and Ordinances of the Interregnum 1642–1660*, vol. I, p. 74, vol. II, pp. 9–10, 18, 66–73.

[31] J. D. Davies, *Pepys's Navy: The Ships, Men & Warfare, 1649–1689* (Barnsley, 2016), p. 104.

made its way from Dutch into English in the seventeenth century. Plunder was finally outlawed by an Act of William and Mary in 1692.[32] The Act also provided for the distribution of prize money. One fifth of the proceeds of the cargoes of prizes taken by privateers was payable to the Crown and the privateers took the captured ship and its equipment. For prizes taken by the navy the proceeds were divided into three. One third went to the ship's crew, one third went to a fund for wounded sailors and the widows, children and parents of those slain, and the remaining third went to the Crown. A bounty was also payable of £10 for each gun on the taking or destroying of an enemy ship of war.[33]

The Crown clearly tried to interfere with the judiciary in relation to prize matters, before and after the restoration. The courts resisted such interference and in 1672 the then Admiralty judge, Sir Leoline Jenkins, threatened to resign if it persisted.[34] Holdsworth suggested that the interference continued into the eighteenth century, at least in the Vice-Admiralty Courts based at British naval stations abroad, but as will be seen below, by the end of the eighteenth century the courts were, within the confines of the English law and its view of the public interest, asserting their independence in matters of the rights of neutrals. Further, the Admiralty was happy to leave issues of distribution of prize money between fractious admirals to the courts, rather than cause further discontent by attempting to determine the disputes by decision of the Board of Admiralty.

Before the Act of Union in 1707 Scotland had its own hereditary Lord High Admiral and Admiralty Court. At times, however, admiralty rights were devolved or usurped while a given admiral was in prison, in exile or out of favour at court.[35] The Scottish legal system has its own roots in a so-called 'civil' version of Roman law, and it is tempting to think that that played a part in the development of British prize law.[36] The evidence suggests, however, that Scotland adopted the practices of the English prize court, rather than the other way round.[37] The abolition of the Scottish Admiralty offices and courts in 1707 in favour of London was a takeover and not a merger.[38] Decisions of Scottish prize courts were 'sunk in the

[32] 4&5 Will. And Mary c.25.

[33] Robinson, *Collectanea Maritima*, p. 193.

[34] Holdsworth, *History of English Law*, p. 566.

[35] S. Murdoch, *The Terror of the Seas? Scottish Maritime Warfare 1513–1713* (Boston, 2010), p. 12.

[36] Cf. Ibid., p. 31.

[37] T. C. Wade (ed.), *Acta Curiae Admirrallatus Scotiae, 6 Sept. 1557–11 March 1562* (Edinburgh, 1937), p. xii.

[38] Murdoch, *The Terror of the Seas?*, p. 10.

volumes of miscellaneous repertories of jurisprudence' and difficult to identify.[39] Despite many Scottish naval officers and lawyers featuring in prize cases, Scottish prize cases are notably absent from both texts on the law of nations and reports of English case law. In keeping with the nomenclature at the time, therefore, references to English and British prize law after 1707 are used interchangeably.

In what has been described as 'the greatest step forward in the whole of prize legislation,'[40] the Cruizers and Convoys Act 1708, in the time of Queen Anne, determined that the whole proceeds of prize captures should be paid to the captors. Whether or not it was the greatest step, it did set the pattern for prize apportionments throughout the eighteenth century and beyond.[41] Gun bounty was done away with.[42] The example set by Queen Anne was followed elsewhere. In 1715, for example, a Swedish Order granted the whole benefit of prizes to Swedish cruisers.[43]

The Eighteenth Century and Neutral Rights

It was no coincidence that there were common provisions in different states. There was an active diplomatic intercourse between European nations on matters of prize law relating to matters of substantive law as well as distribution of proceeds.[44] Countries in favour of free trade had an incentive to recognise a common law of prize with limitations on the rights of captors over the rights of neutrals. They might encourage others to follow an example if it was set at home, and they might avoid turning neutrals into additional enemies. The need to keep hold of trade in times of war rather than losing it to neutrals, however, set up an inherent conflict for those shouldering the financial burden of war. As pressures mounted during war, the rights of neutrals felt the strain: 'Neutrality was a highly contested concept with no firm legal basis for its usage.'[45]

By the time of the Seven Years' War, the Royal Navy was strong enough to strangle French attempts to trade with their own islands in the Caribbean.

39 T. Baty, 'Scottish Prize Decisions of the Seventeenth and Eighteenth Centuries,' *The Yale Law Journal* 27 (1918), 453–78.

40 Peter Kemp, *A Survey of the History and Distribution of Naval Prize Fund* (Aldershot, 1946), p. 14.

41 Annae c. 13.

42 Head money remained, see Chapter 8 below.

43 Robinson, *Collectanea Maritima*, pp. 194 and 175.

44 Carl J. Kulsrud, *Maritime Neutrality To 1780* (Boston, 1936); see Chapter 4 below.

45 Maartje Abbenhuis, *An Age of Neutrals* (Cambridge, 2014), p. 32.

As a result, by 1756 Machault, the French minister of marine and colonies, had to propose that trade with the islands, normally reserved to French shipping, be thrown open to neutral shipping.[46] The French Atlantic merchants protested, but to no avail as they were unable to service the trade. The number of successful voyages by French merchants sank so low that there was no choice but to allow France's commercial rivals, particularly the Dutch and Danish, to undertake the lucrative trade under special wartime passports, or licences. This was not new; France had reluctantly resorted to similar action in earlier wars.[47] By 1756 Britain's naval strength was such that it no longer had to stand by and accept the French use of neutral ships. If a ship of a neutral was not ordinarily allowed to participate in a trade, such as the Caribbean trade, in time of peace, then if it carried on that trade in time of war under a special licence from the enemy it could be condemned as lawful prize with its cargo before a British prize court under what has become known as 'the Rule of the War of 1756'.

In truth, however, the 'rule' had been around for generations and had been relied upon, and objected to, by various states according to their own interests at the time. Indeed, in 1674, when England was a neutral during Dutch wars, she forcefully argued against the rule that became the Rule of the War of 1756.[48] Protestations of claimed principles during peace dissolved in self-interest in time of war.[49] The problem of knowing whether the country would be a belligerent or a neutral in future wars acted as a brake on attempts to codify the rules of war by international agreement, remaining so throughout the nineteenth century, as British policy-makers recognised.[50] The Rule of the War of 1756 enforced by the British courts was created by the government and the courts working together.[51] Pragmatism overcame any constitutional sensitivities about the executive being seen to 'interfere' with the judiciary.[52]

The rule of 1756 came only eight years after the first publication of Montesquieu's *De l'Esprit des Lois*, hailing the separation of powers as at the heart of Britain's success. Montesquieu's work would help inspire constitutional reform in Corsica, and then the American colonies, based on the separation of the three branches of government, the legislature,

46 D. A. Baugh, *The Global Seven Years War, 1754–1763* (Abingdon, 2014), p. 323.

47 Richard Pares, *War and Trade in the West Indies 1739–1763* (London, 1963), p. 343.

48 Kulsrud, *Maritime Neutrality*, p. 84.

49 Ibid., pp. 90, 336–7.

50 E.g. Frei, *Great Britain, International Law, Evolution of Maritime Thought*, p. 72.

51 See Baugh, *Global Seven Years War*, p. 324 and Richard Pares, *Colonial Blockade and Neutral Rights 1738–1763* (Oxford, 1938), p. 180.

52 Pares, *Colonial Blockade*, pp. 100–1.

the judiciary and the executive.[53] It was, however, the culture of respect for separation of powers within the rule of law that he identified, rather than any necessity for purity of formal separation. The judiciary had to be free to accept or reject the ideas of the executive, and the executive had to respect that decision, but they could work together for a common purpose. Indeed, for the entire time that Sir William Scott was the Admiralty judge he was also a Member of Parliament. A seat in Parliament, with the influence that it could bring to bear, was seen as a career-enhancing asset by ambitious lawyers and both aspiring and sitting judges. Many of his friends and colleagues adopted the same route to success.

The unwritten British constitution was not as clear cut as some readers of Montesquieu might have assumed. The supreme court of appeal was nominally at least a judicial committee of the House of Lords, part of the legislature, and the Lord Chancellor was the senior judge as well as a member of the executive and the legislature until the reforms introduced by the Constitutional Reform Act 2005. Strangely, the formal separation of powers at the start of the twenty-first century appears to have done nothing to encourage respect for decisions of the judiciary by the executive. If anything, the trend seems to be in the opposite direction.[54] Indeed, the post-Brexit Conservative government's attempt to restrain judicial review of government actions was seen, for example, as evidence of its 'contempt for the separation of powers in general, and the judiciary in particular'.[55] Prize law offers an historical perspective on government and judiciary working together.

Brinkman has explored the way in which the Lord Commissioners of Prize Appeals, in what she calls the Court of Prize Appeal, were used as an agent of British policy to maintain the neutrality of the Dutch and Spanish fleets during the Seven Years' War. There is little doubt that the public policy of maintaining neutrality played a significant role in the court's deliberations, due in large part to the influence of the Lord Chancellor, Lord Hardwicke.[56] What is notable, however, is that the political pressure applied to decisions of the court was not in favour of oppressing neutrals in

53 Peter Thrasher, *Pasquale Paoli: An Enlightened Hero, 1725–1807* (London, 1970), p. 44; Dorothy Carrington, 'The Corsican Constitution of Pasquale Paoli (1755–1769)', *The English Historical Review* 88:348, 481–503; Linda Colley, *The Gun, the Ship & the Pen* (London, 2021), pp. 21ff.

54 See e.g. R (Miller and Dos Santos) v Sec. of State for Exiting the EU [2017] UKSC 5; 'Enemies of the People', *Daily Mail*, 4 November 2016.

55 *Financial Times* editorial, 4 May 2021, p. 22.

56 Anna Brinkman, *Balancing Strategy, Sea Power, Neutrality, and Prize Law in the Seven Years' War* (Cambridge, 2024).

order to support the war. On the contrary, it was to assist neutrals in order to reduce the chances of them becoming enemies. Even that political intervention came at a cost. It risked embroiling the government in decisions without the protection of being able to distance itself from an independent judiciary, risking encouraging the erroneous view that the release of prizes was a political gesture within the gift of the Crown.

Understanding the nature of such political influence requires considering the role of appeals from the Prize Court and how this changed during the eighteenth century. The Prize Court had grown out of judges taking over the determination of disputes from the king, either in person or in council. The king-in-council retained the right, however, to review decisions of the Prize Court on appeal. This right became an established system of appeal by the sixteenth century.[57] Appeals were heard by members of the Privy Council specifically appointed as Lords Commissioners of Prize Appeals, a system of appeal given statutory authority by the Prize Act 1707.[58] The problem with this system was that the Lords Commissioners of Prize Appeals did not necessarily have any judicial experience to bring to bear on the appeals they heard. To try and improve matters and speed up the process of determining appeals, Lord Hardwicke as Lord Chancellor issued a list of standing commissioners in 1748 that included the names of judges who were not Privy Councillors.[59] The idea of including judges in the hearing of appeals proved controversial, with opponents complaining that the inclusion of judges was unlawful and in breach of treaty obligations such as those of the 1677 treaty with France that provided in terms for a right of review of prize decisions by nine members of the King's Council. The inclusion of judges was eventually authorised by statute, however, so long as they were in the minority.[60]

One of the problems during the Seven Years' War was that the Admiralty Court judge, Sir Thomas Salusbury, did not have a reputation for competence.[61] By the end of the century, however, the Admiralty Court was in the safer hands of Sir William Scott, one of the greatest of all Admiralty judges, who was himself appointed as one of the judges to sit as a Lord Commissioner of Prize Appeals.[62] As Roscoe, the then Registrar of the Admiralty Court, put it in 1924, 'surveying the course of appellate jurisdiction in prize

57 E. S. Roscoe, *History of the English Prize Court* (London, 1924), p. 83.

58 Anne c. 37 s 8; Roscoe, *History*, p. 90.

59 Roscoe, *History*, p. 88.

60 Prize Causes Act, 22 Geo. II c. 3; Roscoe, *History*, p. 89.

61 Brinkman, *Balancing Strategy*, pp. 64, 172; for case studies of agency practice, see A. B. McLeod, *British Naval Prize Law in the Seven Years' War* (Woodbridge, 2025).

62 Roscoe, *History*, p. 89.

the general tendency for the tribunal to become a court of law is marked.'[63] By the Seven Years' War it was still work in progress, although Hardwicke was trying to improve matters. By the end of the century the Lords Commissioners had earned the right to be called a court, although their decisions carried little weight as precedents as the reasons for their decisions were not generally stated.[64] In 1833 the jurisdiction of the Lords Commissioners was transferred to the Judicial Committee of the Privy Council by statute, establishing the jurisdiction as a de jure as well as a de facto judicial tribunal.[65]

The judiciary were not immune from the influence of public policy, however, and were quite capable of reflecting the wartime needs of the state. Brinkman has pointed out the close-knit personal relations between the law and politics in the mid-eighteenth century. So too, the advocates, judiciary and politicians during the wars of 1793–1815 came from a small circle of interrelated men familiar with the levers of power and the arguments over the interests of a maritime state at war. It could hardly be expected that the courts would ignore those interests, nor did they.

The sight of neutral rivals profiting from the war that British merchants were paying for through their losses and their taxes was too much to bear, and the Rule of the War of 1756 was popular at home as it restricted the opportunities for neutrals to benefit from the war. As belligerents in what they saw as a just war, the British considered that they were entitled not only to protect their own trade but also to outmuscle their enemies in trade, without the connivance of neutrals for their own profit. As Nicolas Magens, a German financier in London, expressed it in his 1755 *Essay on Insurances*:

> Might not those who fought the battles ask, what signifies our being masters of the sea, if we shall not have liberty to stop ships from serving our enemy? And when we examine to the bottom of the thing, it appears very evident, that sea battles are fought not so much to kill people, as to be masters of trade, whereby people live; and by stopping their supplies, to compel our enemies in the end to live in friendship with us.[66]

[63] Ibid., p. 91.

[64] Ibid.

[65] 3 & 4 Will. IV c. 41; Roscoe, *History*, p. 90.

[66] Quoted in Pares, *Colonial Blockade*, p. 181.

Under this pressure the traditional distinction between neutrals trading *with* an enemy and trading *for* an enemy broke down and all trade involving neutrals and the enemy became a target for prize-taking.

The Rule of the War of 1756 did not mean that Britain would not make use of neutral ships for trade when it suited her interests. Britain regularly openly allowed trade under licence that would otherwise have been deemed unlawful where the government saw fit and its interests required it, even with an enemy during wartime.[67] Even when Britain was at war with America after 1812, in part over disputed neutral rights, she fed her troops on the Iberian Peninsula with American grain despite American government attempts to prevent it.[68]

When war came in 1793, revolutionary France once again opened its colonial trade to neutral shipping. Indeed, some French colonies, such as Martinique, had opened their ports to neutral shipping in anticipation of the war.[69] In response, the British government once again resorted to the Rule of the War of 1756. Instructions to British ships of war and privateers of 6 November 1793 required them 'to stop and detain for lawful adjudication, all vessels laden with goods the produce of any French colony, or carrying provisions or other supplies for the use of any such colony'.[70] Subsequent instructions attempted to reassure neutrals that their bona fide shipping was not being targeted, but inevitably tensions rose. With the Peace of Amiens in 1801 France again closed its colonial trade to neutrals, only to immediately re-open it on the return of war in 1803.[71] This behaviour strengthened the hand of those supporters of the Rule who argued that opening up trade in war that was closed in peace was itself an act of war, and those neutrals who engaged in the trade were engaging in an act of war.

Any indication that the British might abandon the Rule of the War of 1756 met with public opposition, such as the influential publication in 1805 of a treatise by the Prize Court lawyer James Stephen, an abolitionist who was advising on the drafting of what became the 1807 Act for the Abolition of the Slave Trade. Seeing the practices of the prize courts and the enforcement of blockades as a model for the practical, as well as legal, abolition of

67 Anon., *Notifications, Orders, and Instructions, Relating to Prize Subjects during the Present War* (London, 1815).

68 Andrew Lambert, *The Challenge: America, Britain and the War of 1812* (London, 2012), pp. 199 and 231.

69 James Stephen, *War in Disguise* (London, 1805), pp. 29–31.

70 Ibid., p. 19.

71 Ibid., pp. 173–4.

the slave trade, he argued forcefully for British policing of the seas by the maintenance of the Rule to prevent fraudulent abuse of neutral status.[72]

Whilst the Rule of the War of 1756 dealt with neutral ships trading with French colonies, it did not deal with the suspicious increase in trade from Dutch and Danish islands in the Caribbean. In particular the small Dutch island of St Eustatius operated as a transhipment port for French goods to become neutral goods before the voyage to Europe. St Eustatius felt the backlash for these activities in 1781 when Rodney seized the island, giving rise to a wealth of litigation about the prizes that he took. In 1756, however, Britain was not at war with the Dutch, so the response was not to invade the island, but to seize the dubious trade. To do so the British developed the doctrine of 'Continuous Voyage', a concept borrowed from the developing law of marine insurance. French goods from French colonies that had gone into neutral islands, or to neutral American ports, were not to be treated as neutral goods when they set off again for Europe just because they were carried in neutral ships ostensibly as neutral cargo. The goods, though not the ships, could be condemned as prize.[73] Although the Royal Navy was instructed after 1794 to detain vessels laden with produce from the French West Indies coming 'directly' from the islands to Europe, a call of convenience at a neutral port was insufficient under the doctrine of continuous voyage to break the direct nature of the journey, whatever the evidential problems that arose.[74]

The Rule of the War of 1756 lasted in British policy until 1854 during the Crimean War, when it was abandoned by Britain. A shift away from the mercantilist and protectionist attitudes of the Enlightenment towards the ideals of free trade favoured keeping the global shipping lanes open for neutrals in a limited war as being in Britain's own best interests, so long as they were policed by the Royal Navy.[75] After generations of relying on the Rule as a precedent, however, the change in direction was only achieved with considerable graunching of the gears of state.[76]

[72] Ann Burton, 'British Evangelicals, Economic Warfare and the Abolition of the Atlantic Slave Trade, 1794–1810', in Jeremy Black (ed.), *The Atlantic Slave Trade* (London, 2006).

[73] Baugh, *The Global Seven Years War, 1754–1763*, p. 324.

[74] Stephen, *War in Disguise*, pp. 22ff.

[75] Abbenhuis, *An Age of Neutrals*, pp. 66–7, 91.

[76] Ibid., p. 82.

Prize Money and the Courts

The Admiralty Prize Court had the exclusive jurisdiction to condemn seized ships and goods as lawful prize.[77] Naval officers, however, traditionally mistrusted the Admiralty Court as a place where their efforts were turned to the profit of the law officers, agents and clerks and where their interests were prejudiced by conflicts of interest. Where possible they brought their disputes over shares in prize money outside of the Admiralty Court in the Court of Common Pleas, and on appeal from there to the Court of King's Bench. The main benefit of doing so was that they could have their own representation rather than having to rely on the King's Proctor, an office roughly equivalent to the Treasury Solicitor in Admiralty matters, but with a reputation as 'a place of considerable profit'.[78] They thought that if they could have their own representation by appointing their own legal agents, or proctors, to act for them, then they would pay lower fees and their interests would be better protected.[79] Among those most voluble on the subject was St Vincent, who wrote to Sir William Scott in 1803 that: 'until the officers of the Navy are permitted to nominate their own proctors, a privilege possessed by privateers, their suspicions will remain.'[80]

It was a time when claims needed to be brought within recognised forms of proceedings. One recognised 'cause of action' in the Court of Common Pleas allowed claims for 'money had and received', referred to as *indebitatus assumpsit.* This involved a legal fiction that whoever had received the prize money thereby assumed a debt to whoever was lawfully entitled to it, so claimants could sue the holder of the monies in an action for payment of a debt. The prize fund would normally be paid out to the prize agent appointed by the putative commander-in-chief. If there was dispute as to who the commander-in-chief was then the recipient would in practice be the first to get their claim in. As the holder of the funds, the prize agent could be sued for payments alleged to be due from the fund. For example, in the litigation considered in Chapter 5 between Nelson and St Vincent, the commander-in-chief's share was paid out to St Vincent's secretary and agent, Benjamin Tucker, who effectively held the monies as stakeholder while the claims on the monies were adjudicated. If a stakeholder pays out money to

77 Le Caux v Eden (1781) 2 Douglas Rep. 614.

78 A description from 1745, David J. Starkey, *British Privateering Enterprise in the 18th Century* (Exeter, 1990), p. 27.

79 Hill, *The Prizes of War*, pp. 163–4; Henry J. Bourguignon, *Sir William Scott, Lord Stowell* (Cambridge, 1987), p. 274.

80 *Letters of Admiral of the Fleet The Earl St Vincent*, ed. D. Bonner-Smith, NRS (London, 1926), vol. II, p. 221.

the wrong person and is then faced with a claim by another party, then they may have to pay the money again if the claim is upheld. As the judge at the initial trial of the action in March 1801 advised Tucker:[81] 'take care to pay money into the right hand, in case it might be claimed by somebody else.'[82] Sometimes the holders of prize money did pay out monies without a court order, but if they were wise they obtained a written indemnity against other claims before doing so.[83]

The Bar and Bench

Admiralty Court barristers were members of Doctors' Commons, based near St Paul's churchyard. It was also referred to as 'The College of Civilians' due to their learning in 'Civil Law', i.e. ecclesiastical and admiralty law originating in Roman jurisprudence. They used the phrase 'Civil lawyer' to distinguish themselves from the 'Common lawyers', i.e. those who practised in areas of law originating in the 'common law' of England created through decisions of the king's courts establishing precedents that were followed and became part of English law, 'common' to all. Whatever the origins of any branch of law, however, all the courts considering prize and freight cases applied the common law of England, of which admiralty law, for all its 'Civilian' influences, formed a part. Though they distinguished between themselves, they were all 'common law' courts in the sense that they all applied the common law.

English 'common' law develops through court decisions in individual cases. The points that arise depend on the issues that come before the courts and may be influenced by the individual merits of a case. It is often said of common law decisions that 'hard cases make bad law', meaning that a decision made to avoid an injustice on the hard facts of a single case may result in a bad law as a more general proposition. There is often a tension in common law decisions between factors pulling in different directions. Commonly there is a tension between the desire for sufficient certainty so that parties know where they are in any dispute and can resolve it quickly (and cheaply), and the desire for flexibility so that a 'fair' result can be reached on the merits of a particular case. Decisions may also be influenced by the way

[81] Lord Alvanley, rather than Lord Kenyon as reported in *The Naval Chronicle*, see Aldous, 'Lord Nelson and Earl St Vincent: Prize Fighters', *MM* (2015), 135–55.

[82] *NC*, vol. V, 256.

[83] E.g. Draft deed of indemnity prepared by Booth & Haslewood for Nelson to indemnify John Tyson against claims by others for the chief flag-officer's share of £500 from the capture of *Civita Vecchia* in Italy by HM Ships in September 1799, NMM CRK/6/142.

in which cases are argued before the court. There may be arguments that for some reason the parties or their advocates choose not to argue, but which might have appealed to the court had they done so. This may depend on the attitude of the parties, or the professional capabilities and/or judgement of the advocates. In one case counsel might be arguing for the rights of flag-officers, but in another case be arguing against them.

Cases over shares in prize money in the Court of Common Pleas involved a small number of counsel who as members of Serjeants' Inn enjoyed special rights of audience in that court. The inn was based in premises near the bottom of Chancery Lane and admitted barristers from other inns. The Chief Justice of the Court of Common Pleas was a member of Serjeants' Inn and in court they all referred to each other as 'Brother'. The judiciary, then as now, were drawn from the ranks of the lawyers practising before the courts, often, but not exclusively, those who had distinguished themselves as advocates.

Counsel and the judges they appeared before were all well known to each other and overlapped in their careers both inside and outside the law. It is often tempting to think of the Bar as an elite group all drawn from a privileged background of wealth and social superiority. Then, and now, that is an inaccurate assumption. Successful members of the Bar were, and are, drawn from a variety of backgrounds. William Scott and his brother John, who as Lord Eldon became Lord Chancellor, were the sons of a Newcastle coal trader.[84] Charles Abbott was the son of a Kent barber, and went on to become Lord Chief Justice in 1815, being elevated as Baron Tenterden.[85] Sam Shepherd was the son of a toymaker and jeweller in Cheapside.[86] The fact that there was a social network amongst those working in this field should not be mistaken as a sign that it was social interconnectedness that explained their success. It was their success that led to their interconnectedness. In many ways this was also the social make-up of the Royal Navy; indeed the Scott brothers went to the grammar school in Newcastle with Cuthbert Collingwood, who as an admiral was Nelson's friend and second-in-command at Trafalgar.[87]

We know about the cases these advocates argued because of the contemporary law reports. Whilst some attention has been paid to decisions

84 William C. Townsend, *The Lives of Eminent Judges* (London, 1846), vol. 2, pp. 278–90.

85 Ibid., p. 234.

86 Humphrey William Woolrych, *Lives of Eminent Serjeants-at-Law of the English Bar* (London, 1869), vol. 2, p. 814.

87 Henry J. Bourguignon, *Sir William Scott, Lord Stowell: Judge of the High Court of Admiralty, 1798–1828* (Cambridge, 2004), p. 32; Max Adams, *Admiral Collingwood* (London, 2005), p. 23.

of the Admiralty Court, decisions of the Court of Common Pleas and the King's Bench have not previously been studied in detail, even though they have been available in law libraries. Many historians have relied on reports of cases in *The Naval Chronicle*, though they tend to be less accurate than legal reports. It was said of Isaac Espinasse, who reported nisi prius cases from 1793 to 1807, that he only heard half of what went on in court and reported the other half.[88] This criticism has at times unjustifiably attached itself to his contemporaries. The quality of the reports on prize cases is notably good. The reports of the King's Bench and Court of Common Pleas tend to be factually better than the reports of the Admiralty Court, which are more concerned with facts only to demonstrate the principle that the case establishes rather than as an accurate recital of the facts for their own interest. By cross-referencing the law reports with the evidence of logbooks, muster books, journals and correspondence, a fresh view of prize capture emerges. Indeed, the law reports cite Admiralty letters that cannot be traced in naval archives, maybe because they were taken to court and never replaced.

The English Courts and the Royal Navy

English courts frequently stated their enormous respect for the Royal Navy and its personnel. They recognised that in time of war 'the existence of the country depends upon its fleets'.[89] It is tempting to read into this that the courts were reluctant to interfere with the way that the navy conducted itself and that military law took the navy beyond the reach of the courts, but that was not the case. The courts regularly dealt with applications for writs of habeas corpus to procure the release of men taken by press-gangs, who they did not see as under the exclusive control of the navy, or beyond supervision by the courts. Indeed, the King's Bench Court under Lord Chief Justice Mansfield had developed its procedures in the mid-eighteenth century to provide effective remedies against unlawful impressment. The legal year is divided into four legal terms, separated by periods of 'vacation'. From Mansfield's time the courts were prepared to hear applications during vacation, rather than waiting for the court to sit again at the beginning of the next law term, despite doubts about the enforcement of writs issued out of term time. More significantly they were prepared, based on sworn written

88 Per Chief Baron Pollock, Theobald Mathew, 'Law-French', *Law Quarterly Review* 54 (1938), 358, 368.

89 Per Lord Kenyon C.J., Ex. P. Softly (1801) 1 East 466, 471.

statements called affidavits, to order those detaining impressed men to show cause why the detention was lawful rather than issue a writ of habeas corpus to bring the man before the court. This avoided the problems of producing the men and gave the Admiralty the opportunity to investigate the detention and concede where appropriate without the embarrassment of publicly contested naval recruitment at a time when it might test the loyalty of the nation.[90] It was an opportunity that the Admiralty often took, thereby providing a very real remedy.[91]

Mansfield was succeeded in 1788 by Lord Kenyon, who is generally remembered as the successor who ended or restricted Mansfield's reforms.[92] Indeed, the general use of habeas corpus was heavily restricted in Kenyon's time, but it continued to be used for supervising impressment.[93] In 1801 Kenyon stated publicly that he frequently dealt with applications for the release of impressed men made to him out of court, as had his predecessors.[94] If there was an issue as to the lawfulness of an impressment then judges were prepared to determine the issue in court and give reasoned judgments on the construction of the Acts under which the right to press arose, whatever the need of the navy to impress men.[95]

From time-to-time courts had to consider whether they could interfere in matters of military discipline, and if so on what basis. One case gave rise to extensive litigation on the issue and still casts its shadow on the law today. In 1781, during the war against the French over American independence, Commodore George Johnstone was sent with a British fleet to secure the Dutch Cape before the French could do so. At Porto Praya on the neutral Portuguese islands of Cape Verde, the French fleet under Admiral Suffren attacked the ill-prepared British fleet watering in the bay on 16 April 1781. Although the French ships suffered damage in the exchange, they did not linger but escaped and sailed on for the Cape. The British response in contrast was slow and ineffectual. As a result, Suffren won the race to the Cape. Johnstone blamed Captain Sutton of *HMS Isis* for being

90 Nicholas Rogers, 'British Impressment and Its Discontents', *The International Journal of Maritime History* 30:1 (2018), 52–73.

91 Norman S. Poser, *Lord Mansfield: Justice in the Age of Reason* (Montreal, 2013), p. 314; Paul D. Halliday, *Habeas Corpus: From England to Empire* (Cambridge, Mass., 2012), pp. 114–16; Denver Brunsman, *The Evil Necessity: British Naval Impressment in the Eighteenth-Century Atlantic World* (Charlottesville, 2013), p. 194; Kevin Costello, 'Habeas Corpus and Military and Naval Impressment, 1756–1816', *The Journal of Legal History* 29:2 (2008), 215–51.

92 Poser, *Lord Mansfield*, pp. 388–9.

93 Halliday, *Habeas Corpus*, p. 134.

94 Ex parte Softly (1801) 1 East 466.

95 Ex parte Bruce (1806) 8 East 27, per Lord Ellenborough C.J.

too slow to respond to his order to sail to join battle and placed him under arrest.[96] Johnstone then humiliated Sutton by appointing a Captain Lumley to acting command of the ship, with Sutton still on board. Despite Sutton's increasingly anguished pleas to be brought to a court-martial it was not until December 1783, upon his return to England having sailed to the Indian Ocean as a prisoner on his own ship, that Sutton faced a court-martial on board *HMS Princess Royal* in Portsmouth harbour over his action at Porto Praya, 32 months earlier. Although Johnstone had captured some valuable prizes in Saldanha Bay, an act which itself would give rise to considerable litigation,[97] his failure to take the Cape still stung and he persisted in blaming Sutton. The court-martial, however, acquitted Sutton.

Sutton felt aggrieved and sued Johnstone for malicious prosecution.[98] He succeeded at trial, and at a re-trial where a jury awarded him substantial damages of £6,000, but he could not keep hold of his judgment on appeal and ultimately failed in his claim. During the proceedings there was a lively debate about whether the courts could interfere with military discipline. Some judgments suggested that there might be an absolute immunity for naval discipline, notwithstanding that in an earlier case of Swinton v Molloy in 1783 the King's Bench had entertained an action for false imprisonment by a ship's purser against his captain. The suggested immunity was far from established in law or accepted by the courts. Sutton lost on appeal because the court held that there was insufficient evidence of malice on Johnstone's part, so a finding that the prosecution was malicious was not one that a jury could properly reach. The appeal was not allowed on the basis that Johnstone was entitled to immunity from suit even if he had acted maliciously. Amongst the views expressed in the judgments on appeal, however, the most famous has become that of Lord Mansfield, that the proper remedy was the satisfaction of an acquittal and of an unjust accuser being 'blasted forever' and losing his reputation, and thus no right to damages was needed.[99] This, and other views on the matter, were, however, obiter dicta, i.e. they were not authoritative judgments on the point as they were not the reasons upon which the decision was reached. They therefore offered no

[96] Johnstone's letter book, 22 April 1781, TNA ADM 1/54.

[97] J. P. van Niekerk, 'The First British Occupation of the Cape of Good Hope and Two Prize Cases on Joint Capture in the High Court of Admiralty', *Fundamina, A Journal of Legal History* 11:2 (2005), 155–81.

[98] For a detailed analysis of the complex litigation see J. P. van Niekerk, 'Of Naval Courts-Martial and Prize Claims: Some Legal Consequences of Commodore Johnstone's Secret Mission to the Cape of Good Hope and the "Battle" of Saldanha Bay, 1781 (Part 1)', *Fundamina, A Journal of Legal History* 21:2 (2015), 392–456.

[99] Sutton v Johnstone 99 ER 1215 (1786) 1 TR 510, 550.

binding precedent on the issue and the fact that there was a debate reveals that the point was not a settled one.

The view of this litigation has been coloured, however, by events a century later when the courts again came to consider the issue of military immunity.[100] Despite strong views expressed in the judgments to the contrary, the Victorian courts treated Sutton v Johnstone as having established a doctrine of absolute immunity for naval discipline. The eminence of Lord Mansfield may have blinded later courts to the true status of his comments, or his comments, taken out of context, may have been a convenient authority for views that had risen to popularity a century later. This Victorian view of what Sutton v Johnstone decided has persisted until today.[101] It fits into a narrative that the eighteenth-century English courts were ready to leave the navy alone and overlook injustices committed in the name of naval discipline. The courts, so this narrative suggests, failed to heed Cicero's warning '*silent enim leges inter arma*', 'in times of war, the laws fall silent.'[102] That narrative needs to be questioned, however. As the cases explored in the following chapters reveal, the courts were only too willing and able to resolve questions of naval discipline and regulation. That benefited the navy in that it added authority and respectability to the system of prize payments that it enjoyed.

Chapters 4–6 consider the way in which prize money was distributed, and the dynamics of the changes that were introduced under the pressures of war. Chapter 7 considers the particular significance of the changes in 1808. Before that, however, the next chapter considers how prize agency operated to distribute prize money in practice, and Chapter 3 considers the law of nations in English prize courts, and how we should treat suggestions that the courts were administering 'international law' when applying the rule of law to prize money cases.

100 Dawkins v Lord Rokeby (1866) 4 F & F 806; Dawkins v Lord Paulet (1869) LR 5 QB 94.

101 A. Tettenborn et al., *Clerk & Lindsell on Torts*, 24th edn (London, 2023), paras 15–64, 21–51.

102 Cicero, *Pro Milone*, Section 11.

2. Prize Agency

Prize Office to Privatisation

Until the Crown gave up its entitlement to a share of prize money in 1708 it had a direct interest in getting the money in, and appointed Prize Commissioners to run a Prize Office and bring in the cash. From 1689, at the start of the reign of William and Mary, the Prize Office was responsible to the Treasury and the High Court of Admiralty, rather than the Admiralty.[1] Its duties included receiving prizes sent in by the navy, guarding them pending condemnation by the court and arranging the sale and distribution of proceeds. At the end of each war the Prize Office was decommissioned to save money, but even then the Prize Commissioners continued their work to get in outstanding prize money, even engaging officials of the East India Company to assist.[2] The Prize Office was supervised by six commissioners in London, assisted by sub-commissioners in Dover, Portsmouth, Plymouth, Bristol and Hull. Naval officers sometimes took some persuading to comply with the Prize Office and hand over their prize captures, including threats of courts-martial from the Admiralty. When in 1708 the Crown gave up the whole proceeds of prizes to the captors, it lost its incentive to run the Prize Office. The Prize Act 1708 and its successors gave authority over prizes to the captors as a form of private property. They still had to obtain condemnation of captures as prizes by the Admiralty Court, but once that was obtained the captors could allow their agents to put the prizes up for sale and distribute the proceeds. Thus, the central Prize Office gave way to privatisation in the form of prize agency.[3]

Prize agents came in different forms. Many were merchants or brokers in related lines of business, and those with the contacts, skills, resources and

1 J. S. Bromley, 'Prize Office and Prize Agency at Portsmouth 1689–1748', in Webb, Yates and Peacock (eds), *Hampshire Studies*, 169–200, 170.

2 Frank Fox, 'The Ronas Voe Incident, 1674', *MM* 106 (2020), 408–21.

3 Tony Gutteridge, 'Aspects of Naval Prize Agency 1793–1815', *MM* 80:1 (1994), 45–55.

appetite undertook the work for the generally recognised commission of 5 per cent of the proceeds. Among these was Alexander Davison, Nelson's man of business, prize agent, banker and go-between.[4] In theory the officers and crew could appoint their own agents, with up to three agents appointed by the grant of a power of attorney to deal with any one prize capture.[5] In general, however, the captain of a ship tended to decide on the agent and the ship's officers and men followed his lead. Flag-officers had a considerable interest in getting in their healthy share of the proceeds and often ensured that their own flag-secretaries were appointed by the captains of the capturing ships as prize agent for the captors. Thus, when in 1799 four Royal Navy frigates captured two Spanish treasure ships in circumstances where the flag-officer's share was disputed, St Vincent as one of the flag-officers claiming a share made sure that his secretary Benjamin Tucker went straight on board at Plymouth to take control of the treasure and be appointed prize agent.[6] A particularly pernicious custom involved appointing friends of the captain and/or the secretary to the commander-in-chief as joint agents, taking 2½ per cent commission but performing no practical function. That practice was outlawed after 1803, but the jostling to be appointed as prize agent in lucrative circumstances remained.

Several established firms offered their services to officers to manage the business of getting in prize money. Many, such as Nelson's bankers, Marsh and Creed, were based around the Strand in London. In seaports around the world a group of navy agents with a far inferior reputation touted for business from the lower ranks. They were not prize agents with conduct of the prizes, but for their own profit would extend credit to sailors on the back of prizes or would buy prize shares yet to be paid at a discount from sailors who preferred cash today to promises tomorrow.

The Commission on Frauds

When St Vincent became First Lord of the Admiralty in 1801, he was convinced that the royal dockyards were dens of iniquity and the prize courts full of rogues. The common theme was that those responsible on shore for assisting sea officers were obstructing the success of the navy for their own profit rather than providing the required help. He had been dismissive of previous reforming efforts as 'cant, Imposture, loads of

4 Martyn Downer, *Nelson's Purse* (London, 2004).

5 Geo. III c.66, S 50.

6 See Chapter 5.

precedents, and scraps of Tape & Buckram'.[7] On taking office he set up a commission of enquiry during the short-lived Peace of Amiens. The 1802 Act 'for appointing Commissioners to enquire and examine into any Irregularities, Frauds, or Abuses, which are or have been practised by Persons employed in the several Naval Departments therein mentioned, and the Business of Prize Agency' left little doubt as to what the commissioners were expected to find.[8] When war resumed in 1803 against Napoleon's France, they embarked on an immediate enquiry into the business of prize agency during the previous French Revolutionary war, with a view to recommending improvements for the new war. Between March and July 1803, the commission took evidence from 18 witnesses with experience of the prize system and published its report two weeks after the last witness gave evidence. The report provides a valuable insight into the workings of the prize agency system, due in large part to the evidence from an experienced prize agent, James Primrose Maxwell. The commissioners also heard complaints from naval officers. Nelson gave evidence that 'From my own Knowledge and Experience I am warranted in observing That Prize-money does not get into the Pockets of the Captors so expeditiously as it ought, and in many instances not at all; great Sums of Money having been lost by the failure of Agents'.[9] Evidence was also heard from active 'Star' frigate captains. This included the evidence of Captain The Hon. Alexander Cochrane that 'agents abroad are in general more attentive to their private Interest than to that of their Constituents; and I have not the least Doubt, that in many Cases where Appeals are entered, it is done by the Contrivance of the Agents, in order that they may keep the Proceeds longer in their Hands ... at the Risk of the Captors for should their Commercial Speculations fail and they become Bankrupts, the ultimate loss would fall on the Captain of the Ship who made the Capture'.[10] The following day the commissioners heard evidence from another 'Star' frigate captain, Captain Graham Moore, just days before his appointment to Sir Edward Pellew's former ship *HMS Indefatigable*.[11] The Peace of Amiens had just ended and renewed war meant renewed opportunities for prizes to be taken in a crack frigate. Moore gave more measured evidence to the effect that although he had not personally come across deliberate delays in payments of prize

7 Knight, *Britain against Napoleon*, p. 29.

8 Appointed under the Act of 43 Geo. III ch. 16, Dec. 1802.

9 Evidence on oath 1 April 1803, HC Paper 160, p. 251, July 1803, App. 16, p. 322; N. H. Nicolas, *The Dispatches and Letters of Vice Admiral Lord Viscount Nelson* (London, 1997), vol. V, pp. 53–4.

10 Evidence on oath 23 June 1803, HC Paper 160, July 1803, App. 7, p. 302.

11 Tom Wareham, *Frigate Commander* (Barnsley, 2012), p. 235.

monies, he had not the least doubt that they existed and that it had been the cause of 'much Dissatisfaction in the Service'.[12]

Prize Agency in Practice

When ships of the Royal Navy captured ships as prizes they sent them into port with a Letter of Attorney either to a single prize agent, or to a number of agents to act jointly, unless they had already appointed an agent in anticipation of captures. The prize agent dealt with securing the prize in port, getting it before the court to be condemned as prize, selling the prize property once authorised, distributing the proceeds to those entitled and sending any unclaimed or forfeited shares (for example by desertion) to the Treasurer of the Greenwich Hospital to fund the home for Royal Navy veterans.

On arrival in port the agent arranged for preliminary examinations to be taken and forwarded with the ship's papers to the Admiralty Registrar at the Admiralty Court in London, or to one of the Vice-Admiralty Courts authorised to sit around the world. The preliminary examinations generally consisted of depositions taken from the master and the next two senior persons on board the prize in a standard printed questionnaire prepared by the King's Advocate. In an out-port the examination was undertaken by a commissioner appointed by the Admiralty judge and an official termed an actuary, appointed by the Admiralty Registrar. They examined the witnesses, through an interpreter where required, to record particulars of the property of the ship, cargo and destination.

In London the Registrar delivered the examination papers to the King's Proctor, a legal official who acted as Attorney General in Admiralty matters. They submitted the papers to the King's Advocate, another law officer of the Crown, to provide an opinion that was in practice final as to whether proceedings should be taken (by way of what was called a monition, meaning a caution or warning) to condemn the captured property as lawful prize.

The monition, if issued, warned potential claimants to make their claims to the property. Thus, in theory at least, the owners of the property had an opportunity to object that the property was not lawful prize and should be released. This applied in practice to owners who claimed that the property was wholly or in part owned by British or allied owners, or by neutrals, and was not made up of contraband goods (a flexible category under English law but including war materiel) bound for any enemy. In practice it

12 Evidence on oath 24 June 1803, HC Paper 160, July 1803, App. 8, p. 304.

required such owners to have legal representation in place in advance, or the master and/or his agents to act quickly to find such representation, as they had only 20 days to lodge their claims. After that time the case could be listed for trial to wait its turn to be heard.

If the capture was an enemy ship of war, or similarly obviously enemy property, and no claimant contested the condemnation then an order condemning the prize as lawful would be made in about six weeks. Where property was claimed by a neutral, however, then proceedings could take a lot longer, depending on the nature of the case, the residence of the claimants, and the ease of obtaining evidence to determine whether the property was neutral or not. In some instances, there were long delays, giving rise to considerable complaints by the officers and men awaiting the proceeds, but delays were often inevitable given the problems of adducing evidence in relation to contested claims. Everyone loves knocking lawyers for the time they take to do apparently straightforward things, and the Georgian Royal Navy was no exception. In a disputed case, gathering the necessary evidence when the key witnesses were at sea with no means of contacting them, maybe for months or years, was far from straightforward. The courts could not be relied on to make inferences from entries in logbooks, even where gaps in the evidence were due to the absence of witnesses at sea. Cases could take years to determine, but equally when the courts put their minds to it, claims could be turned round with an alacrity suggestive of political motivation.

Although the agent took possession of the captured vessel and any cargo at the port of arrival, no disposal could be made officially without permission of the court. Once the court could determine the claim, then it would issue an order either of condemnation or for the release of the property. If the cargo was perishable, then the court could grant an order for its appraisement and sale and the proceeds would then be held by the Registrar of the Admiralty Court pending the final adjudication. The ship would not be sold, however, until an order of condemnation, even though they too tended to rot in port. If a neutral claimant wanted to ensure the release of their property, then they could give security for the value of the property as settled by two appraisers appointed by court-appointed commissioners, one nominated by the captor and one by the claimant. Once security was given, the vessel would be released. If a claimant refused to give security, the captors could only sit and watch the ship rotting at anchor while awaiting a court order for condemnation.

These rules were not always followed in practice. In 1799, 44 wagons of Spanish dollars were removed from captured Spanish treasure ships before condemnation and taken under armed guard from Plymouth to London to be sold to the Bank of England for £661,286 13*s.* 9*d.* Whilst a pragmatic step to take, the removal had not been approved by the Admiralty Court, and Sir William Scott, the Admiralty judge, wrote a mild reminder to the Admiralty:

> You may rest assured that I should throw no obstacles in the way of good government being accommodated. But you surprise me extremely by telling me that the dollars are loaded and deposited. Under what authority was this done? No authority but that of the court can sanction it before condemnation. To open the hatches, or break Bulk, in any manner in a prize not adjudged, is a high misdemeanour punishable with severe penalties. Neither the captors nor their agents have acted with sufficient caution in that respect. If the agents consent and accommodate I shall certainly not be forward to impeach ... but if it is inforced upon my notice in any judicial way I shall be compelled to censure the removal of this treasure out of the ships without leave of the court first obtained, as highly irregular and illegal.[13]

No comment appears written on a turned-over corner of the letter, as was the normal procedure of Sir Evan Nepean, the Secretary to the Board of Admiralty. The matter was not brought to Scott's notice 'in a judicial way'.

Once an order for condemnation was made, the property could then be sold, generally at auction if the Admiralty was not going to 'buy in' a ship for service in the Royal Navy at an agreed price. A claimant to the prize goods as lawful goods could appeal against an order of condemnation, and if they did so then they could offer security for the goods and take them pending appeal. If the claimant refused to offer security for the release of the property pending appeal, the captors could choose to give security pending appeal and sell the property, holding the proceeds until the appeal was decided. Thus, although a sale could go ahead, distribution to the captors would be postponed if there was an appeal. Until 1798 claimants had three months after an order of condemnation to appeal. In May 1798, however, a new Prize Act extended the time for appeal to a more practical 12 months.[14]

The extension of time to appeal, whilst more practical in cases where instructions to appeal had to be obtained from owners abroad during a time of war, led to considerable disquiet on the part of captors. As James Maxwell expressed it in his evidence to the commissioners:

[13] Scott to Evan Nepean, TNA ADM 1/3894, see Chapter 5.

[14] Geo. III c.38.

> the Captors were not only kept out of their Prize-money, but in some instances, I fear, Claims have been lodged for the purpose of delaying the Distribution, and with a View to obtain a Consideration from the Captors to drop the Appeal. It also affords the neutral Claimant Opportunity to contrive and bring forward fabricated Evidence in Support of his Pretensions.[15]

Once there was a final order for condemnation or a final decree on appeal then the captors' prize agent would sell the property within three or four months, if they got on with it. Subject to some statutory exceptions, excise duties on importation were still due on goods brought in as prize. Once the property was sold, the agent would make up the accounts for distribution to the captors. A copy of the accounts verified on oath had to be lodged at the court to be exhibited and deposited in the registry, or a fine of £500 was payable to the Greenwich Hospital.

Notice that the account of sales was being lodged was then given, in England in *The London Gazette* or by some other public means elsewhere. Wherever published, the agent then had to give two copies to the Customs Officer or Principal Officer of the port or place where the prize was condemned. The officer would add his name to one copy and send it to the Greenwich Hospital for registration and keep the other copy. Ten days later they would insert another public notice, giving at least three days' notice of when and where payment would be made to the captors. If the ship was in England, the payment would be made on board. Within three months of the date fixed for payment the agent was required by statute to send to the Treasurer of the Greenwich Hospital an account of the proceeds of the prize, the amount of the sums paid, and of the money remaining in their hands.[16] Any default in these requirements was punishable with a £100 fine.[17] The commission found, however, that particularly where prizes were dealt with by agents abroad there were regularly defaults in compliance with the statutory regulations and in particular the requirements to provide notice of payments of shares.

Sums due to parties who were absent at the time of general payment would be available for payment for three years by what were referred to as

[15] Cited in Fourth Report of the Commissioners of Naval Enquiry, 1803, HC Papers 160, p. 253. Abuse in Vice-Admiralty Courts abroad could be even more difficult to prevent; see the activities of Corsican privateers, Joshua Meeks, *France, Britain, and the Struggle for the Revolutionary Western Mediterranean* (Basingstoke, 2017), pp. 132–3.

[16] Geo. III c.66 s. 62.

[17] Geo. III c.66 s. 52.

Recalls. These were generally fixed at the house of the agent, or a sub-agent. Once the three years expired all the unclaimed shares were paid, together with forfeited shares of men who had deserted, to the Treasurer of the Greenwich Hospital. The payment had to be accompanied by a list of the names, qualities and shares of those who remained unpaid, and an account of the gross and net proceeds of the prize and of the charges incurred, verified on oath. From 1803 a new regulation of the Treasurer of the Greenwich Hospital also required details of every person paid to be given, as well as those unpaid, including when and to whom the money had been paid.

In return for undertaking these onerous duties and liabilities, the prize agents received repayment of the numerous disbursements that they had paid out, together with their own commission, generally at the rate of 5 per cent. If the property was not condemned as prize, then the agent received no commission. Until 1803, save in the rare cases where it was expressly agreed to be on the net sum after payment of costs, the commission was calculated on the gross proceeds of the captures. This gave little incentive to minimise the costs that came out of the proceeds. One of the few changes to be implemented in response to the fourth report of the Commissioners of Naval Enquiry was to stipulate that the commission should be based on the net sum.[18] Agents enjoyed the benefit of the money they held, often for many years, enabling them to trade for their own profit, but placing the captors' funds at risk.

The process of distributing the prize money could be the subject of nefarious activities. As the process of paying the money to claimants could last a long time and involve delayed payments of sometimes small amounts, the task was often delegated to sub-agents, and the methods of accounting were open to abuse. Distributions lists were divided into six columns. The first column listed the names of the persons entitled to shares, arranged according to rank. The second column stated the rank and the third the amount of their share. The fourth column was for the time of payment, with a signature for the recipient in the fifth column and a signature of a witness in the sixth. The commission heard that on Recall days persons claiming to be agents for claimants, or to be entitled to payment having advanced money to the claimant, would be allowed to look down the lists and say whose share they were entitled to, without even the elementary check of asking whose share they were claiming before viewing the list. There was then very little check on the veracity of claims to be entitled to the money on behalf of the true beneficiary. Where there were checks the list was signed in advance of the check, so that when enquiry revealed a

[18] See Chapter 7.

lack of authority to claim, it nevertheless appeared that payment had been validly made. Where a list was about to be closed at the end of the three years allowed for Recall payments, agents would sometimes notify officers with unpaid shares in return for a 2½ per cent commission. Thus, officers paid extra commission for a sum that they had been entitled to all along, had they been given notice. Seamen lost their right to payment on Recall even if they had no notice and would have to petition the Greenwich Hospital for payment.

The net effect of the system of prize agency was that it imposed regulation that was ignored or flouted by the ignorant or unscrupulous. Whilst a good prize agent was worth every penny, the system was open to abuse. As the Commissioners put it in 1803:

> The Mischiefs in the present System of Prize Agency, of which we have had proof in the course of this Enquiry, fall under the Description of Abuses and Irregularities, rather than Fraud. We find no Reason for subjecting to general Censure, or involving in general Disrepute, the Persons concerned in this business; but we are satisfied that there exists a Set of Men, who take advantage of the unsuspicious Character, of the Indiscretion and Extravagance which prevail among Seamen, and who, in Time of War, earn a scandalous livelihood by supplying them with liquor, Clothes, and trifling Sums, and getting from them Wills and Powers of Attorney for their Prize-money.[19]

This might seem a generous view of some of the activities of the agents, and a harsh judgement on the character of seamen. The description of the character of seamen, however, was a widely held view, and not limited to seamen in the Royal Navy. English courts have always adopted a somewhat paternalistic and protective approach towards seamen in disputes with their ship owners and employers. Lord Stowell, one of the most influential Admiralty judges in the history of the court, expressed the view in 1822 that 'the common mariner is easy and careless, illiterate and unthinking; he has no resources, in his own intelligence and experience in habits of business ...'[20] In 1825 he described the disparity of bargaining power in the negotiation of contracts for wages on merchant ships in colourful terms: 'On the one side are gentlemen possessed of wealth, and intent, I mean not unfairly, upon augmenting it, conversant in business and possessing the means of calling in the aid of practical and professional knowledge. On the other side, is a set of men, generally ignorant and illiterate, notoriously

19 HC Papers 160.

20 The Juliana (1822) 2 Dods. 504.

and proverbially reckless and improvident, ill provided with the means of obtaining useful information, and almost ready to sign any instrument that may be proposed to them; and on all accounts requiring protection, even against themselves.'[21] These attitudes led the Admiralty Court in 1864 to hold that when construing seamen's contracts it would give the benefit of doubt to seamen.[22]

The report of the commissioners did not find major abuses but did make some recommendations for change. To some extent they followed the changes proposed by Nelson in his evidence. It has been suggested that these may have come from his public secretary, John Scott.[23] Although Scott was experienced in prize agency matters, he was not appointed as Nelson's public secretary until his transfer to *HMS Victory* a month after Nelson gave evidence to the commissioners. He received the invitation to take up the appointment on 16 March 1803 in a letter from Nelson's banker, Mr Marsh of Marsh and Creed, who had recommended him to Nelson.[24] Given the chronology, it seems more likely that it was Davison's views rather than Scott's that influenced Nelson at this time. Nelson's key proposal was for a new regulator, the Prize Office, or as Nelson had called it, a Prize Agency Office. The main advantages of this new body were that it would provide a central registry so that those entitled to prize money could track it down, and within a reasonable time the monies themselves would be lodged with the office for distribution.[25] A throw-back to the old Prize Office, the recommendation could have been transformative, but it was not implemented.

The views expressed by the commissioners, and the evidence they heard, can give the impression that prize agency profited those who stayed on shore without facing the risks of war at sea, but that was not always the case. When Nelson stood on the quarterdeck of *HMS Victory* approaching the combined Franco-Spanish fleet off Cape Trafalgar on 21 October 1805, the man at his side was his public secretary, John Scott. The 41-year-old had served as a purser from the age of 25 before being appointed by Nelson as his secretary.[26] After a long tussle with Nelson's friend Alexander Davison, Scott had manoeuvred himself into position as prize agent to the fleet just

21 The Minerva (1825) 1 Hagg. 347.

22 The Nonpareil (1864) Br. & L. 355.

23 Hill, *The Prizes of War*, p. 144.

24 John Maynard, *John Scott, Nelson's Secretary and Friend* (London, 2024), p. 361.

25 Fourth Report of the Commissioners of Naval Enquiry, HC Paper 160, July 1803, pp. 275–6.

26 Maynard, *John Scott*, pp. 17–39.

as battle was looming.[27] With high expectations of the battle and his role in its aftermath, he was looking forward to a life of domestic happiness on shore, with his wife, Charlotte, and family. As the battle began Scott was cut in half by chain-shot.[28] His body was thrown overboard. He never lived to enjoy the prize agency for the battle, which went to Collingwood's secretary, William Cosway. Preserved in the National Maritime Museum in Greenwich are the breeches that Nelson was wearing when he fell in battle. The blood stains can still be seen. They are the blood of John Scott, Nelson's prize agent.

[27] Downer, *Nelson's Purse*, p. 316.

[28] *The Times*, 7 November 1805.

3.

A Law of Nations?

At the start of each war during the eighteenth century the Crown issued a commission requiring the Admiralty Court:

> to proceed upon all and all manner of captures, seizures, prizes, and reprisals, of all ships and goods, that are, or shall be, taken; and to hear and determine the same according to the course of Admiralty and the law of Nations.[1]

The reference to 'the law of Nations' has given some the impression that the Admiralty Court was bound by some form of international law, rather than English law (what the cases refer to as 'municipal' law). The whiff of a law of nations has lingered over the prize courts ever since, tainting even well-considered histories to the extent that they even suggest that prize law evolved into 'a smoothly functioning system of international law'.[2] 'International law' is frequently used as the modern language equivalent of 'the law of nations', whilst at the same time recognising the contested nature of the concepts.[3] Still today *Halsbury's Laws of England* repeats the time-worn expression that 'The law administered by the Prize Court is international law which originates in the practice and usage long observed by civilised nations in their relations with each other or in express international agreement.'[4] This chapter considers how we should treat suggestions that eighteenth-century prize courts were applying international law.

The eighteenth-century jurist Sir William Blackstone went so far as to state in his *Commentaries on the Laws of England* that the law of nations 'is here adopted in its full extent by the common law, and is held to be part of

1 In the Matter of the Banda and Kirwee Booty, 30 June 1866, p. A2.

2 Kert, *Prize and Prejudice*, p. 36.

3 Suzanne Amy Foxley, *The American Experience of British Prize Law 1776–1804* (Woodbridge, 2025), pp. 2–6.

4 A. X. M. Ntovas (ed.), *Halsbury's Laws of England*, vol. 85A, 5th edn (London, 2024), The Law of Prize, Introduction, Para. 306.

the law of the land'.[5] Blackstone was often cited to support the idea that the Admiralty Court was bound by international rules, and there are numerous examples of English judges purporting to rely on 'the law of nations' or 'international law' when it suited them, but that does not mean that they were in fact applying international rather than English law. The idea that the Admiralty Court was bound to apply international law is wrong for two key reasons – there was no established body of international law in the eighteenth century that the courts could apply, and in any event they applied municipal not international law. The international nature of prize disputes meant that English courts could not ignore the politics of the wars underlying the claims. This included the national interest in furthering the war, but also the legitimate interests of shipowners and neutrals and the potential for enemy retaliation. The fact that English courts reached decisions about what English law was by taking account of the international interests of the nation should not be mistaken for an idea that the courts were bound to apply some external body of international law. In order to see the true role of international law in the Georgian prize courts we need to unpick the embroidery applied over the eighteenth-century framework during the Victorian era. A different picture emerges from under the later layers, revealing the delicate nature of international law.

The idea of a law of nations looked back to Greek and Roman jurisprudence as a foundation for established principles of maritime nations.[6] The ancient kings of Aragon gathered together the ancient ordinances of Greek and Roman emperors and of the kings of France and Spain as well as the laws of the Mediterranean islands and of Venice and Genoa. Their work was originally written in Catalan but was translated into many European languages and became known as the Consolato del Mare. Its original date is not certain, but it was referred to as a code of maritime law during the eleventh, twelfth and thirteenth centuries. It was still being translated and referred to as a source of the law of nations at the end of the eighteenth century, when the ancient tradition behind prize-taking was relied on as usage and custom and proof of its efficacy and acceptability.[7] By the eighteenth century there were plenty of jurists who had been willing to express their view of what the law was, or should be, governing international trade by sea, both in war and peace. Foremost among these was the Dutch jurist, Grotius.

5 Sir William Blackstone, *Commentaries on the Laws of England, 1769*, Book 4, Chapter 5.

6 Duckworth v Tucker (1809) 2 Taunt. 7, 22 (in argument) and 34 (per Mansfield C.J.).

7 Robinson, *Collectanea Maritima*, pp. ii. and iii.

Hugo Grotius

Around the courtroom of the United States Supreme Court in Washington DC there is a painted mural of the great law-givers in history. Among them is Hugo Grotius, as the 'father of international law'. He is in interesting company. King John is there on the basis that he gave us Magna Carta, although he sealed (not signed) it under duress from his barons, and almost immediately repudiated it. Napoleon is there on the basis that he gave his name to constitutions and the Code Napoleon, an exemplar of codified bodies of law copied in Europe and elsewhere.[8] Blackstone makes an appearance as a codifier of the common law. In the Rijksmuseum in Amsterdam, however, a large wooden chest with metal straps provides an insight into a different side of Grotius. The accompanying label explains that it is believed to be the chest which Grotius used to escape from house arrest in 1621. By then Grotius, or Groot (meaning Great) as the Dutch knew him, had fallen out with the authorities in Holland over how uncompromising the version of Calvinism adopted by the republic should be in its own interests, and was regarded as a threat. He was allowed, however, to arrange for his books to be carried into his house in a large chest. When the chest left, he was inside, smuggled out past his guards before escaping to Paris. Grotius, the international law-giver/fugitive, was a curious character, but he made a permanent impact on prize law.

Grotius was a lawyer engaged to provide a justification for retaining prizes seized by force and claimed by the Dutch East India Company (Verenigde Oostindische Compagnie, or VOC).[9] In February 1603 a Dutch captain, Jakob van Heemskerck, captured the *Santa Caterina*, a Portuguese carrack filled with trade goods of immense wealth. This was neither the first nor the last such capture. Only the previous year the Dutch had seized the Portuguese carrack *San Iago*.[10] What set the *Santa Caterina* apart was the value of her cargo. When sold in Amsterdam the goods made 3 million guilders, nearly the annual revenue of the English government at the time, and double the capital of the English East India Company.[11] Grotius was not just the VOC's legal counsel of choice, the rising genius of the Dutch

8 For Napoleon as the Frankenstein of law-givers, see Colley, *The Gun, the Ship & the Pen*, pp. 168–202.

9 Donald A. Petrie, *The Prize Game: Lawful Looting on the High Seas in the Days of Fighting Sail* (New York, 2001), p. 41.

10 Timothy Brook, *Vermeer's Hat: The Seventeenth Century and the Dawn of the Global World* (London, 2009), p. 63.

11 Stephen Neff (ed.), *Hugo Grotius, The Free Sea* (Cambridge, 2012), p. xii.

legal profession, he also had a family interest; Captain van Heemskerck was his cousin.[12]

Grotius' work was undertaken in a wider political context. The conflict with the Iberian maritime powers of Spain and Portugal was not merely commercial. It occurred in the context of the Dutch struggle for independence from the rule of the Spanish throne. The new Dutch republic was still experiencing the internal conflict of working out what sort of a nation it would be. As with Britain, there was tension in the Dutch United Provinces between the rural and commercial worlds, and conflict over the true meaning of the protestant faith. Grotius favoured a version of liberty, stability and virtue, allied with prosperity. This combination was best achieved, he thought, through a closed oligarchy offering a patrician version of a republic.[13] Commercial success of the VOC was part of his vision of the new republic.

In 1604, as instructed, Grotius produced his justification for keeping seized goods in what is now called *De Jure Praedae*.[14] Grotius went beyond a mere justification, however, and attempted a codification of the law of the sea as understood and accepted by European and Mediterranean nations, using Greek, Roman and Christian theological sources to justify his conclusions. Grotius rejected the Portuguese claim to exclusive rights to trade with the East Indies, either by 'discovery', as the islands had already been occupied, or by alleged right devolving from the pope, which he considered to be beyond any legitimate papal authority. He set out a general statement of the rights to freedom of trade, freedom of navigation and freedom of possession, the so-called freedoms of the sea. These rights, he said, were limited by the right to self-defence and self-preservation, but required others to harm no one and to respect property. He also set out two laws of justice, however. They were that evil deeds should be punished and that good deeds should be rewarded. The Portuguese, he contended, had committed evil deeds in the East Indies and deserved to be punished by just acts of war, such as seizing the *Santa Caterina*. This claim was at the least somewhat one-sided. The Dutch had, along with all the other European states who had attempted to seize the spice trade in the East Indies,

12 O. A. Hathaway and S. Shapiro, *The Internationalists and Their Plan to Outlaw War* (London, 2017), p. 8.

13 J. I. Israel, *The Dutch Republic: Its Rise, Greatness, and Fall, 1477–1806* (Oxford, 1998), pp. 421–2.

14 This name, by which the work is generally known, was given to it by its later editor when the text was discovered in the nineteenth century. Grotius called his work *De Rebus Indicis*, or *On the Affairs of the Indies*.

committed terrible atrocities.[15] So far as Grotius was concerned, however, in punishing an evil act van Heemskerck had been undertaking a good deed in seizing the carrack and his good deed deserved to be rewarded. This, he said, was achieved by vesting the goods seized in the VOC, van Heemskerck's employers.

In his original work, Grotius went so far as to assert that even if the war were a private war, it would be just and the prize would be justly acquired by the VOC. This was an awkward position for a company whose existence depended on unfettered global trade, and the original work was not published in Grotius' lifetime. Only his chapter on the freedom of the sea, *Mare Liberum*, was published, although he later supplemented this in *De Jure Belli ac Pacis*, 'On The Law of War and Peace', in 1625. *Mare Liberum*, as the name suggests, set out the case for freedom of trade at sea, and it was that work which heavily influenced the courts of other trading nations. What the nation states tempted to rely on his work took from it was that the power to seize prizes in war was justified, and comes from the state in whose name war is declared, and reprisals and captures are made. Thus, all such prizes seized in war were the property of the captor state. Conveniently, this meant that it was the captor state that was entitled to determine who should take the benefit of the proceeds.

Grotius' views were contested in his own time, especially in England.[16] Having once controlled both sides of what it called the English Channel, the English crown claimed sovereignty of those waters. *Sovereign of the Seas* was more than the name of a ship, it was an expression of a political claim.[17] Indeed, Grotius would happily contest his own ideas if needs be. When it suited the East India Company in England to argue for freedom of the seas in Asia to try and move in on the Dutch monopoly, Grotius was sent to London to persuade James I that the Dutch claim to exclusive dominion of spice islands was justified by their previous investment, and happily did so.[18] Nevertheless, Grotian ideas of 'freedom of the sea' were

15 Giles Milton, *Nathaniel's Nutmeg, or, The True and Incredible Adventures of the Spice Trader Who Changed the Course of History* (London, 2000).

16 Monica Brito Vieira, 'Mare Liberum v Mare Clausum: Grotius, Freitas, and Seldon's Debate on Dominion over the Seas', *Journal of the History of Ideas* 64:3 (2003), 361–77.

17 B. W. D. Redding, 'A Ship "For Which Great Neptune Raves": The Sovereign of the Seas, La Couronne and Seventeenth-Century International Competition over Warship Design', *MM* 104:4 (2018), 402–22.

18 David Howarth, *Adventurers: The Improbable Rise of the East India Company* (Yale, 2023), pp. 323–7; W. S. M. Knight, 'Grotius in England: Problems of War and Peace', *Transactions of the Grotius Society* (1919), vol. 5.

influential in developing the concept of a 'Law of Nations' that could later be prayed in aid to justify English law. A number of commentators adopted and adapted the work of Grotius. Cornelius Van Bynkershoek a century later considered it axiomatic that there was a right to confiscate or destroy all property belonging to an enemy wherever found and that the right to destroy enemy personnel included the right to enslave.[19] The Swiss commentator Emer de Vattel, writing during the Seven Years' War, considered that the right should only be exercised for the purposes of war.[20] Vattel and others even called their works 'The Law of Nations', or some variant thereof. The full title of Vattel's work, however, reveals that, in common with others like it, it was not a statement of extant law, but an attempt to find such a law by the application of supposed laws of nature to international trade.[21] The short title, often used on its own, can be misleading.[22] The concepts of 'international law' that emerged from the commentaries were simply useful concepts that could be adopted where it suited the purposes of an individual state to do so. Care needs to be taken, therefore, when referring to 'international law' or the 'law of nations' in the eighteenth-century as if they were established legal systems in their own right.

In the 1930s the American academic Carl J. Kulsrud attempted to disentangle the mass of treaties and opinions said to amount to a body of law on the rights of neutrals during wars at sea before 1780. It is an impressive work, with a detailed study of numerous treaty provisions. Supported by the American Carnegie Endowment for International Peace, copies were sent to English university libraries to encourage respect for neutral rights at sea in the impending war. Karlsrud's description of the status of this body of 'law' is perceptive:

> ... the European society of nations, composed as it was of a number of independent states whose existence was contingent upon the fostering of a spirit of self-glorification in the several peoples, and upon the adherence of the several governments to a policy of self-interest, was without a universally recognised system of rules to govern the conduct of its sovereign members toward each other, and without an

[19] Cornelius Van Bynkershoek, *Quaest. Juris Publici, L. i. c 3.*; Corbett and Lambert, *21st Century Corbett*, p. 74.

[20] Corbett and Lambert, *21st Century Corbett*, p. 74.

[21] Emer de Vattel, *The Law of Nations; or the Principles of the Law of Nature: Applied to the Conduct and Affairs of Nations and Sovereigns.*

[22] See also *The Law of Nature and Nations: or, A General System of the most Important Principles of Morality, Jurisprudence, and Politics*, 1672, written in Latin by Baron Samuel Von Pufendorf, Counsellor of State to His Swedish Majesty, and the King of Prussia, translated into English, 1703, Book 8, Chapter 6, s. 8, p. 842, 'of the right of war'.

> authority or tribunal to compose individual dissensions when they occurred. A confusion in international affairs, a clash of interests among the dynastic states, with a resort to arms as the final arbiter, were inevitable consequences of the existing conditions.[23]

Mare Liberum placed Grotius in the pantheon of law-givers. His original work, however, only came into the public domain when his papers were auctioned in The Hague in 1864 and were subsequently transcribed and published. Further research since then has revealed more of the context and the background to the work Grotius produced for the VOC.[24] Therefore it is only recently that greater emphasis has been given to the role Grotius had as legal counsel for a private company, the VOC. As a result of the interest Grotius had in justifying private as well as public war, the attention that has been given to him in public international law is regretted by some.[25] Be that as it may, the fact is that attention was given to Grotius in the eighteenth century, or to the version of Grotius that was then understood, and that is reflected in the judgments of the Georgian Admiralty Court. Although we may have a better understanding now as to the true origins of Grotius' work than did the eighteenth-century courts, it matters little in relation to their conclusions. Grotius' perceived views were cited because they were thought to justify the courts' conclusions. As persuasive as Grotius might have been, the English courts did not reach their conclusions because they were persuaded by Grotius; they cited him when he could be used to support their desired conclusions.

Blackstone and Scott

William Blackstone was a lecturer in English law at Oxford when the future Admiralty judge William Scott arrived there in 1761, four years before the first volume of Blackstone's *Commentaries on the Laws of England* was published. Also lecturing at Oxford during Scott's time there was Thomas

23 Kulsrud, *Maritime Neutrality*, p. 107.

24 Martine Julia van Ittersum, 'Hugo Grotius in Context: Van Heemskerk's Capture of the "Santa Caterina" and Its Justification in "De Jure Pradae" (1604–1606)', *Asian Journal of Social Science* 31:3 (2003), 511–48; Peter Borschberg, 'The Seizure of the Sta. Catarina Revisited: The Portuguese Empire in Asia, VOC Politica and the Origins of the Dutch-Johor Alliance (1602–c.1616)', *Journal of Southeast Asian Studies* 33:1 (2002), 31–62.

25 M. Koskenniemi, W. Rech and M. Jiménez Fonseca, *International Law and Empire: Historical Explorations* (Oxford, 2017), p. 10.

Bever, a fellow of All Souls, a doctor of civil law and a member of the body to which Admiralty advocates belonged at the time, known as Doctors' Commons. The manuscripts of Bever's notes of Blackstone's lectures and of his own lectures on jurisprudence and the civil law survive at All Souls.[26] They include the history of Roman law and the classical 'natural law' school of Grotius and those who followed in his wake. As Scott's modern biographer has put it: 'We can probably safely assume that Scott faithfully attended the entire course of more than thirty mind-numbing lectures.'[27] Bever, like Blackstone, introduced his students to the law of nations as it was understood in the eighteenth century, deriving 'from the same law of nature which God in the act of creation had engraved in the minds and hearts of men.'[28] According to this view the relations between 'civilised,' i.e. Christian, nations must be regulated by fixed rules derived from natural reason and which being confirmed 'upon the daily occurrences of the World and being approved by frequent experience, are now become by general consent and acquiescence, the fixed rules for regulating the mutual intercourse between the several Nations of the Universe.'[29] Scott, who joined Doctors' Commons as an Admiralty Court advocate in 1779 but remained as Camden Reader in Ancient History at Oxford for 20 years, took on board such ideas, but used them pragmatically.

In 1799, for example, shortly after he had been appointed as the Admiralty judge, Scott had to determine whether a British ship had been validly sold as a prize to new owners so that they acquired title to the ship against the original British owners.[30] A British ship, *The Favourite*, had been captured by French privateers who sailed her into Bergen, a neutral port in Norway. There she had been condemned by the French Consul and sold at auction, but without a formal sentence of condemnation. The circumstances of the sale were suspicious. Although supposedly sold to a neutral Danish merchant, she was bought by the same general agent who had put her up for sale acting for the French, and there were no other bids. The dubious nature of the transaction was compounded by evidence that the ship was then loaded and sent to sea with written instructions to sail to St Maartens, the Dutch half of a Caribbean island shared with France, and effectively under French control since the invasion of the Netherlands by revolutionary France, but with oral instructions to try and put into the

26 All Souls Library, Oxford, MS 300 and 109 respectively.

27 Bourguignon, *Sir William Scott, Lord Stowell* (Cambridge, 2004), p. 36.

28 Ibid., p. 36.

29 Thomas Bever, *A Course of Lectures on the Civil Law*, Lecture 31, All Souls Library, Oxford, MS 109c, pp. 27–8.

30 The Flad Oyen (Martenson) (1799) 1 Rob. 135.

blockaded French port of Le Havre. Although a formal sentence of condemnation was officially required by British law, there was evidence that the sale was in accordance with the practice carried out by a number of countries, including on occasion the British. It was argued that the general practice was sufficient for the court to recognise the sale as in accordance with the law of nations. The dubious nature of the transaction did not make the submission an attractive one. Scott's view of the law of nations could in this case be prayed in aid of a result that reflected the merits of the case. Scott considered that 'a habit of irregularity' was insufficient to establish a practice 'conformable to the usage and practice of nations'. Scott cited the law of nations to dismiss it as an argument against his decision on the merits, not because he was bound by an extraneous body of law. Scott could give effect to the ideas in forming the English law as and when he saw fit, but it was a British view of the law of nations.

In theory, international law would be the same whether the court administering it was a court of the belligerent power or that of the person aggrieved, and equally binding on both parties to the litigation. The clearest statement of this ideal position appears in another judgment of Sir William Scott in 1799.[31] The *Maria* was part of a fleet of Swedish merchant ships, neutrals in the war between Britain and France, that had sailed for ports in France, Portugal and the Mediterranean under convoy by a Swedish frigate. Their cargoes included hemp, iron, pitch and tar; naval supplies, which if bound for an enemy port in France would be contraband goods liable to seizure. In the English Channel the fleet was intercepted by a British squadron under Commodore Lawford. Having sent an officer on board the Swedish frigate and ascertained the cargoes in the convoy, Lawford sent a message to the Admiralty for instructions and meanwhile kept the convoy in view. The Admiralty's orders when they arrived were to detain the merchant ships and take them into the nearest English port. Captains Sir Charles Lindsay and Henry Raper were sent on board the Swedish frigate to explain the Admiralty orders, but in response the Swedish officer showed them his instructions, which were to repel by force any attempt to board the convoy, and declared that he would defend them to the last. To back up his declaration, the Swedish crew were stood to quarters, with matches lighted, ready for battle. In response the British squadron was sent to quarters and readied for battle. It had overwhelming force compared with the single Swedish frigate guarding a disparate fleet of merchantmen but wanted to exercise caution over how it used that force.

[31] The Maria, Paulsen master (1799) 1 Rob. 340, 350.

Night then intervened, during which Lawford, on his larger, 50-gun flagship *HMS Romney* with her lower guns run out and every man at his quarters, watched the Swedish frigate's 'many movements', keeping her to windward and away from the convoy. Meanwhile, the rest of the squadron took possession of most of the Swedish fleet. In the morning the Swedish frigate officer, seeing what had happened, sent an armed boat to one of the seized merchantmen and took the British officer from her by force, and sent an officer to Lawford on *Romney* to complain that he had taken advantage of the night to get possession of the convoy unobserved by its escort, declaring that had he been aware he would have defended it to the last. In reality there was little he could do in the face of Lawford's overwhelming force, so he agreed to sail with the convoy, now under British control, to Margate Roads, and returned the British officer who had been seized. In Margate Roads the Swedish officer lamented that he had not exchanged broadsides, that he did not consider his convoy as detained and would resist any further attempt to take possession of it. His protestations were, however, all in vain. The British had seized his convoy and there was nothing he could do about it. His complaints merely demonstrated a hostile intent in the face of a demand to submit to a search of the convoy, which added to the justification for seizing the ships rather than the opposite.

For much of the eighteenth century commentators on the law of nations from neutral countries had been suggesting that if neutral powers provided a naval escort for their convoys, then belligerents should recognise that protection and accept the legality of the ships and cargoes protected by the sovereignty of the neutral state. When the case of The Maria came before the Admiralty Court the arguments centred on whether the law of nations recognised the protection of neutrals by a convoy, or whether belligerents retained the right to search for contraband.

The right of protection under convoy had been supported by neutral European states taking trading advantage of that status when major powers were at war. English opinion, as one of the major powers who relied on naval power over trade at sea as an instrument of war, was against respecting the protection of ships under convoy and giving up the right to search. Indeed it was the temerity of the suggestion that the right to search should be curtailed by the mere promises of neutral states about their convoys that led Christopher Robinson, the Admiralty lawyer and future Admiralty judge in whose reports we read of Scott's judgment in The Maria, into print in 1801 to reassert the right of prize-taking and search.[32] The law report of The Maria contains a series of footnotes about the historic right to search

[32] Robinson, *Collectanea Maritima*.

that were reflected in Robinson's later work, but as Robinson was a follower of Scott's they represent Scott's thinking whether they originated with Scott or his amanuensis. Scott applied his mind to the right to search in The Maria. Having reminded himself that his role was not 'to deliver occasional and shifting opinions to serve present purposes of particular national interest, but to administer with indifference that justice which the law of nations holds out without distinction to independent states', the part of the judgment most quoted afterwards, Scott then went on, however, to outline what he described as 'a special consideration':

> the nature of the present war does give this country the rights of war, relatively to neutral states, in as large a measure as they have been regularly and legally exercised, at any period of modern and civilized times. Whether I estimate the nature of the war justly I leave to the judgment of Europe, when I declare that I consider this is a war in which neutral states themselves have an interest much more direct and substantial than they have in the ordinary, limited, and private quarrels, if I may so call them, of Great Britain and its great public enemy.[33]

Thus, Scott was declaring, this was no ordinary war, but a fight for the future civilisation of Europe and if the French were not defeated then neutrals such as Sweden would be among the first to suffer. For that reason, so Scott thought, it was important to uphold the long existing right to search neutral shipping on the high seas. Scott described this as a special consideration in favour of Britain. Though he said that he would allow Sweden the same consideration in the same or similar circumstances, the fact was that Sweden was never going to undertake the role of world policeman that Britain was exercising at the end of the eighteenth century. Scott went on to dismiss the arguments for limiting the right to search and held that the ships resisting the right to search had been lawfully seized.

The economic war increased after the Peace of Amiens, when war resumed against Napoleon. This brought conflict with neutrals, including the USA, that the Admiralty Court had to deal with. In 1807 Scott heard the case of the *Recovery*, an American ship which had been seized with her cargo. Her cargo had originally been loaded in India under an exemption from the British ban on such trade under the Navigation Act. The exemption permitted such trade so long as the cargo was unloaded at a US port. The *Recovery* had sailed to the US, but in breach of the Navigation Act had not unloaded her cargo, sailing instead for Europe. An action by the American owners of the cargo was resisted on the ground that the Admiralty

[33] The Maria, Paulsen master (1799) 1 Rob. 340, 350.

Court should not entertain the claim as the owners were in breach of the Navigation Act. The Admiralty Court did not have jurisdiction over the breach of the Navigation Act, but it had to consider whether any such breach affected the jurisdiction of the Admiralty Court over the cargo that had been seized. Scott rejected the argument that he should not restore the goods as neutral goods, leaving it to the proper court to take any action that was considered appropriate over the breach of the Navigation Act. Whilst he may have considered that the objection would have force in the case of a British subject who had disregarded the law of his own country, in the case of a foreigner, who could be dealt with in the proper court rather than the Admiralty Court, he said:

> It has to be recollected that this is a court of the Law of Nations, though sitting here under the authority of the King of Great Britain. It belongs to other nations as well as to our own, and, what foreigners have a right to demand from it is administration of the Law of Nations simply, and exclusively of the introduction of principles borrowed from our own municipal jurisprudence, to which, it is well known, they have at all times expressed no inconsiderable repugnance.[34]

On the face of it this is once again a strong expression of the independence of the Admiralty Court from municipal interference. The case could easily have been decided the other way, but Scott clearly did not want the Admiralty Court in 1807 to trespass on the tricky issue of neutrality of American ships and the Navigation Act, to which the Americans had 'at all times expressed no inconsiderable repugnance'. By 1807 the US was already objecting to what it saw as British assaults on the rights of neutrals. The former president, John Adams, in retirement at Quincey, summarised the US debate about its relationship with Britain in 1807: 'War? or no War? That is the question.'[35] Although Britain considered that the US was benefiting at the expense of Britain, who by her considerable sacrifices was saving the world from Bonaparte, she did not want to have to deal with another war at that stage. No tea was to be spilt in Boston harbour in 1807 on Scott's account. Although war with the US would eventually come in 1812, it was not to be encouraged by the Admiralty Court in 1807.

By 1811, however, the economic war had reached a new level. Just as Scott had been considering the case of the *Recovery*, Napoleon began his attempt to enforce his Continental System through the Berlin and Milan decrees,

[34] The Recovery (1807) 6 Rob. 348, 349.

[35] Letter, John Adams to Benjamin Rush, 1 September 1807, Founders online, National Archives, http://founders.archives.gov/documents/Adams/99-02-5211.

purporting to place the whole of the continent under blockade from British ships. Tensions between Britain and America also rose to a new level with the clash at sea between *USS Chesapeake* and *HMS Leopard*, an indication of the war that would eventually come in 1812.[36] Britain responded to Napoleon's Continental System with reciprocal orders-in-council. In November 1810 the American ship *Fox* was captured by the Royal Navy on a voyage from Boston to Cherbourg as a result of an order-in-council of 26 April 1809. Once again, the British sentiment was that while they fought to protect the world, neutrals such as the Americans were taking advantage of the British sacrifices to improve their own trading position. The validity of the order-in-council was challenged when the seizure of the *Fox* came before Scott in the Admiralty Court in 1811.[37] Britain's interest had traditionally been to support the international view that a valid blockade must be enforced by ships at sea, rather than mere paper declaration. As the major naval power, she had the ability to impose such blockades, where others did not. Scott held that although the order-in-council would not have complied with the generally accepted, i.e. British, view of the law of nations as to a valid blockade had it been made without provocation, its retaliatory nature meant that it was not repugnant to the law of nations. Understandably, he was referred to his own comments in The Maria about the duty of the prize court in relation to the law of nations. In that case there had been no express order-in-council:

> In the case of the Swedish convoy, which has been alluded to, no order or instruction whatever was issued, and the Court therefore was left to find its own way to that legal conclusion which its judgment of the principles of law led it to adopt.[38]

Although Scott had held that there was no conflict between the order-in-council and the law of nations, he nevertheless sought to clarify his views on the role of the prize court:

> this Court is bound to administer the Law of Nations to the subjects of other countries in the different relations in which they may be placed towards this country and its government. This is what other countries have a right to demand for their subjects, and to complain if they receive it not. This is its unwritten law evidenced in the course of its decisions, and collected from the common usage of civilized states.

36 Lambert, *The Challenge*, pp. 7–46.

37 The Fox [1811] Edw. 311.

38 The Fox [1811] Edw. 311, 315.

So far, so good, and following the approach outlined in The Maria, but then he turned to the effect of orders-in-council:

> [The] two propositions, that the Court is bound to administer the Law of Nations, and that it is bound to enforce the King's Orders in Council, are not at all inconsistent with each other; because these Orders and Instructions are presumed to conform themselves, under the given circumstances, to the principles of its unwritten law. They are either directory applications of those principles to the cases indicated in them – cases which, with all the facts and circumstances belonging to them, and which constitute their legal character, could be but imperfectly known to the Court itself; or they are positive Regulations consistent with those principles, applying to matters which require more exact and definite rules than those general principles are capable of furnishing.

So where did that leave the court in any particular case? In this case Scott concluded that:

> The constitution of this Court, relatively to the legislative power of the King in Council, is analogous to that of the Courts of Common Law relatively to that of the Parliament of this kingdom. Those Courts have their own unwritten law, the approved principles of natural reason and justice – they have likewise the written or statute law of Acts of Parliament, which are directory applications of the same principles to particular subjects, or positive regulations consistent with them, upon matters which would remain too much at large if they were left to the imperfect information which the courts could extract from mere general speculations.[39]

This could be seen as a very naïve view of the relationship between the courts and the executive, but Scott was not a naïve judge. There was, is, and always will be, a tension between the courts and the executive. That tension has given rise to the whole body of law that we now call Judicial Review. The task of the courts is to decide when, and with what tools, to push back against the legislature in pursuit of justice. Scott clearly took the view that the war was a fight for the survival of civilisation, and he was not alone in that view. It was not the role of the court to decide how that war should be fought. The king-in-council was in the best position to make that assessment and the court should assist. The law of nations was useful where it gave a reason to find as the court wished to find, as in The Maria, but was

[39] Ibid.

of less significance where it was the basis of a submission that the court did not want to accept, as in The Fox.

To some, however, there was a clear conflict between the views that Scott had expressed in the two cases, 12 years, mainly years of war, apart. That conflict came before the courts in The Zamora in 1916.[40] The dispute in The Zamora arose out of the tension between the courts and the executive arm of government attempting to govern by order-in-council under the pressures of the First World War. Ships captured as prizes had to be brought into port to be condemned as such by the Admiralty Court before they could be considered as legitimate prizes to be disposed of by the Crown. In the meantime, the duty on the court was to preserve ships and their goods unless they needed to be sold to preserve their value from deterioration, in which case it preserved the proceeds of sale for whoever was found to be entitled. In response to the exigencies of war the British government introduced a power to requisition goods within its territory for the war effort. By prize court rules made by order-in-council under the Prize Court Act 1894, which gave power to make rules as to the procedure and practice of the prize courts, the king-in-council created rules to govern the workings of the prize courts. Order 24 of the rules provided that 'where it is made to appear to the judge on the application of a proper officer of the Crown that it is desired to requisition, on behalf of His Majesty, a ship in respect of which no final decree of condemnation has been made, he shall order that the ship be appraised, and upon an undertaking being given ... the ship shall be released and delivered to the Crown.' That provision was all well and good where the ship was already within the jurisdiction, and therefore liable to be requisitioned. What was the position, however, where the ship could not have been requisitioned out of the jurisdiction at sea, and was only brought within the jurisdiction to be assessed by the court as to whether she should be condemned as prize or not? Could she be requisitioned when no determination had yet taken place, and therefore it had not been determined whether she had been brought within the jurisdiction lawfully or not?

On 8 April 1915 the *Zamora*, a neutral Swedish steamship, was bound from New York to Stockholm with a cargo of grain and copper. She had reached a point between the Faroes and the Shetland Isles when she was intercepted by the Royal Navy. At that point, as a neutral ship on the high seas, she could not have been requisitioned by the British. Suspicious of her real intentions, the Royal Navy escorted her first into the Orkney Isles and then to Barrow-in-Furness, where she was seized as prize and handed over

[40] The Zamora [1916] 2 AC 77.

into the custody of the Admiralty Marshall and the Prize Court. Whether the ship or the cargo were prize or not depended on whether the ship had a concealed or ulterior destination in an enemy country (i.e. Germany), or whether the copper (as potential contraband of war if destined for an enemy) was destined for the enemy, by way of transhipment or otherwise. If that had not yet been established, then how should the courts deal with a claim by a neutral that might have serious international consequences.

The Zamora is generally remembered by the first half of the first sentence in the head note to the case in the main, Appeal Cases, law report, even though the head note is no part of the judgment in the case. The head note began: 'The Crown has no power by Order in Council to prescribe or alter the law which Prize Courts have to administer ...' This has been taken as a statement that the law of nations had supremacy over municipal law before the prize courts. Holdsworth in his 1942 article for the *Minnesota Law Review* construed the judgment in The Zamora in this way.[41] He surmised that the decision, if correct, meant that the prize court 'is not bound by an Order-in-Council which purports to alter a rule of international law, whether or not it is a rule of international law which has been accepted by the common law'. In his view, however, the decision was doubtful in law and politically inexpedient. Holdsworth's disdain for the decision in The Zamora would have been justified had his description of the decision been correct. The decision created excitement in the newspapers of 1916 in the same way that the decisions of the High Court and the Supreme Court on Gina Miller's challenge to the triggering of Article 50 to start the UK's withdrawal from the EU without parliamentary authority did a century later in 2016.[42] Much of it was, however, equally misconceived. As the *Harvard Law Review* of 1916 pointed out, the decision in The Zamora did not hold that the rule that had been included in the Prize Court Rules was invalid as repugnant to the law of nations or because of any 'dominant quality of the law of nations'. It was invalid because the rule was made without authority.[43] The king-in-council had authority under the Prize Court Act 1894 to make rules as to the procedure and practice of the prize courts, but that did not give authority to dictate matters of substantive law that the court had to decide.

Those on the receiving end of British policy and Scott's judgments could be less than charitable about them. A later Lord Chancellor summarised

41 William S. Holdsworth, 'The Relation of English Law to International Law', *Minnesota Law Review* 26:2 (1942), 141–52, pp. 151–2.

42 R (Miller and Dos Santos) v Sec. of State for Exiting the EU [2017] UKSC 5, 'Enemies of the People', *Daily Mail*, 4 November 2016.

43 'The Case of The Zamora', *Harvard Law Review* 30:1 (November 1916), 66–8.

their view of the traditional British stance as 'a Machiavellian policy'. He was arguing unsuccessfully in the build-up to the Great War of 1914–18 in favour of a Liberal government's attempt at giving up Britain's traditional right to take prizes. In doing so he contended that 'from the time of Lord Stowell we have stored up a quiver full of legal quibbles and precedents by which we can recover whatever we profess to concede' on matters of capture at sea.[44]

In the eighteenth century the courts reflected the British stance of at least purporting to uphold international law, even if it was their version of international law that they were upholding. In making use of concepts of international law Scott looked to them as a source for justifying municipal law when it suited. He always maintained that he was respecting what he called the law of nations, but it was his own notion of what that law was, or ought to be, and he was not automatically incorporating it into English law. Scott's robust dicta on the topic sometimes suggested a different view, but his comments need to be seen in context in order to understand his approach.

Scott was not alone in giving the impression that English courts applied international law as part of English law. In Lindo v Rodney, for example, Lord Mansfield considered the nature of the prize jurisdiction in a claim against Admiral Rodney for goods seized by him in 1781 on the Caribbean island of St Eustatius. Lord Mansfield is commonly regarded as a founder of modern commercial law, enfolding 'into the ancient common law of England the customs and usages of the merchants and industrialists'.[45] Applying this process he declared that:

> By the law of nations, and treaties, every nation is answerable to the other for all injuries done, by sea or land, or in fresh waters, or in port. Mutual convenience, eternal principles of justice, the wisest regulations of policy, and the consent of nations, have established a system of procedure, a code of law, and a court for the trial of prize. Every country sues in these courts of the others, which are all governed by one and the same law, equally known to each.[46]

On its face this appears to be a clear representation that there existed an established code of law that governed the courts of all nations. In truth, however, Mansfield was simply acknowledging that prize disputes inevitably ended up in the courts of the captors and that by custom and usage

44 Earl Loreburn, *Capture at Sea* (London, 1913) p. 155.

45 Poser, *Lord Mansfield*, p. 4.

46 Lindo v Rodney (1781) 2 Doug. 613, 615.

there were mutual interests in affording access to those courts. He was also recognising that the English courts had an interest in promoting their rules and procedures as fair to all in order to gain recognition of English law as the preferred law of international trade, especially with the neutral merchants whose governments Britain did not wish to antagonise.

The international nature of prizes meant that the English courts would even recognise the prize judgments of enemy courts as conclusive in transferring title.[47] It could thus appear that the English courts were enforcing the orders of enemy courts as a result of some international rule applicable even in war. In fact, however, they were not enforcing the orders of foreign courts but were determining issues of title before their own courts as they saw fit in accordance with English municipal law. The municipal law that they were applying was subject to the control of Parliament, not international law. Thus, in 1808, as economic warfare with Napoleon intensified, Parliament acted to change English law to reduce the market for ships taken by the French as prizes. The Prize Act 1808 provided that British ships captured by the enemy, but which afterwards became the property of British subjects again, would no longer be entitled to the privileges of British ships.[48] The aim was to reduce the value and the market for captured British ships, and so remove the incentive to capture them. Although French privateers did not disappear completely, the financial incentive to equip a privateer was reduced, so reducing the main French weapon against British trade through financial pressure. Thus, although the English courts might recognise title to ships obtained through sales under the authority of foreign courts, that did not mean that they were doing so under a discrete body of international law. They did so under, and subject to the control of, English municipal law. As this change demonstrates, Britain applied its own law as it chose and in its own interests.

Mansfield's reference to 'the law of nations, and treaties' reveals the problem. A network of treaties did not create a body of international law that existed apart from those treaty provisions. If there existed a body of international law apart from the treaties then the treaties would have been unnecessary, or exceptions to the rule rather than proof of it. Although treaties may have sought to justify their provisions by reference to the law of nations, no attempt was made internationally to define the supposed law, or to find a common formula for the conflicting principles of various

[47] Oddy v Bovill (1802) 2 East 473; Baring v The Royal Exchange Assurance Co. (1804) 5 East 99; Bolton v Gladstone (1804) 5 East 155.

[48] Geo.3 c.70.

treaties.[49] More accurately, 'widespread conventions of prize and credit often stood in for the law of nations'.[50] Further, compliance with any principles established by treaty lasted only until a party became involved in war.[51] Britain's naval policy indicated her true indifference to questions of supposed international law. Britain's interest in the enforcement of a claimed 'international' law through its naval policy was limited to cases where to do so served to advance Britain's immediate commercial interests, an approach that the courts were only too ready to support.[52] Writing in 1801, the Admiralty Court lawyer Dr Christopher Robinson, amanuensis of the great Admiralty judge Sir William Scott and himself a future Admiralty Court judge, confided that 'the great defect' of the 'public law of nations' was 'the want of some coercive authority to compel the performance of the most acknowledged duties'.[53]

The Rise of International Law in the Nineteenth Century

What we now call Public International Law, the law of states and their relationships with each other, became an academic legal subject during the nineteenth century.[54] Sir Travers Twiss QC, the compiler of the Black Book of Admiralty who we met in Chapter 1, taught international law at King's College London before becoming Regius Professor of Civil Law in Oxford in 1855, but Oxford only created its first chair in International Law in 1859, Cambridge in 1866.[55] Study of 'Natural Law' and 'The Law of Nations' moved away from philosophy towards the study of law, and the Victorians tried to look to eighteenth-century decisions as a basis for asserting that international law had a long history and a direct role before the English courts.

The issue of how English law should embrace international law came to a head in 1876 in a decision of 13 judges sitting in the court of Crown Cases reserved. The German captain of *The Franconia* was charged with

49 Kulsrud, *Maritime Neutrality*, p. 315.
50 L. Benton and L. Ford, *Rage for Order* (Cambridge, Mass., 2016), p. 6.
51 Kulsrud, *Maritime Neutrality*, p. 336–7.
52 Ibid., p. 316.
53 Robinson, *Collectanea Maritima*, p. ii.
54 For attempts by academic jurists to 'codify' international law, see Frei, *Great Britain, International Law, Evolution of Maritime Thought*, pp. 88–110.
55 Arthur Nussbaum, *A Concise History of the Law of Nations* (New York, 1947), p. 237; S. A. Keefer, *International Law and Britain's Quest for Naval Security: International Law and Arms Control, 1898–1914* (Basingstoke, 2016), p. 63.

manslaughter of a passenger after negligently running down *The Strathclyde* and causing a fatal collision within the three-mile territorial limit. The question that arose was whether the English court had jurisdiction to try him on the basis that the English courts would recognise the rule of international law that was 'established as solidly as any proposition of international law can be' that the sea within the limit was for all purposes part of the territory to which it was adjacent.[56] By a majority of seven against six they concluded that rules of international law did not apply automatically as part of English law.[57] It was Parliament that had the power to claim jurisdiction over territorial waters, which it did in the Territorial Waters Jurisdiction Act 1878.

By 1913 Lord Loreburn, the active advocate for doomed attempts to use international law to abolish capture at sea, still questioned whether the phrase 'international law' was 'a proper appellation for a mass of customs, precedents and conventions, a great part of which are by no means uniform and some of which are the subject of vehement dispute'.[58] He identified the issue of a lack of a legislature: 'There is no Parliament of nations in which a predominant opinion may be imposed upon the minority.'

Focused on solving the issue that arose in each particular case, English courts treated the law of nations as a potential source of municipal law where they wished to but were not bound by some external international law as such. They were neither blind to the policies of the British government, nor required to frustrate such policies by rigid application of some alien law. As the retired law lord, Patrick Devlin, put it in his 1968 Rede Lecture at Cambridge University:

> One great difficulty in the way of establishing a common law of the seas lay in the diversity of attitudes adopted by the prize courts of different nations. Prize law was accepted as international law, that is to say, it was based on treaties, customs or practices which were (or which in the opinion of the prize court hearing the case ought to be) adopted by all maritime nations. But it is asking a great deal of even the most conscientious judicial mind to invite it to condemn as illegal the measures which its government is taking for the prosecution of a war in which the nation's life is at stake. It is not necessary to suppose that on such an issue a conflict of duty arises in the judge's mind; it

[56] The three-mile limit was notionally based on the distance that a cannonball could be fired so as to exercise control over the seas visible from land.

[57] R v Keyn (1876) 1 Ex. Div. 63.

[58] Earl Loreburn, *Capture at Sea*, p. 15.

> is simply that he is predisposed to find the same sort of reasons for justifying the measure as his government has found.[59]

That concepts of international law, or a law of nations, have played a role in both international affairs and in the formation of municipal law of states is beyond dispute. The contentious issue is what the nature of that role has been. It is easy for any analysis to be affected by the ambiguities in the historical origins that are relied on. Even the Roman law of Justinian could be viewed in differing ways. For some it was a natural law based on instinct or reason, for others it was a kind of positive law in force among all civilised nations. English courts in the eighteenth century enjoyed using the ambiguity of the law of nations to suit their judgments when it suited them, and nineteenth-century jurists exploited them in an effort to create a modern idea of 'international law', but the English courts applied the laws that they decided upon as municipal, English law. So a proposal to create an International Prize Court was always going to ruffle feathers.

An International Prize Court?

In the build-up to the First World War there was a doomed attempt to set up an International Prize Court, making English prize courts subject to a right of appeal to an International Prize Court applying international law. Far from it being a proposal for a court to apply an established code of international law, however, it was a proposal to establish a court because of, or despite, the absence of such a code.

The seizure of prizes had caused international problems for Britain both in the Boer Wars in South Africa, when Britain was a belligerent with overwhelming naval strength, and in the Russo-Japanese War, when Britain was a neutral.[60] In 1907 the 2nd Hague Conference, which had been called by the US in 1904 to discuss the rules of war before the outbreak of actual war between Russia and Japan, resumed its work. Article 12 of the 1907 treaty provided for the establishment of an International Prize Court that would sit automatically in the event of war to hear appeals from, or in some cases in lieu of, national courts. The court was to have 15 judges. Great Britain, whose empire owned half the mercantile marine of the world, would be a

59 Lord Devlin, *The House of Lords and the Naval Prize Bill 1911* (Cambridge, 1968), p. 4.

60 Alan Anderson, 'The Laws of War and Naval Strategy in Great Britain and the United States 1899–1909 (unpubl. PhD thesis, King's College London, 2016), p. 267; Frei, *Great Britain, International Law, Evolution of Maritime Thought*, p. 203; Abbenhuis, *An Age of Neutrals*, pp. 194–209.

permanent member through its appointed judge, along with those of seven other great naval powers. The remaining seven judges would be drawn in turns from countries with either no or very little naval presence, but all would have the same voting rights in the verdict.

As an additional response to the Russo-Japanese War, the British Foreign Secretary in the Liberal government, Sir Edward Grey, called a conference of naval powers to effect a codification of the laws of naval war. The 1909 London Declaration attempted to codify the concepts of blockade and contraband in prize captures. The British, who had not fought a major naval war for nearly a century, achieved a tightening of its traditional policy of choice, the close blockade. Britain had argued unsuccessfully at the Hague for the abolition of the right to seize contraband but had more success in the Declaration of London. The British government was aware that it might soon face a naval war against Germany but thought that success would lie in securing supplies for herself rather than in seeking to cut off supplies from other, more self-sufficient, nations which had land as well as sea supply lines. Against this background 'in exchange for what she considered a satisfactory statement of the law on blockade she agreed to, and indeed advocated, severe restrictions on seizure in the law of contraband.'[61] The effect was to take away the unrestricted right that Britain had previously enjoyed to determine what counted as contraband.

Both the idea of an International Prize Court and the provisions of the Declaration of London proved controversial in Britain. Some pressed acceptance of their terms as an act of international humanity, others on pragmatic grounds contended that Britain, with the world's greatest merchant fleet, had more to gain than to lose from limiting the right to capture.[62] Sir Robert Reid, shortly before becoming Lord Chancellor as the ennobled Lord Loreburn, wrote to *The Times* in 1905 advocating the abolition of capture at sea, but accepted that 'no operation of war inflicts less suffering than the capture of unarmed vessels at sea.'[63] Cited against him by Sir Julian Corbett in his 1907 rebuttal of Loreburn's argument,[64] Loreburn omitted the concession when he later published his newspaper correspondence in the form of a book.[65]

Many regarded the reforms as giving away Britain's maritime supremacy. They included the Imperial Maritime League,[66] Admiral Lord Charles

61 Lord Devlin, *The House of Lords and the Naval Prize Bill 1911*, p. 6.

62 Earl Loreburn, *Capture at Sea*, p. 16.

63 Sir Robert Reid, 'The Capture of Private Property at Sea', *The Times*, 14 October 1905.

64 Corbett and Lambert, *21st Century Corbett*, p. 77.

65 Earl Loreburn, *Capture at Sea*.

66 Lord Devlin, *The House of Lords and the Naval Prize Bill 1911*, p. 7.

Beresford,[67] Lord Ellenborough, whose ancestor as Lord Chief Justice had sat in judgment of Nelson's prize matters during the Napoleonic Wars,[68] and the former Lord Chancellor, the Earl of Halsbury.[69] The President of the Steamowners' Association spoke in favour of ratification of the Declaration of London in the Port of Liverpool, but the President of the Association of Chambers of Commerce reported that the majority of its members were opposed.[70] Many tangled explanations for the British attitude to the Declaration have been advanced, including the notion that the old concepts of close blockade were no longer relevant with the advent of torpedoes and submarines.[71] What is not in doubt, however, is that the Declaration was controversial.

Despite considerable opposition to implementation of the International Prize Court and the Declaration of London, the Liberal government whipped the Naval Prize Bill through the House of Commons to implement them in English law. Against an available majority of 120, it achieved only majorities of 70 on the second reading and 47 on the third.[72] Within a week, however, the Bill had been defeated in the House of Lords, despite the government's attempts earlier in the year to bring the House of Lords to heel with the Parliament Act 1911. The House of Lords voted to postpone consideration of the Bill for three months, and it never came back. It has become fashionable to explain the defeat as the House of Lords seizing 'an opportunity for revenge' for successive humiliations at the hands of the Liberal government.[73] As can be seen, however, the Bill was already struggling in the Commons and with a naval race with Germany looming, the argument was being lost. The International Prize Court never materialised, and the Declaration of London was never ratified.

When war came in 1914 both the British and the Germans breached the Declaration, even though the Royal Navy had incorporated the substance of the Declaration in its 'Handbook for Boarding Officers and Prize Officers in War Time' at the outbreak of war.[74] The US objected to the breaches, but in the absence of an International Prize Court, it was the attitude of Germany that finally provoked the US to take up arms for the allies. Claims that the House of Lords had saved Britain from defeat in the First World

67 Quoted by Earl Beauchamp, Hansard, HL Debate 12 December 1911, vol. 10, c 809.

68 Hansard, HL Debate 12 December 1911, vol. 10, cc 809–95.

69 Ibid.

70 Earl Brassey, Hansard, HL Debate 12 December 1911, vol. 10, cc 809–95.

71 Anderson, 'The Laws of War and Naval Strategy', pp. 253–63.

72 Marquess of Lansdowne, Hansard, HL Debate 12 December 1911, vol. 10, cc 809–95.

73 Rodger, *The Price of Victory*, p. 185.

74 Anderson, 'The Laws of War and Naval Strategy', p. 260.

War by opposing the Bill were used as evidence to support the revising role of the House in the 1960s.[75]

Had the English prize court really been a purveyor of a law of nations independent of municipal law then there could have been very little objection to an appeal to an international court applying those self-same settled and ascertainable principles of international law. That, however, was far from the position. The drive for reform had come about not because there was an accepted law of nations, but because there was none, and the Declaration had not addressed the critical legal questions that an International Prize Court would have to address.[76] Speakers both for and against the Bill complained that in naval matters international law was in a state of complete uncertainty and chaos. The British courts had sought to create some order out of the chaos, and American courts had largely followed that lead due in large part to their respect for the views of Lord Stowell. The rest of the world had not embraced such ideas of a law of nations, however. When Earl Beauchamp presented the Bill to the Lords for second reading on 12 December 1911, he quoted the Lord Chief Justice, Lord Alverstone, that 'British prize law was practically the prize law of the world,' but continued 'it is sufficient to point out that although British prize law figures largely in the text-books and although it has a very real importance in deciding what international prize law may be, other countries do not accept the same view of British prize law as we do ourselves. It is unfortunate it should be so, but there it is; and, therefore, it is impossible for us to expect, without a convention or some negotiation, that we should get our rules and principles universally accepted throughout the world.'[77] Lord Alverstone added that 'The prize law of the civilised world has been built up by the Courts of this country, and subsequently followed by the Courts of America, particularly the United States, and ... the judgments of Lord Stowell and Dr Lushington, and of all the distinguished Judges of the Prize Courts, have been treated as forming the foundation of the principles of international law.' It was not so much that the English prize court was following an established law of nations, it was the English prize court establishing what it thought the law of nations should be and expecting it to be followed by others.

Thus, decisions in the prize court had an inevitable international flavour given the subject matter of the disputes. The prize court had a role that was recognised by other nations as the court of remedy for alleged wrongs in the course of prize seizure. There was a public interest in being

75 Lord Devlin, *The House of Lords and the Naval Prize Bill 1911*, pp. 20–8.
76 Rodger, *The Price of Victory*, p. 185.
77 Hansard, HL Debate 12 December 1911, vol. 10, cc 809–95.

able to claim that the prize court performed that task independently of the executive and respecting the international norms accepted by 'civilised' nations. The court protected its independence more vigorously than might have been the case in earlier periods, but ultimately it was an English court of law and applied English law, where the law was within the powers given to those who made them. In so far as 'international' law was applied, it was applied because the court chose to incorporate such ideas into English law, not because it was bound to do so, nor because it was functioning as some form of 'international' court beyond the power of the British constitution. In coming to their decisions, the prize court and the common law courts looked to what they perceived to be the national interest. In time of war that included the effective pursuit of the war against the enemy and the maintenance of peace with neutrals. How the English courts struck the balance between the competing national interests varied with the course of the war, and with national and international events. That was a feature not only of the prize courts, but of the English judicial system as a whole. When English courts applied a law of nations, it was a British law of nations.

The next chapter will begin to consider how the English courts applied their own municipal law to the distribution of prize money. Who got what, and why.

4.
Who Got What: Captains, Officers and Crew

During the eighteenth century a series of Prize Acts at the start of hostilities granted the proceeds of all prizes to those involved in their capture 'for the encouragement of the officers and seamen of his Majesty's ships of war'.[1] Royal Proclamations issued by the king-in-council stipulated the distribution between the officers and men, which changed over time, revealing the evolution of the navy. Disputes about entitlement to payouts under the terms of the Royal Proclamations were determined by the courts. Those disputes, and the attitudes of the courts, influenced the way in which the terms of the proclamations changed, and the records of those disputes give an insight into the sometimes bizarre ways in which the navy organised itself.

By the outbreak of war with revolutionary France in 1793 the division of the proceeds of prizes into eighths, distributed more thinly as they went down in seniority, had become settled practice. With the open declaration of war against France, George III in council ordered his ships to commence 'General Reprizals' against the ships, goods and subjects of France on 11 February 1793, and on 17 April 1793 set out the distribution of the proceeds. A new Prize Act was passed by Parliament on 17 June 1793, implementing the earlier proclamations. The 1793 proclamation largely replicated the provisions that had applied during the previous war against the rebel American colonies and their French, Spanish and eventually Dutch allies.[2]

Two small amendments to the previous provisions reflected the increasing complexity of naval fleets. For the first time express provision was made for a physician to a fleet or squadron, who would henceforth be entitled to a share ranking as a naval lieutenant. For the first time also, flag-captains

[1] E.g. Prize Act 1793, 33 Geo3 c.66.

[2] Respectively, orders-in-council dated 22 December 1775, 16 September 1778, 25 June 1799 and 27 December 1780.

to flag-officers in command of significant fleets or squadrons were to be treated as junior flag-officers for prize share purposes (see Chapter 6).

The April 1793 proclamation divided the proceeds of prizes among the officers and crew of HM ships of war as follows:

The Captain	Three-eighths
Flag-officers where ship under their command	One of the captain's three-eighths divided between them
Navy or 'sea' lieutenants, captains of marines and land forces, the Master, and physicians to a fleet or squadron, counting as equal to a sea lieutenant if actually on board	One eighth between them
Lieutenants and quartermasters of marines, lieutenants, ensigns and quartermasters of land forces Secretaries of flag-officers (admirals or commodores with a captain under them) Warrant officers: boatswains, gunners, carpenters, pursers, chaplains on board, ship's chirurgeons (i.e. surgeons), master's mates and pilots	One eighth between them
Petty officers: midshipmen, captain's clerks and master sailmakers Assistants to warrant officers: carpenter's mates, boatswain's mates, gunner's mates, surgeon's mates Master at Arms, corporals, yeomen of the sheets and the powder room, coxswain, quartermasters, quartermaster's mates, serjeants of marines and land forces on board	One eighth between them
All the rest: trumpeters, quarter gunners, carpenter's crew, steward and steward's mate, cook and cook's mate, armourer, gunsmith, cooper, swabber, barber, able seamen, ordinary seamen, marines and other soldiers and all other persons doing duty and assisting on board	Two eighths between them

Captains, Officers and Crew 'On Board'

To qualify for the prize share attributable to a particular role, the person had to be performing that role as part of the ship's crew. During Anson's voyage round the world in 1743 (that we met in the Introduction), he abandoned his ships *Gloucester* and *Tryal* as unseaworthy and took their remaining officers and men on board his own ship, *Centurion*, as supernumeraries. While on board their commander-in-chief's ship the men were involved in the capture of the Spanish treasure ship, the *Nostra Signora de Cabadonga*. In March 1745 the Admiralty Court decreed that the officers from *Gloucester* and *Tryal* were 'officers in His Majesty's service on board the *Centurion* at the time of capture' and so were entitled to share according to their ranks with the officers of the *Centurion*.[3] The officers of the *Centurion* appealed, however, and in May 1747 the Lords Commissioners of Appeals in Prize Causes reversed the Admiralty Court decision. They held that being 'on board' as an officer within the royal proclamation meant more than merely being 'corporally on board' and involved 'belonging to the ship' as an officer. Thus, they held that the officers from the abandoned ships who were on board *Centurion*, but not part of her complement of officers, shared only as persons 'doing duty and assisting on board', along with ordinary sailors.[4]

The dispute over shares in a fortune estimated at over £50 million in present values was seen as a squalid legal struggle. One supernumerary complained colourfully that 'we had more terrible engagements in the courts of law than we ever had on the high seas'.[5] Philip Saumarez, who had been fortunate to embark on the voyage as 3rd Lieutenant on the *Centurion*, was deeply disturbed by the outcome:

> This fatal law suit lays me under, and all my friends by restraining and preventing my assisting them in the manner I could wish is a most scandalous thing. And was I in the room of that prudentially scheming jesuitical person who first involved us in it, I should be most miserable being alive and ashamed to show my head.[6]

William Murray, later Lord Mansfield, the famous and highly regarded eighteenth-century Lord Chief Justice, appeared as counsel on the *Centurion* appeal. Trying a similar case, Wemys v Linzee, in 1779 in the Court

3 (1808) 6 Rob. Adm. Rep. 305n.

4 Ibid.; and Wemys v Linzee (1780) 1 Doug. 324, 327 per Lord Mansfield.

5 Leo Heaps, *Log of the Centurion* (Leeds, 1973), p. 249.

6 Ibid., p. 248.

of Common Pleas he said that he had always thought the outcome on the appeal was a very hard one.[7] Wemys was a captain of marines on board the frigate *Surprise* as a supernumerary en-route to join his own ship, when a prize was captured. Although as a captain of marines he was senior to the lieutenant commanding the frigate's marines, Wemys had not taken command of the marines. Indeed, there was no regulation that permitted a frigate such as the *Surprise* to carry a captain of marines as part of her complement. Wemys nevertheless sought a share of the prize, the French merchant ship *Les Deux Freres*, as a captain of marines rather than as a passenger 'doing duty and assisting on board.' Despite his view that the outcome was harsh, Mansfield considered the decision in the case of the *Centurion* to have been 'solemnly decided' and summed the matter up to the jury by indicating that they should find against Wemys. The jury, however, refused to follow the summing up and decided in favour of Wemys. Matters did not end there as the following year the Court of King's Bench ordered that the case be re-heard. It did so based on evidence from Lord Amherst, who had been on board *HMS Dublin* with his brother on their way from England to America to fight the French when a prize was taken and they had shared in the prize, but only as passengers rather than in their rank as army officers. That evidence was of dubious relevance, but further evidence was also produced from the Admiralty that no captain of marines could have been appointed to a ship of under 50 guns, such as the *Surprise.* In May 1780, with Mansfield presiding once again, the case was re-heard with a jury and judgment was finally entered against Wemys.

These decisions were followed in two later disputes during the Napoleonic Wars, both of which arose from events in December 1804. They were both therefore determined under the Royal Proclamation of 1803, but this time in the Admiralty Court by Sir William Scott. In December 1804, Lt Robert Nicholas of *HMS Niger* was on board *HMS Tribune* courtesy of her captain, Captain Bennett, who had sought his officers' consent before agreeing to give Nicholas passage home. En-route *Tribune* lost her master, the senior navigating officer on board. A Lt Box was detailed to carry out the master's navigating functions, but was not appointed as master, even in an acting role. Box's extra duties, however, left the officers stretched, even though the ship still had its full complement of lieutenants. Bennett therefore sought the help of Nicholas with the words 'Mr Nicholas, your services are now become necessary, you will therefore keep watch.' In February 1805, at the end of the voyage, Bennett provided Nicholas with a certificate

[7] Wemys v Linzee (1780) 1 Doug. 324, 327. The law report gives the year of trial as 1769, but from the context this is a Georgian printing error, and the year was in fact 1779.

of his service which read 'These are to certify that Lieutenant Robert Nicholas of his Majesty's ship *Niger*, served by my order as Lieutenant on board His Majesty's ship under my command, from 28th December 1804 unto the date hereof.' The certificate was addressed to 'Lieutenant Robert Nicholas of *HMS Niger*' and signed by Captain Bennett on 12 February 1805. While Nicholas had been standing watches, *Tribune* captured the *Nostra Signora Del Carmen* as a prize. To the dismay of the lieutenants belonging to the *Tribune*, who had consented to the hospitality shown to Nicholas, Nicholas claimed a share of the prize as a lieutenant, thus reducing their shares, rather than as a passenger assisting on board. Applying the previous cases, Scott found against Nicholas in May 1806.[8]

These decisions were again followed in cases that raised similar issues in circumstances that demonstrate the sometimes bizarre approach to discipline in the Royal Navy. In December 1804, *HMS Agamemnon* was serving in Sir John Orde's squadron off Cadiz. Orde's station had been excluded from the Mediterranean command by the Admiralty and as a result Orde was reaping a 'golden harvest' of prizes that Nelson thought should have been his as commander-in-chief of the Mediterranean fleet.[9] On 8 December, Orde sent *Agamemnon* on a two-week cruise off Portugal. Britain was about to declare war on Spain, but hostilities had already started. On 5 October 1804, a British squadron led by Captain Graham Moore had, on Admiralty orders, intercepted a Spanish treasure fleet off the same cape.[10] Although one of the Spanish ships exploded and was lost, the remaining three ships and their treasure were seized and taken to England; to the value of some £900,000. As war against Spain had not been declared, the seizure was not technically prize, but when war was finally declared on 14 December the seized ships and their cargo became vested in the Admiralty as what was known as Droits of the Admiralty. The Admiralty eventually agreed to make ex gratia payments to the captors, although not for the full value of the seizures.

On the day before *Agamemnon* left on her cruise, Orde took two lieutenants from her and sent only one replacement in return, leaving a vacancy for a lieutenant unfilled. Under the Admiralty Instructions in force at the time her captain, Sir John Harvey, had authority to appoint someone as an acting-lieutenant in the event of a death, but not merely because there was a vacancy.[11] Only a commander-in-chief could make temporary appointments

[8] The Nostra Signora Del Carmen (1808) 6 Rob. Adm. Rep 302.

[9] Nelson to Sir Alexander Ball, 5 December 1804, Nicolas, *The Dispatches and Letters of Vice Admiral Lord Viscount Nelson*, p. 285.

[10] Wareham, *Frigate Commander*, pp. 250ff.

[11] Naval Instructions S. 4 c. 2 art. 24 and 2, recited at (1808) 6 Rob. Adm. Rep. 310.

to fill vacancies, and then only pending an appointment by the Admiralty. Nevertheless, once Harvey sailed out of sight of Orde, he took it upon himself to appoint Samuel Whiteway as an acting-lieutenant on the imaginative basis that he was the commander-in-chief of his detached force of one ship. *Agamemnon* then captured the *Nostra Signora Del Coro*, which was condemned as a prize by the Admiralty Court. When *Agamemnon* finished her cruise, Orde approved of Whiteway's appointment, but did not confirm it. Instead, he took Whiteway into his own ship and sent someone else to take his place. Whiteway claimed a lieutenant's share of the prize. Two of the undisputed lieutenants contested his claim, objecting that Harvey had no authority to appoint a lieutenant. Even Sir Edward Berry, it was said at the trial in March 1808, went into battle at Trafalgar without his full complement of lieutenants, and Harvey had not been on detached duty but only temporarily absent from the admiral who had seen fit to leave the vacancy. Whiteway claimed that as he had done the duty of a lieutenant, messed and been paid as a lieutenant, all under the authority of his captain, he should receive a lieutenant's share. Scott held that Harvey had no authority to appoint Whiteway as a lieutenant, so could not make Whiteway a lieutenant for the purposes of the royal proclamation.

Conversely, however, a person who did hold a position on a ship could be entitled to the share that went with that position even if he was unable to perform the duty that went with it. If a captain of a ship was on board at the time of capture, then he was entitled to the captain's prize money even if he was under arrest pending a court-martial and another officer had been sent aboard to command as acting-captain. This issue came before the court in the tortuous litigation that arose from the failure of Commodore Johnstone and his fleet to engage properly with the French fleet under Admiral Suffren at Porto Praya, Cape Verde Islands, in 1781 in the race for the Cape during the war with France over the American War of Independence. Johnstone blamed the failure to engage on Captain Evelyn Sutton of *HMS Isis*, placed Sutton under arrest on his own ship, and sent Captain Lumley on board *Isis* to take acting command as she sailed on towards the Cape. When Johnstone's fleet reached the Cape, Suffren had beaten them to it, but four rich prizes were taken in Saldanha Bay. Sutton remained on *Isis* until 2 June 1782, when he returned home for his court-martial. Although he was acquitted, Sutton could not forgive Johnstone's actions and sued him for false arrest. As seen in Chapter 1, the court at first instance accepted Sutton's claim, but on appeal it was held that there was insufficient evidence of malice on Johnstone's part.[12] Deprived of the opportunity to sue Johnstone for lost

12 Sutton v Johnstone 99 ER 1215 (1786) 1 TR 493, 508 and 544.

prize money, Sutton claimed and, after 17 years of dispute and litigation, won the captain's prize share.[13] It was poor Captain Lumley who lost out, however, not Johnstone or his estate. Johnstone had died on 24 May 1787, but his estate was entitled to retain the flag-share of the prize money as a commodore with a captain under him, whichever captain was entitled to the captain's share.

Where two captains were appointed to command a single ship, they were entitled jointly to the captain's share. The strange idea of concurrent appointments as captain was adopted for the convict transport fleets to Australia. In 1786 Captain Arthur Phillips was ordered to take a fleet of convict ships to Australia, and to found a colony with himself as governor, in what became known as the First Fleet. As it was intended that Phillips would go ashore and remain in Australia, the Admiralty appointed Captain John Hunter as a second captain of Phillips' ship, *HMS Sirius*. Phillips was not granted the flag-rank of commodore with Hunter serving under him as his flag-captain. Although Hunter was subject to Phillips' command, he was appointed not as Phillips' first lieutenant to be promoted to captain once Phillips went ashore, but as a second captain. Once Phillips went ashore as governor, Hunter became the sole remaining captain on *Sirius*. Eight years later, in 1794, Captain Hunter was sent back to Australia to take over the vacant governorship, Phillips having returned home. Hunter was sent out with another fleet of convict ships, and in command of *HMS Reliance*. Once again, the Admiralty appointed a second captain, Captain Waterhouse. In 1795, after the French takeover of the Netherlands, *Reliance* captured some Dutch prizes, and a dispute arose over who was entitled to the captain's share.[14] The court held that both Hunter and Waterhouse were entitled jointly to the captain's share of the prizes. They distinguished the facts in Lumley v Sutton, on the basis that Lumley had only been appointed as an acting command and carried as a supernumerary, and Sutton had remained on board and in the ship's books as captain, even though under arrest.

Where someone was validly appointed to acting command of a ship following the dismissal of her commanding officer, however, then the acting commander became entitled to the commander's share even if the original commander was subsequently reinstated. In 1803 the revenue cutter *Hinde*, under an acting commander, captured some prizes on the resumption of war after the Peace of Amiens. Her original commander, J. M. Allen, had been dismissed by the Commissioners of Customs for inactivity and

13 Lumley v Sutton (1799) 8 TR 224.

14 Under Royal Proclamation of 25 November 1795, *London Gazette* No. 13836, pp. 1255, 1257.

inattention to the service based on information they had been given. The Commissioners cancelled Allen's commission and ordered the mate, Mr Pill, to assume command until a new commander was appointed, paying Pill the commander's allowance for victualling. Allen challenged the dismissal and was reinstated, but in the meantime the cutter had captured prizes in his absence. Applying the principles that applied to the Royal Navy in cases such as Lumley v Sutton, the Court of King's Bench held that Pill was entitled to the commander's share of the prizes.[15]

Thus, it can be seen that the validity of an appointment mattered. Where an officer was promoted into a command by the commanding officer of a squadron, he could only be sure of a captain's prize share if the promotion was valid, and within the powers of his commanding officer. In 1805 Captain Sir Home Popham was appointed by the Admiralty under Lord Barham as commodore of a fleet to capture the Cape from the Dutch. Popham sailed as captain on board *HMS Diadem* with William King as his first lieutenant. His fleet included *HMS Diomede* under Captain Downman and *HMS L'Espoir* under Captain Edwards. Popham's instructions were to hoist his broad pennant as commodore on *Diadem* once he left Madeira. His instructions made no mention of any authority to appoint a captain of *Diadem* under him as commodore. When Popham left Madeira, however, he not only hoisted his commodore's pennant, but appointed Downman as captain of the *Diadem* under himself as commodore. He then appointed Edwards to command of *Diomede* and King to command of *L'Espoir*. None of the officers thus promoted were aware that Popham's instructions gave no authority to make the promotions. Thereafter they all acted as if the appointments were valid and even entered into a number of prize-sharing agreements as commanders of their vessels. Popham sailed and took the Cape, but then, without orders, sailed to the Rio Plata in South America and captured Montevideo and Buenos Aires, in the process taking a large quantity of prizes. When the Admiralty heard about the promotions, it refused to ratify them. Popham was out of favour with the new Admiralty that had taken office after Barham and faced a court-martial for his unauthorised expedition to South America. All this left poor William King in an unfortunate and impecunious state, and he and Popham both petitioned the Privy Council for relief.[16] Lord Barham, though out of office, wrote to the Privy Council on Popham's behalf saying that he had intended Popham to have a captain under him, and he considered Popham's instructions to

15 Pill v Taylor (1809) 11 East 414; see below for prize distribution for revenue cutters.

16 Donnelly v Popham (1807) 1 Taunt. 1; Papers relating to Property captured at Buenos Ayres, HC Misc. Accounts and Papers 1812 Vol. X.

be authority to appoint one.[17] Barham's memorial was dated only 13 days before a related dispute between Popham and Captain Donnelly was heard in the Court of Common Pleas, but Barham was not called to give evidence and Popham lost the case.[18] Sir James Mansfield, Chief Justice of the Court of Common Pleas, ruled that Popham had no authority to appoint a captain under him and was not entitled to a flag-officer's share. An application in November 1807 to set the judgment aside was rejected, and it was 1809 before the Admiralty relented in part and authorised payment of extra allowances to Popham.

Whether a member of a ship's company could ever be entitled if he was not actually on board the ship was a potential moot point. When the *Guillaume Tell* was captured off Malta in 1800, after her escape from the French defeat at the Battle of the Nile in 1798, one of the officers who first sighted her was a Lt Oliver of the *Northumberland*, one of the ships blockading Malta. Oliver had been sent ashore to a signal post known felicitously as Belvidere and sent rockets up to alert the fleet that *Guillaume Tell* was at sea. Although *Northumberland* was slow to react, she was held to be a joint captor with *HMS Foudroyant*. Lt Oliver benefited from the prize as he was able to get back on board *Northumberland* by the time of the capture. Whether he would have been entitled had he not made it back on board, merely on account of the intelligence he was the means of conveying, was described by Sir William Scott as a question of 'some nicety'.[19] As the question did not need to be answered, no answer was given. Scott may well have found a means of treating him as 'constructively on board', sent ashore as part of his service on-board, rather than on a detached service.

Joint Capture

It is commonly, but inaccurately, supposed in naval literature that a ship shared in a prize if it was 'in sight' at the time of the capture, and not otherwise. Initially 'actual cooperation' in the capture had been required, but the courts extended joint capture to include 'constructive assistance, for the purpose of preserving harmony and a good understanding in the navy'.[20]

17 Memorial dated 14 June 1807 written from Barham Court, see Papers relating to Property captured at Buenos Ayres, HC Misc. Accounts and Papers 1812 Vol. X, p. 16 enclosure No. 1.

18 See Chapter 8.

19 The Guillaume Tell (1808) Edw. Adm. Rep. 6, 7.

20 The Vryheid (1799) 2 Rob. 16, per the King's Advocate, 16 and Sir William Scott, 21–2.

What was required was either a sufficient form of association between the vessels, or sufficient cooperation in the form of some presence at the capture. Both rested on the same principle, that of encouragement to the friend and intimidation to the enemy. Cooperation, but not association, required a ship to be within sight of the capture, although being in sight was not necessarily enough in itself.

In 1866 the Admiralty judge, Dr Stephen Lushington, reviewed the eighteenth-century law of joint capture in a seminal judgment for a case that involved no ships at all. The Admiralty Act 1840 had given the Admiralty Court jurisdiction to determine questions concerning booty of war. The court thus acquired for the first time jurisdiction to determine issues relating to assets seized in war solely on land, and to do so 'as in cases of Prize of War.'[21] The first test of the new jurisdiction came with seizures made by Crown land forces acting with the East India Company in campaigns to suppress the Indian mutiny in 1857. In order to decide how he should deal with the various claims, Lushington reviewed the principles upon which the court proceeded in matters of prize.[22] Lushington was not a complete stranger to the world of Indian politics. When he was a young man his father, Sir Stephen Lushington, had been chairman of the East India Company.

Unfortunately, Dr Lushington considered that it would 'be very difficult, and would serve no practical purpose, to explore the ancient history of Prize Law,' but nevertheless his approach is enlightening.[23] In considering who were 'the takers' for prize purposes, Lushington identified two grounds for a joint claim: association and cooperation.

Association

If naval vessels were associated together then a capture made by one was treated as for the benefit of all, whether in sight at the time of capture or not. So long as each vessel was at the time discharging the part of the service assigned to it for the purposes for which they were associated, then no further cooperation or contribution to the capture was required. Thus, *HMS Audacious* was permitted to share with the fleet at the battle of 1 June 1794 where, having engaged with the fleet on 28 May, she had been sent to

[21] & 4 Vict. C. 65, s. 22.

[22] In the Matter of the Banda and Kirwee Booty, 1866.

[23] Ibid., p. 6.

chase a single French ship, the *Revolutionaire*, thereby reducing the enemy fleet and contributing to success on 1 June.[24]

'Association' was recognised where vessels were cruising together under a common authority or deployed together to conduct a chase. While under orders from Admiral Dickens to cruise within sight of his fleet blockading Holland, *HMS Director* captured the *Forsigheid*, but when she was out of sight due to fog that had closed in. Sir William Scott held that the fleet shared in the prize as *Director* was associated with the fleet and not on a detached service.[25] Where *HMS Beagle* and *HMS Rover* joined in a chase and the commander of *Beagle*, as the senior commanding officer, ordered *Rover* to chase a new ship that was sighted, *Beagle* was held to be entitled to share in the prize taken by *Rover* out of sight of *Beagle*.[26]

'Association' included ships serving together as a fleet or squadron, so long as they had not been detached on some separate and distinct service.[27] Where they were associated, then so long as they were playing their allotted part, 'Whether that part is important or not, is not so material, the part is performed and that is all that was expected' and 'by the very fact of their Association, there exists that which is of the very essence of the claim, encouragement to the Friend and intimidation to the Enemy'.[28]

In a case in 1784, Admiral Pigot had detached two ships in the West Indies to chase two strange ships. The chasing ships captured both these ships plus a third vessel, about which a dispute arose. As the fleet had continued in the same direction and was treated as having been known to be at hand and ready to support if needed, the court decreed the third prize a joint capture.[29]

Scott rejected a claim for joint capture where a ship, having been in sight of the enemy Dutch fleet, was detached from a squadron off Holland to take dispatches to England and missed being present at the capture of the Dutch, only returning afterwards and helping bring two of the prizes into the Humber.[30] Scott distinguished between a ship being detached in sight of the enemy, and under preparations for a chase, and a ship being sent

[24] Quoted as an example in The Vryheid (1799) 2 Rob. 16, 20.

[25] The Forsigheid (1801) 3 Rob. 311, 317.

[26] The Empress (1814) 1 Dods. 368.

[27] The Vryheid (1799) 2 Rob. 16, 22, The Island of Trinidad (1804) 5 Rob. 92, The Stella del Norte (1805) 5 Rob. 349.

[28] Per Sir William Scott, The Dordrecht (1799) 2 Rob. 65 and L'Etoile (1816) 2 Dods. 106.

[29] Sir William Scott appeared as counsel and recited the case in The Vryheid (1799) 2 Rob. 16, 25–6.

[30] The Vryheid (1799) 2 Rob. 16.

away after the enemy had been sighted but before any preparations for a chase, or other hostile movements.

Association had its limits, and at times was out of favour. Scott noted that the notion of constructive capture had 'already travelled a considerable way beyond the meaning of the Act of Parliament' and accordingly 'the disposition of the Court will lean, not to extend it still further, but to narrow it, and bring it nearer to the terms of the Act'.[31] There was a tension between the claimed practice of the navy and the wording approved by Parliament. In Scott's view 'the practice of the navy, in opposition to the words of the Act of Parliament, or a Proclamation, or to the established practice of law cannot weigh or be of any authority: at the same time the Court would be extremely unwilling to break in on any settled and received notions of the navy, or to disturb a practice generally prevailing among themselves'.[32] Where two ships, *Emerald* and *Amethyst*, joined in a chase but *Emerald* lost sight of the chase, she lost a claim as joint captor even though she had continued searching and *Amethyst* engaged the chase before a third ship, *Arethusa*, came up and made the actual capture.[33]

Where ships operated together to maintain a blockade they could be treated as associated.[34] The concept of association by unity of a blockade worked with a traditional blockade, where ships were ordered to carry out a close blockade of a specific port acting together, but that simple pattern did not always apply. Where ships were stationed at different outlets to Port au Prince to catch a French ship that had to pass through one of them, a claim of joint capture by the ships who were guarding the outlets the enemy did not choose was rejected in 1760, during the Seven Years' War.[35]

Sir William Scott had to consider a new and different type of blockade arising from the British response to Napoleon's Continental System in 1806.[36] The 'usual and regular mode of enforcing blockades, by stationing a number of ships, and forming as it were an arch of circumvallation [circling within walls] round the mouth of the prohibited port', Scott noted, meant that 'if the arch fails in any one part, the blockade itself fails altogether'. In those circumstances being engaged in a blockade of the same port could properly amount to association for the purposes of joint capture. By the Berlin Decree of 21 November 1806, Napoleon purported to place the whole of Britain under a blockade. Britain responded with a series of

31 The Vryheid (1799) 2 Rob. 16, 22.
32 The Vryheid (1799) 2 Rob. 16, 26.
33 Le Niemen (1811) 1 Dods. 9.
34 La Henriette (1815) 2 Dods. 96, The Guillaume Tell (1808) Edw. Adm. Rep. 6.
35 The Mars (1760), quoted by Sir William Scott in The Vryheid (1799) 2 Rob. 16, 22.
36 The Arthur (1814) 1 Dods. 423, 425.

orders-in-council tightening its blockade on all the coasts of Europe, and declaring that neutral vessels had to call at a British port before sailing to the continent.[37] As Scott described the position, under the modified provisions of the order-in-council of 26 April 1809 the new policy imposed a blockade 'applicable to a very great extent of coast, and was never intended to be maintained according to the usual and regular mode'.[38] The change had 'arisen out of the violent and unjust conduct of the enemy' and 'was maintained by a ship stationed anywhere in the neighbourhood of the coast' or 'the river itself, observing and preventing every vessel that might endeavour to effect a passage up or down the river'. Scott noted that 'the principle of association had not been of late favoured' in either the Admiralty Court or the Court of Appeal, but that in The Forsigheid it had been held that 'where ships were acting together for the maintenance of the same blockade, there is, in the nature of such an association, an identity of service that forms a just foundation for the joint-interest in prizes taken for the violation of the blockade; because it could not be supported without unity of operation. The connexion between the ships so employed is of so intimate a nature, that they may be considered as forming links in the same chain.' The same consideration, Scott held, was not applicable to the newer, looser, form of blockade, where:

> no circumvallation is necessary; and although a number of different ships may be engaged in maintaining the blockade, yet they are not so connected and continued as to form one mass of obstruction to the communication which may be attempted to be carried on with the prohibited port.[39]

Scott was considering the capture of an American ship, *The Arthur*. Two British ships, *HMS Paz* and *HMS Blazer*, had each independently been ordered to blockade the river Ems. *Blazer* succeeded in intercepting *The Arthur* and detained her for breach of the blockade. *Paz* claimed to have been in sight, but that claim was rejected. To succeed, therefore, she had to establish a right by association. Both ships had independently been

[37] J. Davey, *In Nelson's Wake: The Navy and the Napoleonic Wars* (Yale, 2015), p. 238; L. E. Davis and S. L. Engerman, *Naval Blockades in Peace and War: An Economic History since 1750* (Cambridge, 2006), pp. 25–52; E. F. Heckscher, *The Continental System: An Economic Interpretation* (Oxford, 1922); Frank Edgar Melvin, *Napoleon's Navigation System: A Study of Trade Control During the Continental Blockade* (New York, 1919).

[38] Anon., *Notifications, Orders, and Instructions, Relating to Prize Subjects during the Present War*, p. 113.

[39] The Arthur (1814) 1 Dods. 423, 425.

instructed to mount the blockade by orders from Lord George Stuart, the commander-in-chief of the inshore squadron in charge of the blockade. In the light of Scott's distinction between the forms of blockade, *Paz* failed in her claim.

Cooperation 'In Sight'

If ships were not 'associated' then, to share as a joint captor, they had to show that they were in sight at the time of capture. For a capture to be 'in sight' so as to be a joint capture, the joint captor had to be in sight of both the actual captor and the prize: 'A vessel out of sight of the Captor cannot give encouragement to the captor, and, out of sight of the Prize, cannot cause intimidation to the Prize.'[40]

Earlier in the eighteenth century the courts awarded prize shares between the ships in sight at the time of capture on a 'quantum meruit' basis, i.e. according to the contribution they made to the capture. Thus, in 1746 the Admiralty Court dealt with the capture of the *Margaret Martyn* by three ships, the *Queen of Hungary*, the *Trial* and the *Terrible*, during the War of Austrian Succession. The *Queen of Hungary* was present at the capture but did nothing. The *Trial* was in sight, but at a distance from the scene of the action and doing nothing. It was the *Terrible* who engaged the enemy for three hours and made the capture. Sir Henry Penrice awarded three quarters of the prize to the *Terrible*, one quarter to the *Trial* and none to the *Queen of Hungary*.[41] By the end of the century, however, division on a quantum meruit basis was no longer made. If a vessel was deemed to have played a part, she shared fully, if not then she did not share at all.

For ships of the Royal Navy being in sight gave rise to a rebuttable presumption that they had encouraged the capture and been ready and willing to assist so that their presence contributed to the intimidation of the captured vessel. A ship claiming to have been in sight was required, however, to prove it. In 1802 the Admiralty Court heard a claim to be entitled as joint re-captor of the East Indiaman *Lord Middleton*, that had fallen into enemy hands.[42] The Royal Navy armed cutter *Viper* saw and chased a ship that turned out to be the British privateer, *Maria*. They parted company in light airs, and the next morning both vessels saw the *Lord Middleton* at a distance. *Viper* stood to and reconnoitred before continuing on her own

40 Per Dr Lushington, In the Matter of the Banda and Kirwee Booty, 30 June 1866, p. 9.
41 Recited in the judgment of Sir William Scott in La Melanie (1816) 2 Dods. 122, 125.
42 The Lord Middleton (1802) 4 Rob. Adm. Rep. 153.

way. The *Maria,* however, came up to *Lord Middleton* by labouring with her sweeps in a perfect calm and recaptured her. At the time of capture a sail of a ship proceeding on its own way was visible in the distance from *Lord Middleton.* Sir William Scott found that not only had *Viper* not participated in the capture, but it had not even been proved that she was the sail in sight. *Viper*'s claim as joint captor was rejected.

The same rules applied to claims to join in the naval share of the proceeds of expeditions that captured land and ships in joint land and naval operations. In 1804 Sir William Scott heard a claim for shares in the proceeds of an expedition to capture the island of Trinidad commanded by Admiral Harvey and General Abercrombie. He was not satisfied with Admiral Harvey's evidence that in his opinion the claimant vessels 'must have been in sight on the evening' in question as the court expected direct evidence of the vessel being in sight.[43] Neither presence within sight at the first overtures to a surrender, nor at the aftermath of a capture, would amount to sufficient presence if the vessel was not there at the time of surrender or capture.

Even a witness to a capture might not succeed in claiming to be a joint captor, however. In March 1813 Sir Thomas Staines commanded *HMS Briton* off Bordeaux when she saw and gave chase to the French schooner *La Melanie,* laden with cotton from New Orleans and making for Bordeaux. The pursuit brought the two ships within sight of the British squadron under Admiral Sir Harry Neale, anchored in Basque Roads, blockading French ships at the Isle de Aix. The tops of the squadron's masts were visible from the chase and her pursuer. *La Melanie*'s master had seen the mastheads of the British squadron, but the court concluded that if he had just come from New Orleans, he could not have known for sure that they were British. When *Briton* saw the squadron, she made her number by flag to the admiral and continued the chase. *La Melanie* could not make for the Basque Roads to escape the pursuit without being captured by the squadron, but the squadron could not sail from the Basque Roads to assist the capture even though it claimed to have been ready to assist if needed.

Briton fired at the chase, brought her to and captured her, just within sight of the squadron, about 12 to 14 miles distant. The barricade of *Briton*'s quarterdeck was described as just visible. The fully laden *La Melanie* would have been even lower. As Sir William Scott described it, 'I think I have scarcely seen a more indistinct account of sight in any case that has here

[43] The Island of Trinidad, and its Dependencies, with the Saint Damaso, captured in port, and other ships destroyed, during the late war (1804) 5 Rob. Adm. Rep. 92.

been brought to my notice.'[44] Nevertheless the squadron claimed to share in the capture. Scott dismissed the claim and found exclusively for *Briton*. The chase, he held, had been commenced by *Briton* alone and it was only the efforts of *Briton* that had brought the chase within the distant sight of the squadron. The squadron was engaged in a blockade that it could not desert, and they were lying at anchor with their sails furled in the bottom of a bay into which the wind was blowing strong. They were not in any position to do anything to aid the chase other than preventing refuge in the roads or port of La Rochelle. Scott accepted the presumption that a claim for joint capture would generally be sustained by a king's ship in sight but held that it was rebutted on the particular facts.

Although not strictly a prize case, the same principles were applied in a case dealing with events just before the outbreak of war with the US in 1812. In August 1812 six ships of the Royal Navy were escorting about 300 merchant ships out of the Baltic. The convoy was under the command of Captain Wilkinson of *HMS Courageux*, and included seven American ships, including the *Galen*, laden with cordage, iron, canvas and tar bound from Cronstadt to Rio de Janeiro. Formal reprisals against American ships were not ordered by the Prince Regent until 13 October 1812.[45] Thus, the American ships could not be seized as prizes, but the British government ordered that American ships be detained unless they held British licences permitting them to sail. Once war came, any detained ships would be forfeit to the Crown as Droits of the Admiralty. The Americans in the convoy had no British licences. As neutrals and unaware of the British order, they had not thought they needed them and freely sought the protection of the British convoy. As the convoy sailed into the Great Belt, between the Danish islands, it was joined during the night by the frigate *HMS Pyramus* under the command of Captain Charles Dashwood, who brought news to Wilkinson of the order to detain American ships. The following day, while the convoy was becalmed and at anchor off the island of Femerin, *Galen* and the other American ships were quietly seized by boats from *Courageux* and the squadron. As the ships were being seized, two other groups of Royal Navy ships were sailing into the Baltic and within sight. A claim by the first squadron, five ships led by *HMS Cressy*, was accepted, but claims by a further group of three ships, the frigate *Aquilon* and the bomb vessels *Devastation* and *Meteor*, were challenged. As with the seizure of the Spanish treasure ships by Graham Moore's squadron before the outbreak of war with Spain in 1804, there was strictly speaking no entitlement to

44 La Melanie, Lafitte (1816) 2 Dods. 122.

45 Order-in-council 26 Oct. 1812, *London Gazette* 1812, No. 16661, p. 2139.

the proceeds of the seizures as prize, although there was an expectation of reward.[46] The King's Proctor submitted the claims for adjudication by the Admiralty Court on the same principles as a claim relating to prize.[47] The commanders of the three new ships knew of the order to detain American ships, and that there would be American ships in the convoy. They assumed that the convoying ships would not know of the order, as one of them had been ordered to convey it to Captain Wilkinson in command of the convoy. When they saw the convoy, they had every intention to pick up prizes, as they termed them. Although they had no particulars of the American ships being seized, and were unaware that the seizures were being undertaken, they were in sight and intending to seize the ships. Sir William Scott upheld their claim to be joint captors.

For private ships claiming a share of a capture there was no presumption that they had contributed to the capture by their mere presence. They had to prove not only that they were in sight, but that they had contributed to the capture. Claims were investigated with a degree of scepticism, especially if they were not made promptly and smacked of opportunism. A claim by a British privateer to a joint share in the capture of the Spanish treasure ship *Santa Brigida* in October 1799 was rejected. She claimed to have been in sight at the time and in a position to have cut off a retreat by the Spanish frigate, which was desperately seeking a friendly Spanish port having nearly made it across the Atlantic from Mexico. The claim was rejected on the basis that the claimed involvement was too remote. The privateer claimed she was driven off the Spanish coast by four Spanish ships, and the captors had seen four Spanish ships approaching and prepared to defend their prize until they turned back. It may well be that the privateer did play a role in distracting the Spanish ships and so preserving the prize, but Sir William Scott was not willing to give a privateer the benefit of the doubt.[48]

Cutters, Schooners and Other Armed Vessels

The crew of cutters, schooners and other armed vessels commanded by lieutenants shared in the same proportion as persons of like rank on board HM ships if they were involved in a capture and present or within sight of a ship or vessel of war and aiding to the encouragement of the captors and terror of the enemy. If no ships of war were present then the crew shared

[46] Wareham, *Frigate Commander*, pp. 250ff.

[47] The Galen (1815) 2 Dods. 19.

[48] The Santa Brigada (1800) 3 Rob. Adm. Rep. 52 (the name is misspelt in the report).

in a way that again reflected the hierarchical distribution of proceeds, as follows:

Lieutenant in Command	3 eighths
Flag-officers where vessel under their command	One of the above eighths
Master or other person second in command and the pilot if one on board	Master: 1 eighth, or Master and pilot: Master; 2 thirds Pilot; 1 third
Chirurgeon (chirurgeon's mate if no chirurgeon), midshipmen, clerk and steward	1 eighth between them
Boatswain's mate, gunner's mate, carpenter's mate, yeoman of the sheets, sailmaker, quartermaster, quartermaster's mate	1 eighth between them
Seamen, marines and other persons on board assisting in the capture	2 eighths between them

Proclamations 1795–1805

Further proclamations were added as the war expanded in scope to embrace additional hostile countries. When France subsumed the Netherlands as a subject state, the prize provisions were extended to the ships, goods and subjects of the United Provinces by a proclamation dated 25 November 1795.[49] A proclamation dated 25 January 1797 brought Spanish prizes under a similar regime, and a proclamation of 12 February 1800 dealt with prizes seized from Genoa, the Papal territories and the Ligurian and Roman republics. These proclamations mirrored the provisions of the 1793 proclamation concerning France.

With the resumption of war against Napoleon in 1803 after the Peace of Amiens, a Royal Proclamation of 7 July 1803 made new provision for the distribution of the proceeds of prizes seized from both France and the

[49] *London Gazette* 1795, No. 13836, p. 1255.

Batavian Republic, the Dutch republic that had become a Napoleonic client republic. On 17 August 1803 a proclamation dealt with reprisals against the Italian and Ligurian republics. The 1803 proclamations contained a number of changes from those of 1793. As will be seen, the changes reflect the changes that were happening in the Royal Navy.

Conjoint Captures with Land Forces

The earlier proclamations of 1793, 1797 and 1800 did not expressly exclude conjoint expeditions between the Royal Navy and land forces despite the fact that, where major joint expeditions were planned, the distribution of the spoils was generally provided for separately in the orders given to those leading the expedition. The proclamations after 1803 expressly excluded conjoint expeditions with the army, reserving the division and distribution of all prize and booty taken to the king.

Hired Armed Vessels

Many smaller vessels were brought into Crown service as part of the war effort. In 1759, during the Seven Years' War, the Admiralty had used a combination of available frigates and hired privateers to cruise the north coast of Brittany, disrupting the French trade supplying the French invasion force being assembled there.[50] When the Admiralty anticipated war they would authorise the seizure of ships belonging to potential enemies, as we have seen. Hired armed vessels were useful for detaining slow-moving, unarmed, lightly manned merchant ships, particularly where they were unaware of hostile intent at the outbreak of war. Thus, for example, in 1807 in anticipation of war in the Baltic an order-in-council on 2 September provided for Danish ships to be detained. On 10 September the Danish merchant ship *Knud Terkelson* was detained laden with salt by *HM Hired Armed Ship The Duchess of Bedford* and taken into Lisbon. Urgent repairs were carried out to the Danish ship, paid for in part by sale of her cargo. The captain of *The Duchess of Bedford* then took on a cargo for his detained ship to sail to England, and took the precaution of insuring the vessel, its cargo and the freight. *Knud Terkelson* sailed from Lisbon on 3 November 1807,

[50] Baugh, *The Global Seven Years War, 1754–1763*, p. 427.

a day before reprisals were ordered against Danish ships. Before reaching London, and before any condemnation by a prize court, she foundered in bad weather on the coast of France and she and her cargo were lost. Her fate gave rise to a dispute about the validity of the insurance that had been taken out. One of the arguments raised was that the captain of *The Duchess of Bedford* could not have known about the order to detain Danish ships, and acted speculatively, and unlawfully, in detaining the Dane. The court rejected that argument, holding that even if the captain had not known of the lawful authority, it was enough that lawful authority existed.[51]

As a result of the growth in the use of hired armed vessels, the 1803 proclamation dealt expressly with prize shares for them. The distribution of prize shares for hired armed vessels depended on whether the vessel had a commissioned officer on board in command.

Where a commissioned officer was in command on board, the division was:

Commissioned commanding officer on board	3 eighths
Flag-officers where vessel under their command	One of the commanding officer's 3 eighths
Any commissioned sea lieutenant in king's pay	1 eighth
Master Mate	1 eighth divided 2 thirds 1 third
Unless there are midshipmen or those classed above with midshipmen in the pay of the king in which case:	
Master Mate, Midshipmen etc	1 half of the eighth Shared equally the remaining half of the eighth
Other officers and the rest of the crew	3 eighths between them

If there was no commissioned officer in command on board, the division was:

51 Routh v Thompson (1809) 11 East 428, (1811) 13 East 274; log of *The Duchess of Bedford*, TNA, ADM 51/4051.

Flag-officers if under command of a flag	1 eighth
Master and mate	2 eighths divided: 2 thirds to master, 1 third to mate
Other officers and crew	3 eighths between them

Any surplus remained at King's disposal and if not disposed of within 1 year after final adjudication then to the Greenwich Hospital

If hired armed vessels were involved in joint captures with HM ships of war, the officers and crew of the hired vessel shared as follows:

Commissioned officers on board hired vessel	Share with commissioned officers of same rank on HM ships as joint captors
Master of hired vessel	Share with warrant officers of HM ships
Mate of hired vessel	Share with petty officers of HM ships
Seamen of hired vessel	Share with the seamen on HM ships

Unless the vessel was commanded by a commissioned master and commander with no commissioned lieutenants on board, or by the master, then the master and mate would share as follows:

Master	Share with lieutenants of HM ship
Mate	Share with warrant officers of HM ships

It was anticipated that even this provision might not cover all eventualities involving hired armed vessels, so the proclamation provided that in case of dispute it was to be referred to the Lords of the Admiralty and their direction was to be final, a provision that the Admiralty avoided applying to their own ships, preferring to leave the determination of disputes to the courts.

Revenue Cutters

The royal proclamations expressly excluded 'the produce of such prizes as are or shall be taken by ships or vessels belonging to or hired by or in the service of the Commissioners of Customs or Excise', reserving them to the king's 'further pleasure' once the Admiralty Court had condemned a prize. In practice this meant that distribution was under warrants issued by the king, or in his name. The prize position was complicated where revenue cutters were specifically co-opted to prize-taking service and Royal Navy officers and sailors were sent on board to assist both in prize-taking and providing prize-crews. In anticipation of the resumption of war in March 1803, for example, Lt Senhouse RN was sent on board the revenue cutter *Hinde* from *HMS Conqueror* in Plymouth with some of *Conqueror*'s sailors to assist in capturing prizes when war resumed. In May 1803 *Hinde*, under the command at the time of her own acting commander appointed by orders from the Commissioners of Customs, captured a number of prizes that were condemned by the Admiralty Court. The distribution of these prizes was provided for by King's Warrants of 4 July and 26 November 1803.[52] If there were no Royal Navy personnel on board, the distribution would have been:

The commander	One half
The mate	One quarter
The remaining mariners	One quarter between them

If Royal Navy sailors were sent on board but no Royal Navy officer, the proceeds would have been divided into 32 parts and distributed:

[52] Set out in Pill v Taylor (1805) 11 East 414. The King's Warrant of 4 July 1803 was issued three days before the 7 July 1803 royal proclamation of the king-in-council dealing with other prizes.

The commander	14 parts
The mate	7 parts
The deputed mariners	3 parts between them
The other mariners	8 parts between them

As there was a Royal Navy officer on board, the proceeds were divided into eighths and the distribution was:

To the Port Admiral Plymouth, under whose orders the men from *Conqueror* had been sent on board *Hinde*	One eighth
To the captain, officers and crew of *Conqueror*, incl. Lt Senhouse and the men put on board *Hinde*	Three eighths divided between them as prize money
To the commander of *Hinde*	Two eighths
To the mate of *Hinde*	One eighth
To the other mariners of *Hinde*	One eighth between them

Thus, the half remaining after the Royal Navy had taken its half was distributed to the men from *Hinde* in the same shares as if they had been sailing without the assistance of men from the Royal Navy and had taken the prize without assistance.

A small addition to the provisions for distribution among the crew of line-of-battle ships indicates the increasing sophistication of such vessels. For the first time, the 1803 proclamation included the second masters of line-of-battle ships as entitled to share in the one eighth apportioned to warrant officers, junior marine and land forces officers and flag-officer secretaries.

The 1803 proclamation also dealt expressly with another problem that had caused difficulties in practice, namely captures that the Royal Navy made together with ships of allies, such as the Portuguese Navy. It provided that a share of prizes equal to that which the allied ships would have had if they had been HM ships was set apart and at the king's disposal. As will be seen in Chapter 5, this did not deal with potential claims by flag-officers in allied fleets attached to British fleets to a flag-officer's share of fleet captures even if they were not present at the capture. That issue was left to be determined by the courts.

When war with Spain resumed in 1805, reprisals were ordered on 11 January 1805. A royal proclamation of 31 January 1805 then provided for the distribution of proceeds of prizes seized from Spain and the Italian and Ligurian republics. It did so on the same terms as the proclamation against France and Batavia of 1803, thus maintaining a consistent approach whoever the enemy might be. There was one small change in 1805 in respect of smaller vessels in the king's service that gave a slightly larger share to sub-lieutenants serving alongside masters or pilots. Unusually, it also made that change retrospective, so that it altered the distribution under the previous 1803 proclamation.

In 1807 war came again in the Baltic and reprisals were ordered against Denmark and Russia on 4 November and 18 December 1807 respectively. The war in the Baltic was an economic war to break the Continental System that Napoleon sought to impose on Russia and the Baltic states, and the reprisals expressly excluded vessels under licence from the British. Proclamations apportioning the proceeds of prizes followed on 11 November and 23 December 1807. In the haste to draft the proclamations for the king to make in council at the Queen's Palace,[53] the wording of the 1803 declaration was used, overlooking the 1805 amendment relating to sub-lieutenants on small ships of war.

1808

The most significant change to the pattern of distribution of prize money came in June 1808 when all the previous proclamations were revoked and replaced with a new distribution. Why and how this change was made in 1808 is the subject of Chapter 7.

The 1808 proclamation effected a significant shift in the rewards away from captains and admirals in favour of the petty officers who formed the middle management of ships of war. The captain's share was reduced from three to two eighths. Where flag-officers took a share, that was reduced

[53] The name given to Buckingham House, on the site of the present-day Buckingham Palace.

from one of the three eighths previously taken to a one third share of the captain's two eighths. Thus, the proportions as between the captains and the flag-officers remained the same, but the shares of each were reduced.

The categories of petty officers were also redefined, introducing for the first time two separate classes of petty officer, petty officers first and second class. The increasing sophistication of ships of war was recognised with the first express mention of men such as schoolmasters and captains of the forecastle (both first class) and captains of the foretop, maintop, afterguard and mast (all second class). The new allocation of the proceeds of prizes was as follows:

The captain actually on board	Two eighths instead of three
Flag-officers where the ship was under the command of a flag or flags, the flag-officer or officers actually on board, or directing and assisting in the capture	One third of the captain's two eighths (i.e. one twelfth of the whole)
[Navy, or] 'Sea' lieutenants, captains of marines and land forces the master A physician to a fleet or squadron if actually on board at the time of taking	One eighth between them, as before
Lieutenants and quartermasters of marines Lieutenants, ensigns and quartermasters of land forces, secretaries of admirals or commodores with captains under them, second masters of line-of-battle ships Warrant officers: ship's surgeons, boatswains, gunners, pursers, carpenters, master's mates, pilots, chaplains on board	One eighth between them, as before

The remaining half of the proceeds was then divided into shares as follows:

Petty officers first class: midshipmen, surgeon's assistants, secretaries-clerks, captains' clerk, schoolmasters, masters at arms, captain's coxswain, gunners' mates, yeoman of the powder-room, boatswains' mates, yeomen of the sheets, carpenters' mates, quartermasters, quartermasters' mates, ship's corporals, captains of the forecastle, master sailmakers, master caulkers, master ropemakers, armourers, serjeants of marines and land forces	4½ shares each of the remaining half of the proceeds

Petty officers second class: midshipmen ordinary (graduates of the Royal Naval Academy without a midshipman's sea-time), captains of the foretop, the maintop, the after guard and the mast, sailmaker's mates, caulker's mates, armourer's mates, ship's cook, corporals of marines and land forces	3 shares each of the remaining half of the proceeds
Quarter gunners, carpenters' crew, sailmakers' crew, coxswains' mates, yeomen of the boatswain's store room, gunsmiths, coopers, trumpeters, able seamen, ordinary seamen, drummers, private marines and other soldiers doing duty on board in place of marines.	1½ shares each of the remaining half of the proceeds
Landsmen, admiral's domestics, all other ratings not enumerated above, together with all passengers and other persons borne as supernumeraries and doing duty and assisting on board (NB acting officers received the share of the rank they were ordered to act in)	1 share each of the remaining half of the proceeds
Young gentlemen volunteers and boys of every description	½ a share each of the remaining half of the proceeds

After 1808 cutters, schooners and other armed vessels commanded by lieutenants involved in a capture where a Royal Navy ship or vessel of war was 'present or within sight and aiding to the encouragement of the captors and terror of the enemy' once again shared in the same, amended, proportion as allowed to persons of like rank on board HM ships, but did not in respect of such captures 'convey any interest or share in the Flag eighth to the Flag-officer'. Where no other ship was in sight, the amended shares were:

Lieutenants in command	Two eighths, instead of three
Flag-officers	One third of the captain's two eighths share

Sub-Lieutenant, master and pilot if one on board	1 eighth, divided if all 3: 2 fourths sub-lieutenant 1 fourth each to master and pilot If only 2 then: 2 thirds to person second in command and 1 third to the other If only a sub-lt or a master, then they took the whole eighth If there was only a pilot, then he took one half of the eighth and the remainder went to the Greenwich Hospital
Surgeon or surgeon's assistant if no surgeon, midshipmen, clerk and steward	1 eighth

The remaining half of the proceeds was then divided into shares as follows:

Boatswain's mate, gunner's mate, carpenter's mate, yeoman of the sheets, sailmaker, quartermaster, quartermaster's mate, serjeant of marines	4½ shares each of the remaining half of the proceeds
Corporals of marines	3 shares each of the remaining half of the proceeds
Able seamen, ordinary seamen and marines	1½ shares each of the remaining half of the proceeds
Landsmen, passengers and other supernumeraries doing duty and assisting on board	1 share each of the remaining half of the proceeds
Boys of all descriptions	½ share each of the remaining half of the proceeds

Hired Armed Vessels after 1808

Commissioned commanding officer on board	2 eighths instead of the previous 3
Flag-officers where applicable	1 third of the commanding officer's two eighths share
Any commissioned 'sea' lieutenants in king's pay	1 eighth
Master Mate Unless there are midshipmen or those classed above with midshipmen in the pay of the king in which case: Master Mate & midshipmen etc	1 eighth divided: 2 thirds 1 third Master 1 half of the eighth Share equally the remaining half of the eighth
Other officers and crew	4 eighths distributed as above

If no commissioned officer in command:

Flag-officers if under command of a flag	1 eighth
Master Mate	1 eighth divided: 2 thirds 1 third
Other officers and crew	4 eighths divided as above
Any surplus	Remained at king's disposal and if not disposed of within 1 year after final adjudication then to the Greenwich Hospital

If joint capture of hired vessel and HM ships of war, then:

Commissioned officers on board hired vessel	Share with commissioned officers of same rank on HM ships as joint captors
Master of hired vessel	Share with warrant officers of HM ships
Mate of hired vessel	Share with first class of petty officers of HM ships
Seamen, landsmen and boys of hired vessel	Share with persons of the same description on HM ships

Unless the vessel is commanded by a commissioned master and commander with no commissioned lieutenants on board or by the master, then:

Master	Share with lieutenants of HM ship
Mate	Share with warrant officers of HM ships

1812 and 1815

In 1812, when war broke out with the United States of America, the same provisions were applied to prize captures in that dispute by a proclamation of the Prince Regent at Carlton House on 26 October 1812, 13 days after reprisals against the ships, goods and citizens of the USA were ordered.

When Napoleon escaped from Elba and resumed his war against Britain, reprisals against France were ordered on 21 June 1815 and the previous provisions for the distribution of the proceeds of French prizes reintroduced by a proclamation of the Prince Regent at Carlton House on 29 June 1815. These lasted until Napoleon's surrender to the Royal Navy on *HMS Bellerophon* after Waterloo, bringing an end to the war.

The most contested disputes were those between flag-officers over their shares, which is the subject of the next chapter, including the court battle between Nelson and St Vincent.

5.

Who Got What: The 'Flag-share', Nelson v St Vincent

Prize Money and the 'Flag-share'

By the outbreak of war with France in 1793 the division of prize proceeds into eighths distributed more thinly as they went down the seniority was settled practice. A captain operating under the command of a flag-officer did not get the entire share allocated to him but accounted for one third of his share to his flag-officer, or officers. Where two or more flag-officers were on a station, they divided the flag-share between them, with a larger share to the commander-in-chief than the junior flag-officers. Details of the allocation of prize shares to, and between, flag-officers changed over time, but continued to cause some of the most bitter and prolonged disputes.

Seniority

A recurrent feature of the disputes over flag-officers' prize money was the notion of 'seniority'. An officer in command of a ship who had not achieved the permanent rank, or post, of captain was referred to as a 'master and commander'. He was entitled to be called captain while in command of his ship. But when his command ended and he came ashore, he was no longer a captain. Once an officer was appointed to a ship of sufficient size, he was 'made post', i.e. he was a post-captain, entitled to be called captain even if he was not in command of a ship. Once an officer was 'made post' he ranked in seniority as against all other post-captains by reference to his date of appointment, working his way up the list of seniority of post-captains until he reached the top and could be appointed an admiral. There was then a rigid system of seniority among admirals, with nine grades of admiral before 1805, and ten thereafter.[1] Admirals would work their way up from rear-admiral to vice-admiral and then to admiral. Within each rank there were sub-categories of seniority, originating from the mid-seventeenth-century practice of dividing a fleet into three divisions, each flying a different colour flag. In order of seniority the divisions were blue, then white and finally the most senior, red. Those divisions were in turn divided into three squadrons each under a flag-officer, with the rear-admiral in charge of the rear squadron, the admiral in the centre squadron and the vice-admiral in charge of the van. Before 1805 the admiral of the red was called Admiral of the Fleet, but after 1805 the proliferation of admiral appointments led to the creation of admirals of the red, with a separate post of Admiral of the Fleet. In practice, not all ranks were necessarily present in a fleet. At his death, Admiral Nelson had reached vice-admiral of the white but was commander-in-chief of the fleet at Trafalgar. This system of seniority created problems with putting the right people in charge, leading to work-arounds to permit flexibility. Captains could be appointed to the temporary position of commodore. They could then be placed in command of a squadron without being appointed as a permanent flag-officer. They reverted to being a captain once their appointment as commodore ended. Even within the ranks of commodores there were seniorities. A commodore with the right to appoint a captain of his ship under him was treated as a full, albeit temporary, flag-officer, but a commodore without that right was not. He was referred to by his derisory additional daily allowance as a 'ten-shilling commodore' and was not entitled to a flag-officer's share of prize money. In order to make captains who had not reached the top of the list of seniority up to permanent flag rank as an admiral, captains above him in the list could be appointed as admirals as well to clear the path. Appointment as an admiral, though, contained no assurance that they would actually be employed. An officer who was appointed an admiral but not assigned to one of the active squadrons could be appointed to an 'unspecified' squadron, and would be known popularly, but unflatteringly, as an admiral 'of the yellow'.[2]

The Flag-share Rules

Until June 1744 a flag-officer's entitlement to share in prizes began as soon as he was appointed to a command regardless of when he actually arrived

[1] Brian Lavery, *Nelson's Navy* (London, 1989), p. 98.

[2] Lavery, *Nelson's Navy*, p. 99.

on station to take up the command.[3] That simplistic approach caused disputes between flag-officers, so a new set of rules was proclaimed by George II on 14 June 1744, during the Wars of Austrian Succession.[4] It was expressed to have been made 'in order to prevent disputes arising among the Flag-officers, who have been, or may hereafter be employed in our service'.[5] It was a vain hope. The seven rules introduced in 1744 were amended in 1756[6] and in that form they were the basis for the rules included in the 1793 proclamation.

The 1793 proclamation contained eight separate articles setting out the rules for allocating shares to, and between, flag-officers. By 1808 this had risen to 12 separate articles, intended to restrict the scope for further disputes. Some provisions addressed the problems that arose with exercising command in remote places round the world with poor, seriously delayed communications. An appointment to a command signed in the Admiralty might take months or years to be carried into effect, if ever. A sign of the change to a global naval establishment during the age of sail appears in the changing wording of the proclamations. In 1793 references to flag-officers sent to command overseas still appeared as 'at Jamaica or elsewhere', but by 1803 had become 'any station', as Britain became a global naval power.

All of the proclamations dealing with prizes taken by ships under the command of flag-officers referred to flag-officers 'being actually on board, or directing and assisting in the Capture'.[7] This wording was given a wide interpretation and where a ship was sailing under the orders of a flag-officer that was regarded as sufficient to amount to the flag-officer directing or assisting in captures, though captains may have disagreed with the idea that their remote flag-officers were directing or assisting in captures made by their hard efforts. Indeed, it may seem a generous

3 Per Lord Mansfield, Pigot v White, Easter 25 Geo. 3 B. R., noted in Johnstone v Margetson (1789) 1 H. Bl. 265n.

4 *London Gazette*, 12–16 June 1744, No. 8336, p. 6; the history of the provisions was considered during counsel's submissions recorded in Johnstone v Margetson (1789) 1 H. Bl. 261, 264. Cf. the proclamation of 9 March 1744 without the flag provisions at *London Gazette*, 27 March 1744, No. 8314, pp. 7–9.

5 The proclamation by the King's Lords Justices, dated 19 June 1740, made in the absence of King George II, who was in the habit of spending his summers in Hanover; *London Gazette*, 21–24 June 1740, No. 7921 p. 1, and for explanation see *London Gazette*, 12–16 June 1744, No. 8336, p. 6.

6 Royal Proclamation of King George II, 7 July 1756, *London Gazette*, 6–10 July, No. 9598, p. 1.

7 Such wording had pre-dated even the 1740 and 1744 proclamations referred to above, see Proclamation of George I, 19 March 1718, *London Gazette*, 21–24 March 1718, No. 5731, pp. 1–2.

interpretation of the proclamation. It was, however, in line with the view in English law at the time of the authority that servants had from their masters. In a leading authority from 1698 it had been held that a master could be found liable for a fire set by his servant which had got out of control and damaged a neighbour's property, even though the master had not given express authority for the fire to be set. Chief Justice Holt said of the fire, 'it shall be intended that the servant had authority from his master, it being for his benefit.'[8]

Even where a ship was sailing under the orders of a flag-officer who had been superseded, that was enough for the ship to be under the command of the new flag-officer and for that new flag-officer to be 'directing and assisting' in the capture.[9] If a captain was sailing under direct orders from the Admiralty, however, then no flag-officer was entitled to share in prizes, although that too led to disputes.

The Flag-officer Articles[10]

1st Article: When was a Captain under the Command of a Flag-officer?

The 1793 proclamation, like its predecessors, attempted no definition of when a captain came under the command of a flag-officer for prize purposes, simply awarding a flag-officer a flag-share of 'Prizes taken by Ships and Vessels under his Command', even though disputes had already arisen over when a ship was under the command of a flag-officer. On 14 February 1758 Captain Lane Falkner of *HMS Windsor* received an order from the Admiralty to cruise between Cape Ortugal and Ushant, returning to Plymouth a month after his departure.[11] The purpose of such a 'cruise' was to hunt for enemy ships to be captured as prizes. On 13 March 1758, within the month allowed, Falkner captured the vessel *La Pacifique*. Meanwhile, on 5 March 1758 Sir Edward Hawke, on *HMS Ramilles*, had been appointed by the Admiralty to command a squadron in the Channel which included the *Windsor*, which was then on its cruise between Cape Ortugal and Ushant. Falkner arrived back in Plymouth with his prize on 26 March 1758. Then,

8 Turberville v Stampe (1698) 1 Ld Raym. 264, 265; 91 ER 1072, 1073.

9 Pigot v White, Easter 25 Geo. 3 B. R., noted in Johnstone v Margetson (1789) 1 H. Bl. 265n, see below.

10 The articles in the proclamations between 1793 and 1815 will be considered below in the order that the 12 articles appeared after 1808.

11 During the Seven Years' War, the royal proclamation in force at the time was dated 7 July 1756, *London Gazette*, July 1756, No. 9598.

and only then, did he receive an order from Hawke to place himself under Hawke's command. Thus, at the time of the capture Falkner was acting under the order from the Admiralty, although Hawke had been ordered to take the *Windsor* under his command. *La Pacifique* was condemned as a prize by the Admiralty Court on 6 May 1758, and Hawke claimed a one-eighth flag-officer's share of the prize. It was three years before the Admiralty Court reached a decision. On 13 May 1761 the not very highly regarded Admiralty judge, Sir Thomas Salusbury, allowed Hawke's claim on the basis that at the time of capture *Windsor* had been under Hawke's command. Falkner appealed and the decision was reversed on 28 July 1764 on the basis that at the time of capture Falkner had been acting solely under the orders of the Admiralty and so did not have to account to a flag-officer.[12]

In 1759 another dispute had come to court over a prize taken by Captain Taylor while sailing from the Downs under orders from Lord Harry Powlett during the Seven Years' War.[13] By the time the prize was taken Powlett had been superseded in command of the Downs station by Admiral Smith. Taylor claimed that as Powlett was no longer entitled to the flag-share having been superseded he, Taylor, should receive the whole captain's share. Powlett was a controversial commander, having been court-martialled in 1755 for abandoning a rendezvous with Admiral Hawke and returning to Spithead without orders. His defence that he had relied on the advice of his ship's carpenter that *Barfleur*'s stern-post was dangerously loose earned him the nickname of 'Captain Stern-Post', and the poor carpenter dismissal from the service.[14] He was also thought to be the inspiration for Captain Whiffle in Smollett's satirical novel, *The Adventures of Roderick Random*, but Powlett had his supporters. Having served with Boscawen in the East Indies, 1746–50, Powlett was Boscawen's choice as his second-in-command in the Mediterranean in 1756, but the appointment was overruled by George II, who shared popular anti-Powlett views. Powlett was appointed a rear-admiral in June 1756, but his temporary command in the Downs was the only

12 La Pacifique (1764) Burrell 158, ER 167, 518.

13 Taylor v Lord H. Paulett (1789) 1 H. Bl. 264n. Misspelling of names in case reports at the time is not unusual and part of the family used the spelling Paulet. By 1789, when the case was reported in a note added to the report of Johnstone v Margetson, the spelling was easily confused. Powlett's remote, and younger, cousin, Lord Harry Paulet, made a successful career in the French Revolutionary and Napoleonic Wars and ended up as an admiral.

14 P. K. Crimmin, Powlett [Paulet], Harry, sixth duke of Bolton (1720–1794), ODNB (accessed 3 May 2016). This entry suggests that Powlett remained unemployed once he reached flag rank, but the report of the disputed flag-share would suggest otherwise. N. A. M. Rodger notes that Powlett 'did in fact serve a few months as relief commander-in-chief in the Downs', *The Wooden World* (London, 1988), p. 300.

time he flew his flag.[15] Admirals Boscawen and Knowles gave evidence for Powlett in his dispute with Taylor, speaking to the 'discipline of the Navy' on the determination of an officer's command. They agreed that if a ship was detached on business on instruction from the Admiralty, then if the admiral was superseded, he had no further charge of the ship and she was transferred to the superseding admiral, who was entitled to all prizes taken thereafter even if he had conveyed no further order to the ship. Where the ship was undertaking a task on the original admiral's own initiative, however, they agreed that the original admiral remained accountable and entitled to the prizes until the ship returned to the fleet, even though he may have been superseded in his command of the station and its fleet in the meantime. The court did not have to determine whether the evidence of navy 'discipline', or custom, represented the position in law. At no time had there been a break in command. There had always been a flag-officer in command, and one of them was entitled to the flag-share. Taylor had always been under the command of a flag-officer, whoever that flag-officer may have been. That was enough to defeat Taylor's claim to the whole share.[16] Had there been a dispute between Powlett and his successor, Smith, then it is likely that Smith would have won. As the evidence Powlett called had shown, Powlett would have remained accountable for his decision as commanding officer to give orders to Captain Taylor, despite having been superseded, and could have faced a court-martial over his decision if he had got it wrong. That would not, however, have resolved the issue of entitlement to prize money from prizes taken while those orders were being acted upon. The approach that the courts adopted was that the prize share attached to the territory of the station and to the commander at the time of capture.

The Admiralty could remove a flag-officer from a station for another duty without appointing a new flag-officer to succeed him. In December 1780, during the American War of Independence, Captain George Johnstone was flying a commodore's broad pennant as flag-officer in command of the Lisbon station and entitled to the flag-share of prizes taken on the station.[17] On 16 December 1780 Johnstone, while at Spithead but acting as the commander-in-chief of the Lisbon station, sent a written order to Captain Mann of *HMS Cerberus* to cruise on the Lisbon station patrolling for enemy vessels. Mann received the order on 17 January 1781 and sailed on 28 January 1781. On 25 February 1781 Mann captured the Spanish frigate

[15] William Laird Cowes, *The Royal Navy: A History from the Earliest Times to the Present* (London, 1898), vol. III, p. 565.

[16] Taylor v Lord H. Paulett (1789) 1 H. Bl. 264n, per Lord Mansfield.

[17] For entitlement of commodores to a flag-share, see Article 11 in Chapter 6 below.

Grana and took her as a prize into Plymouth on 3 March 1781, writing to Johnstone at Spithead to tell him of his arrival. On 19 January 1781, however, the Admiralty had appointed Johnstone to command a fleet, not including the *Cerberus*, to capture the Dutch Cape. Johnstone received his new commission on 3 February 1781, before the capture of the *Grana*. From 19 January 1781 the Admiralty addressed no new orders to Johnstone as commander on the Lisbon station and even though no new commander was appointed to supersede him, they treated Johnstone's command of the Lisbon station as at an end. Nevertheless, Johnstone claimed the flag-share of the *Grana* prize on the basis that he had not been superseded on the Lisbon station and therefore Mann had been acting under his order at the time of the capture. By the time the case came to court in June 1789 Johnstone had died, but the claim was pursued by his executor.[18]

The court held that, absent any indication to the contrary, the appointment of Johnstone to a new command terminated his command of the Lisbon station. At the time, therefore, Johnstone was not the commander on the station and neither he nor his estate were entitled to the flag-share. Had he survived then Johnstone might have felt hard done by. His new fleet had only sailed for the Cape on 13 March 1781 and no one else was in command of the Lisbon station until then, and he had given up the Lisbon station for a dream of gold that turned to dust. The expedition to the Cape had originally been intended to be followed by a raid on the river Plate to capture Spanish treasure ships said to be shipping $4 million, and then a prize-taking trip to the South Seas.[19] These lucrative additions to the plan were abandoned, however, when the need to reinforce America was given priority.[20]

The dispute over the Lisbon prizes was far from being the only litigation that the expedition gave rise to. The dispute between Johnstone and Captain Sutton over responsibility for allowing Admiral Suffren and the French fleet to reach the Cape first has already featured in Chapter 4. Having discovered that Suffren had beaten him to the Cape, Johnstone abandoned the assault to take the Cape but did capture four rich Dutch East Indiamen in Saldanha Bay as a consolation. Even that, however, led to yet further

[18] Johnstone v Margetson (1789) 1 H. Bl. 261. Johnstone died on 24 May 1787.

[19] Not a 'privateering expedition' as suggested by Prof. J. P. Van Niekerk in his otherwise excellent article on the Saldhana Bay litigation, J. P. van Niekerk, 'Of Naval Courts-Martial and Prize Claims: Some Legal Consequences of Commodore Johnstone's Secret Mission to the Cape of Good Hope and the "Battle" of Saldanha Bay, 1781 (Part 1)', *Fundamina, A Journal of Legal History* 21:2 (2015), 392–456, at p. 397 n. 15.

[20] Piers Mackesy, *The War for America 1775–1783* (London, 1964), p. 376.

litigation over the division of the spoils.[21] Johnstone did at least resist the temptation to flout his orders and redirect his forces to the river Plate as originally intended, a temptation that would later be too great for Captain Home Riggs Popham after capturing the Cape in 1806, leading to more litigation, as we will see below.

Despite these disputes, it was not until after war with revolutionary France in 1793 that the Admiralty attempted to clarify the royal proclamation wording.

1793, New Wars, More Problems

Problems arose if a captain received orders from flag-officers on two different stations. Whose orders was he acting under at the time of a capture? In June 1797 Captain Linzee was serving on *HMS L'Oiseau* under Admiral Pringle at the Cape of Good Hope. *L'Oiseau* needed repairs at the East India Company's facilities, and in June 1797 Pringle sent her to India for repair. India was within the East Indies station under the command of Admiral Rainier, so Pringle wrote to Rainier requesting that *L'Oiseau* be repaired at Bombay. The precise chain of command between the officers appointed to the Cape and India was often unclear and confused, placing Rainier at times in a difficult position, though nothing of this can be detected in the law report.[22] When *L'Oiseau* arrived in Madras in August 1797, Linzee reported to Rainier, who placed Linzee under his orders and ordered him to Calcutta, rather than Bombay, for repairs. When Linzee had finished his repairs and was ready to sail back to Pringle, Rainier ordered him to accompany a convoy to the Cape. While following Rainier's order to escort the convoy in July 1798, *L'Oiseau* became detached from the convoy and bore away for Prince of Wales Island. When near the island, and still within the limits of Rainier's station, *L'Oiseau* captured the *Angelique*, a prize worth £21,600. By then Admiral Christian had superseded Pringle in command at the Cape.

The law report does not recite that Prince of Wales Island was the name then given to Penang, an island in the Malacca Straits that is part of modern Malaysia. Thus, it would appear that Rainier was doing more than just sending *L'Oiseau* back to the Cape. Constantly short of ships for the protection of trade and having to cater for a threat of invasion by the French via Egypt, he took the opportunity to use her to protect trade from the Far East. If

21 Sam Willis, *The Struggle for Sea Power* (London, 2015), pp. 429–36; Mackesy, *The War for America 1775–1783*, p. 390; G Rutherford, 'Sidelights on Commodore Johnstone's Expedition to the Cape (1942) Pt 1', *MM* 28:3, 189–212, and 'Pt 2', *MM* 28:4, 290–308.

22 Peter Ward, *British Naval Power in the East, 1794–1805* (Woodbridge, 2013), p. 4.

Linzee was still acting under Pringle's orders as commander-in-chief at the Cape when he captured the prize, then Christian, as Pringle's successor, was entitled to the flag-share. On that basis he and his executors laid claim to the flag-share, but without success. The action got to court in 1807, when the Court of Common Pleas decided that by being sent out of the limits of the Cape station into the limits of the East Indies station and under the command of Admiral Rainier, the command of the Cape station over *L'Oiseau* had been suspended and the commander-in-chief of the Cape was not entitled to the flag-share.[23]

The first provision providing further definition of when a ship was under the command of a flag-officer appeared in the 1803 proclamation, to deal with ships joining and leaving stations commanded by a flag-officer. The first part of the 1803 provision was that a captain was deemed to be under the command of a flag 'when he shall actually have received some order directly from, or be acting in the execution of some order issued by a flag-officer'.[24]

The second part of the 1803 provision was that a captain was deemed to:

> continue under the command of such Flag so long as the Flag-officer by whom the Order was issued, or any other Flag-officer acting upon the same station shall continue upon such station or until such Captain shall have received some Order issued by some other Flag-officer or the Admiralty.

The first part was supplemented in 1808 by additional wording that provided that in the event of a captain 'being directed to join a flag-officer on any station he shall be deemed to be under the Command of such flag-officer from the time he arrives within the limits of the station'. Thus, a captain was now deemed to be under the command of a flag-officer by arriving within the limits of the station to join the flag-officer there, even without actually receiving an order from the flag-officer on the station. The second part of the provision dealing with continuing under a command was therefore simplified, to provide simply that a captain would 'continue under the command of the flag-officer of such station until [he] received some Order issued by some other Flag-officer or the Admiralty'.

The reasoning in Holmes v Rainier presupposed that the flag-officer providing the new orders was entitled to do so. Rainier had been entitled to give his orders to Linzee because of the implied transfer of authority

[23] Holmes v Rainier (1807) 8 East 502, Lord Ellenborough, Grose J., Lawrence J. and Le Blanc J.

[24] Proclamation of 7 July 1803, *London Gazette*, 15599, p. 801.

when *L'Oiseau* was sent to India. The decision in Holmes v Rainier did not mean that flag-officers could assume command of a ship from another station without authority and thereby acquire a right to share in the prizes that the ship might take. That did not stop them trying. In 1805 Admiral Lord Gardner was appointed by the Admiralty to temporary command of the Channel fleet. To do so he handed over command of the Irish station at Cork to Rear-Admiral Drury.[25] On 3 May, as commander-in-chief of the Irish station, Drury ordered Captain Maitland of the frigate *Loire* to cruise for a month in the western Channel 'for the protection of the trade of his Majesty's subjects, and the annoyance of the enemy', the standard wording of an order for a month of hunting for prizes. Once the month was over, he was to return to Cork, but if Maitland should see the enemy fleet, or hear of their being at sea, he should either return to Cork to report it to Drury or report it to the Channel fleet off Brest and then return to Cork 'without loss of time'. Whilst on his cruise Maitland received intelligence that the enemy were at sea and, pursuant to his orders from Drury, sailed to meet Gardner off Ushant to tell him, falling in with him on 25 May 1805. On 28 May, three days later, Gardner ordered Maitland to take Captain William Brown and his followers from *HMS Polyphemus* to join *HMS Ajax* off Ferrol, northern Spain, where he was also to deliver Gardner's despatches to Vice-Admiral Sir Robert Calder. Ferrol was outside the limits of both the Irish and the Channel stations. Meanwhile, a convoy accompanied by *HMS Desiree* and a sloop had left Jamaica on 20 April and was expected in the Channel. Accordingly, Gardner gave Maitland the private signals for the convoy and directed him 'while in the execution of the order you have already received from Rear-admiral Drury, to keep a good look out for the convoy'. Should he fall in with it then he was 'to afford it every protection and assistance' in his power to see the ships safely bound up the St George's and the Bristol channels.

On 1 June 1805, supposedly while on his way back from Ferrol to Cork after delivering Brown and the despatches, Maitland captured one French and two Spanish prizes worth £3,000 in Muros Bay. Muros Bay is south of Ferrol, and not on any direct route back to Cork from a fleet off Ferrol. Maitland had taken the opportunity of being in prime prize-hunting territory

[25] Admiralty orders to Gardner dated 25 February 1805 to shift his flag into one of his frigates at Cork and sail to Plymouth to await further orders, handing over command to Drury in Cork, Admiralty to Drury dated 27 February 1805 to take up the command, Gardner to Drury dated 5 March 1805 handing over command of the station and its frigates, including *Topaze*, and Admiralty to Gardner dated 20 March 1805 to assume command of the Channel fleet, cited in Lady Gardner v Lyne (1811) 13 East 574 and Drury v Lady Gardner (1813) 2 M&S 150.

off Spain. The flag-share of the Muros Bay prizes was paid to Edward Lyne, Drury's prize agent in Plymouth. Lyne was accustomed to the tussles of the prize agency business. His brother-in-law, Benjamin Tucker, was St Vincent's secretary and the prize agent involved in litigation with Nelson. Lyne had also been Captain Thomas Hardy's prize agent in Plymouth when Hardy sent in a Dutch prize, the *Orion*, captured by *HMS Victory* in the Channel. Nelson's prize agent Alexander Davison, jealous of his position and rightly seeing it under threat, protested about Lyne's appointment. Hardy was forced to write an apology to Davison, who was appointed in Lyne's place.[26] Gardner did not replace Lyne, but did claim the flag-share for himself. Gardner had been a tenacious frigate captain used to hunting down prizes. His fighting spirit had received hard-earned praise from St Vincent, who described him as 'a zealous and brave man.'[27] Gardner had felt slighted in the spring of 1800 when command of the Channel fleet was given to St Vincent as successor to Lord Bridport. St Vincent had returned from the Mediterranean fleet supposedly for reasons of his health and then picked up the plum job in the Channel. In correspondence with his sister, Gardner admitted to enduring 'mortification and chagrin' at the decision.[28] Spencer, the First Lord of the Admiralty, tried to make amends to Gardner with the Irish station in August 1800, and an Irish peerage in December 1800.[29] The two months in command of the Channel fleet in May and June 1805 must have had the taste of a sweet fruit previously denied him. He was not going to let prizes go without a fight, especially where the rival claim was from the station that he had given up in order to take the temporary position with the Channel fleet.

As the prize dispute rumbled on, Gardner was reappointed to the Channel fleet in 1807, but ill health forced him to resign in 1808, and he died at the turn of the year before the legal action over the Muros Bay prizes was heard. Gardner's widow, Susanna, as tenacious as her late husband in pursuing his outstanding prize claims, took this and other claims to court after his death. Susanna was used to handling the reins of wealth. She was the sole heir of her father's Jamaican fortune at 14 and had been widowed

26 Downer, *Nelson's Purse*, p. 239.

27 ODNB/10371, J. K. Laughton, rev. Christopher Doorne, 9 August 2016. This entry does not include Gardner's brief spell in command of the Channel fleet in 1805 recorded in the law report.

28 Francis Davey (ed.), *Heart of Oak: Letters from Admiral Gardner (1742–1809)* (Exeter, 2015), p. 111.

29 An Irish peerage did not entitle the holder to a seat in the House of Lords, and Gardner continued to represent Westminster as an MP. He was granted a UK peerage in 1807, with the title Baron Gardner of Uttoxeter.

in her first marriage at 17.[30] At 20 she married 27-year-old Captain Alan Gardner, who named Susanna in his will as his joint executrix unless and until she remarried.[31] Thus, when the claim over the captures by Captain Maitland in the *Loire* came to court in May 1811 after Gardner's death her name appeared as the first named plaintiff along with her co-executors.[32]

Lord Ellenborough delivered the judgment of the court that Lady Gardner had lost her late husband's claim. The court held that Gardner's order to Maitland did not keep the *Loire* under his command after delivery of his despatches off Ferrol, but was a modification of, or addition to, Drury's orders, for the purpose of the more beneficial execution of them. It was to be seen not as 'a supersession or abrogation' of them, but as requiring 'a coincident and not a contradictory service'. That disposed of the claim, but the court went on to consider whether Gardner would have been entitled to the prize-share if he had intended to oust Drury's orders and replace them with orders putting the *Loire* under his own command. They decided that in those circumstances a flag-officer could not create for himself an entitlement to a flag-share. They doubted whether a commander on one station could annex a ship from another station to his own command, but if it could be done then he could not create a right to prizes taken outside of the limits of his station, unless the chase began within the limits. The idea of a station, said Ellenborough:

> implies that the limits of that station are to be under the superintendence and control of the commander of that station, and that he may place his cruizers within the limits of that station, wherever, in his judgment, the interest of the service may require: but to allow him to place his cruizers beyond his own station, for the purpose of cruising out of that station, is inconsistent with the idea of a station, and is making the whole ocean from one extremity to the other eventually within the limits of any one particular station.[33]

The victory was too late for Drury, who had also died, suddenly on 6 March 1811 while on the East Indies station, although the news had not yet reached the court. He left behind him not only his legal battles with Gardner's estate, but also a string of squabbles with Admiral Albemarle Bertie

30 http://gale-gaylefamilies.com/gale-gayle-families-of-the-west-indies.html (accessed June 2016).

31 TNA, PROB 11/1495/204.

32 Lady Gardner v Lyne (1811) 13 East 574.

33 Lady Gardner v Lyne (1811) 13 East 574, 585.

of the Cape station, whose successful invasion of Isle de France (Mauritius) Drury had claimed as his own, amidst complaints that Bertie rather than Drury was rewarded with a baronetcy.

Ellenborough and the Court of Common Pleas developed the territorial theory of a station in a further claim between the estates of Gardner and Drury, arising again out of the departure of Gardner from the Irish station in 1805.[34] It came to court two years later, in November 1813. Mr Gifford was again counsel for the Drury family, but Mr Brougham, who had previously appeared for Lady Gardner, was replaced by Mr Horner as her counsel. When Gardner left Cork in 1805 he handed over command of the station to Drury, but as ordered by the Admiralty he left for Plymouth flying his flag in one of the frigates from the station.[35] He chose *HMS Topaze* under Captain Willoughby Lake, which had just returned to Cork.[36] Having convoyed a Spanish prize from Cork to Plymouth, *Topaze* had left Plymouth on 11 February 1805 to cruise the same hunting ground to which Drury would later send Captain Maitland and the *Loire*.[37] On her way, however, she had captured a prize, which she took into Cork on 22 February 1805. There was no dispute that Gardner was entitled to the flag-share of that prize as it was taken under his orders, within the territory of the Cork station and while he was still in command of that station. Instead of continuing on her cruise as originally ordered, however, *Topaze* sailed from Cork with Gardner on board on 15 March 1805, arriving in Plymouth on the 17th. Gardner received his appointment to the Channel fleet on 20 March. Then came the controversial order from Gardner to Lake, dated 30 March 1805. The Admiralty had received a letter from the merchants at Lloyds Coffee House about the unprotected state of a homeward-bound convoy from Surinam.[38] Having told Lake about the Lloyds letter, Gardner gave Lake an order that:

[34] Drury v Lady Gardner (1813) 2 M&S 150.

[35] Admiralty orders to Gardner dated 25 February 1805 to shift his flag into one of his frigates at Cork and sail to Plymouth to await further orders, handing over command to Drury in Cork, Admiralty to Drury dated 27 February 1805 to take up the command, Gardner to Drury dated 5 March 1805 handing over command of the station and its frigates, including *Topaze*, and Admiralty to Gardner dated 20 March 1805 to assume command of the Channel fleet, cited in Lady Gardner v Lyne (1811) 13 East 574 and Drury v Lady Gardner (1813) 2 M&S 150.

[36] Dated 21 January 1805.

[37] 'between lat. 48N and 53N and Long. 10 to 25 W'.

[38] Drury v Lady Gardner (1813) 2 M&S 150, 152.

> you are hereby required and directed in obedience to their Lordships' directions, to proceed to sea, and cruise for one week to the westward for the protection of the said convoy, and at the expiration of that time it is their Lordships' directions that you proceed in execution of the former orders which you received from me,[39] and at the expiration thereof you are to return to your former station at Cork, and follow the orders of Rear-admiral Drury.

The terms of the order suggest that Gardner had orders from the Admiralty to send *Topaze* on the voyage that he prescribed, but no evidence of such an order was before the court, who criticised the state of the evidence and were disinclined to fill in any gaps by inferring facts in the absence of direct evidence.[40]

Topaze left Plymouth on 1 April 1805 as a result of Gardner's order and arrived within the limits of the cruising ground that he had prescribed on 21 April. On 7 May 1805, *Topaze* captured a Spanish prize, the *Napoleon,* a privateer from St Sebastian, pierced for 20 guns and mounting ten nine-pounders and four 18-pounder carronades, with 108 men on board. She was no match for the French-built *Topaze* of 32 guns.[41] In a 57-day cruise from Bordeaux, however, she had taken as prizes the *Westmoreland* from Liverpool and the *Brunswick,* a brig from Honduras.[42] The capture was made within the limits of the Cork station and the area prescribed by Gardner in his order of 21 January 1805, but outside of the six-week period covered by his original orders.

On 20 May 1805 *Topaze* captured a second prize, the Spanish privateer *El Fenix* of St Sebastian, a brig of 14 guns and 85 men. She had sailed out of Vigo but not made a capture in the ten days she had been at sea before capture.[43] Once again, her capture was outside the six-week period covered by Gardner's order for a cruise. Her capture was also made just outside the limits of the Cork station and the area prescribed by Gardner's order of

39 i.e. the orders dated 21 January 1805 to start a six-week cruise.

40 Per Lord Ellenborough, Drury v Lady Gardner (1813) 2 M&S 150, 161.

41 *Topaze* was one of the vessels taken by Hood at the siege of Toulon in 1793.

42 *London Gazette,* 11 June 1805, No. 15815, p. 773, letter 7 May 1805 Lake to Gardner copied to the Admiralty. The law report gives the date as 8 May but such confusion was not unusual due in part to the naval practice whereby a day ran from noon until noon and was thus 12 hours behind the calendar date, much to the frustration of William James when he wrote his *Naval History of Great Britain,* vol. 2, p. 521, referring to 'this silly and perplexing custom'.

43 *London Gazette,* 11 June 1805, No. 15815, p. 773, letter 20 May 1805 Lake to Gardner copied to the Admiralty. The law report adopts the Anglo-Greek version of her name, *Phoenix.*

21 January. During the hearing enquiries were made to discover whether the chase had begun within the limits of the Cork station, but the logbook did not provide an answer and Captain Lake was abroad. It was argued on behalf of the Drury family that the court should infer that the chase began within the limits of Drury's command rather than presume that the captain was guilty of a breach of his orders in straying out of his stipulated limits. Once again, however, the court refused to do so. The Spanish ships were condemned as prizes and the flag-share was paid to Lord Gardner in the sum of £1,961 17*s*. As Drury had taken over command of the Cork station, including the *Topaze*, at the time of the captures he claimed the flag-share from Gardner and the action between their respective estates was eventually heard in November 1813.[44]

The court held that any claim by Drury was reliant on his appointment to succeed Gardner as commander of the Cork station. As *El Fenix* had been taken outside the limits of that station, and there was no evidence that the chase began within the limits of the station, the court held that Drury's appointment to the Cork station could give him no right to the flag-share as his right was 'coextensive with the limits of the station'. As to the *Napoleon* that was taken within the limits of the station, the court held that Drury rather than Gardner was entitled to the flag-share. Gardner's authority over the *Topaze* had been limited to ordering her to take him to Plymouth. They refused to infer any further authority from the Admiralty without proof of an order. When the *Topaze* sailed from Plymouth, therefore, she had been a ship of the Cork station returning to her commander-in-chief in Cork, despite Gardner's order of 30 March 1805. As the *Napoleon* had been taken as a prize by a ship attached to the Cork station under the command of Admiral Drury and within the limits of the station, he and his estate were entitled to the flag-share of that prize.

One of the features of this case is that the intelligence gained via the insurance market at Lloyds Coffee House was openly referred to in court and reported. There was no need for the intelligence or its source to be named, yet it was. The Admiralty was happy for all the world to know; to say to the world 'We know who you are and where you are, we will find you and capture you.' That in itself was a weapon in the economic war being fought at sea.

44 After a trial of the facts before a jury in Hilary term in early 1813. Drury v Lady Gardner (1813) 2 M&S 150.

The Curious Incident of the Ship that Passed in the Night

Fear that rival flag-officers would seek to take ships from neighbouring fleets under their control meant that subterfuge would occasionally be used to defeat their attempts. Such subterfuge offers a window into the delicate relationships upon which the operation of the fleets depended.

At the end of 1804 Nelson was off Toulon watching for the French fleet to emerge in the cat-and-mouse game that would end the following year off Cape Trafalgar. Nelson was in command of the fleet in the Mediterranean, but the lucrative area between Gibraltar and Cape Finisterre along the Atlantic coast of Portugal and Spain, which had previously been included in the Mediterranean station, had been hived off and placed under the command of Admiral Sir John Orde, with his own squadron of ships. The rivalry between Nelson and Orde went back to 1798 when Nelson had been sent into the Mediterranean in command of the squadron that fought the French at the Battle of the Nile. Several of the more senior officers felt slighted by the appointment, including Orde. St Vincent had sent Orde home, and Orde then challenged St Vincent to a duel, a challenge that St Vincent contemptuously refused to accept. When the Admiralty made the decision to divide the Mediterranean station between Nelson and Orde there was little hope of cooperation, and none ensued. Orde did not communicate with Nelson for weeks after he arrived on station.[45] Orde's area of command was apt to provide rich pickings in terms of prizes as ships to and from the Mediterranean and further afield had to pass through it, leaving them open to capture. This was not lost on Nelson, who complained that Orde had been sent 'to reap the golden harvest' at his expense.[46]

Enemy and merchant ships were not the only ones who had to sail through Orde's area of command. If Nelson wanted to send his dispatches to the Admiralty, then he had to send them through those same waters. When he did so he instructed the ships sent to carry the dispatches to keep out to sea and avoid contact with Orde's ships. Gibraltar and the coast beyond were sickly places for a ship to call and there was a 'dreadful malady' raging at the time.[47] That might have justified a wide berth on voyages to Lisbon with dispatches bound for the Admiralty in London, but Nelson had

[45] Nelson to Sir Alexander Ball, 5 December 1804, Nicolas, *The Dispatches and Letters of Vice Admiral Lord Viscount Nelson*, vol. VI, p. 286.

[46] Nelson to Sir Alexander Ball, 5 December 1804, Nicolas, *Dispatches*, vol. VI, p. 285.

[47] Nelson to Capt. Robert Pettet, H.M. Sloop *Termagant*, 4 November 1804, Nicolas, *Dispatches*, vol. VI, p. 259.

another problem in mind.[48] He had to get dispatches to Lisbon and called the then Captain William Parker, in command of the frigate *Amazon*, on board *Victory* to give him orders to carry them. Parker was a favourite of Nelson's and a nephew of St Vincent. The orders, dated 30 December 1804, contained the injunction that 'In proceeding and returning from Lisbon, you are not to approach within fifty leagues [150 miles] of Cape St Vincent, and on no account go near Cadiz, or in any manner interfere with the Squadron under Sir John Orde.'[49] Nelson also provided a private, unsigned memorandum in his own handwriting that required Parker to pass Cape Spartel, on the African side of the Straits of Gibraltar, in the night, steering to the southward and westward to avoid Orde, and ended with 'Bring-to for nothing, if you can help it. Hoist the signal for quarantine, and that you are charged with dispatches. If you are forced to speak by a superior officer, show him only my order for not interfering with you; and unless he is an admiral superior to me, you will obey my orders instead of any pretended ones from him.'[50] Nelson added in conversation with Parker that 'Sir John Orde takes my frigates from me, and sends them away in some other direction from what I wish. I cannot even get my despatches home. You must contrive to get to the westward and go into Lisbon, and avoid his ships. I have not signed your orders [alluding to the private memorandum] because Sir John Orde is my senior; but if it should come to a Court-Martial, Hardy can swear to my handwriting, and you shall not be broke. Take your orders, and good-bye; and remember, Parker, if you cannot weather that fellow, I shall think you have not a drop of your old uncle's blood in your veins.'

Parker complied with the private instructions in the memorandum and passed Cape Spartel, at night, but was spotted in the moonlight by one of Orde's outlying frigates, who gave chase. Fortunately, when the *Amazon* was overhauled it turned out that the pursuing frigate was under the command of Captain William Hoste, who was junior in seniority to Parker, but more importantly was a fellow devotee of Nelson.[51] Hoste had served as a midshipman with Nelson on *Agamemnon* and it was Nelson who had made Hoste a commander after the Battle of the Nile. Hoste came aboard *Amazon* and was ushered below by Parker, out of earshot of the quarterdeck. 'Captain Hoste', Parker is reported to have said, 'I believe you owe all

48 Captain A. T. Mahan, *The Life of Nelson: The Embodiment of the Sea Power of Great Britain* (London, 1897), pp. 261–3; Sir Augustus Phillimore, *The Last of Nelson's Captains* (London, 1906), pp. 125–9.

49 Nicolas, *Dispatches*, vol. VI, p. 308.

50 Ibid.

51 Hoste is remembered for his victory at the Battle of Lissa in 1811 when he went into battle displaying the signal 'Remember Nelson'.

your advancement in the service to my uncle, Lord St Vincent, and to Lord Nelson. I am avoiding Sir John Orde's squadron by desire of Lord Nelson.' Showing Hoste Nelson's handwritten note, he said: 'you know his handwriting; I must go on.' Had Parker disobeyed an order from Orde once it had been passed on by Hoste, then Parker would have risked a court-martial. 'The question of a court-martial would be very mischievous,' Parker pointed out, 'Do you not think it would be better if you were not to meet the *Amazon* this night?' Hoste left the *Amazon* and Nelson's dispatches sailed on unmolested. Parker won more than Nelson's gratitude from the expedition. On 27 January 1805 he took the Spanish ship *Gravina* off Cape St Vincent with a valuable cargo of colonial goods and 330,000 Spanish silver dollars. The capture earned him £24,000, enough to set him and his parents up in style.[52] What would have pleased Nelson just as much was that, by avoiding coming under Orde's orders, Parker had avoided the flag-share of £12,000 being claimed by Orde instead of Nelson.

Acting Contrary to a Flag-officer's Orders

There were limits to the extent to which a commander-in-chief could claim that a captain was acting under his direction. Where a captain was acting inconsistently with his orders, because his actions were outside the orders he had received, he had been ordered to do something else, or even not to do the things that he was doing, then his commander-in-chief was not entitled to a share of prizes taken in the course of such actions.

In July 1796 Captain Milne of the frigate *HMS La Pique* was attached to the Leeward Island station with orders to protect Demerara, a Dutch colony on the north coast of South America in what is now Guyana. French depredation of the British trade in the area was a real problem and British merchant ships had insurance that was only valid if they sailed in convoy with a Royal Navy escort. On 1 June 1796 Admiral Christian, then commander-in-chief of the station, had written to the Governor of Demerara that he would direct a Royal Navy ship to escort a convoy to Europe on 15 July 1796 as the ships needed to sail then to make the rendezvous in St Kitts for the onward convoy to England. He told the governor to tell the merchants to load their ships and be ready to put to sea. By 21 July 1796 the merchant ships had responded and were ready for sea, but no escort ship had arrived. Under pressure from the governor and the merchants, Milne decided to escort the ships to St Kitts, where they could join a convoy to England, anticipating that he would make a speedy return to Demerara.

52 Andrew Lambert, *Admirals* (London, 2009), p. 207.

While sailing to St Kitts, however, Milne received a letter from Admiral Christian dated 23 June 1796 explaining that he had appointed the *Madras* to relieve Milne off Demerara. The letter was written on the day that Christian handed over command to Admiral Harvey, and contained no further orders for Milne, either releasing him from his previous orders or providing for what he was to do next. On 27 July, while off St Lucia, Milne dispatched a tender with a letter to Christian explaining why he was sailing for St Kitts, hoping that Christian would approve. Milne told Christian that should the convoy have left St Kitts before he arrived, he would wait there for Christian's orders. Some of the convoyed ships needed repair, which might detain them in St Kitts for two days in any event. Milne arrived at St Kitts on 31 July 1796. His letter to Christian arrived in Martinique on the following day, although Milne feared that the tender had been captured or lost as he received no orders from either Christian or his replacement, Harvey.

The St Kitts convoy had in fact departed for England already, so the Demerara ships were in St Kitts without an escort to England. Enemy ships were ready to prey upon them, and the hurricane season was coming. The convoy captains again pressed Milne to act, this time to continue his escort of the convoy fleet all the way to Europe. Expecting orders at any time from his commander-in-chief, Milne held off until 9 August. By then the weather was so threatening that it was unsafe for the merchant ships to remain at anchor, and they had to get underway. Milne, therefore, wrote to Harvey, having heard that Harvey had now taken over command from Christian. He explained the dangerous position of the merchant fleet and that, whilst he had no wish to leave the Leeward station, he had no orders. He added that if he had received none by the following morning, he would take charge of the convoy again and sail with it for England. Milne stood over towards Guadeloupe and off Nevis Point on the morning of 10 August in the hope of intercepting some orders for him, but orders came there none. Accordingly, Milne sailed with the convoy on 10 August without orders and set course for England.

Unknown to Milne, Harvey had in fact ordered the *Ariadne* to St Kitts to convoy the Demerara ships to England, but she only sailed on 16 August and arrived at St Kitts ten days after Milne had sailed. Writing to the Admiralty to explain what had happened, Harvey confirmed that Milne had sailed for England out of anxiety for the safety of the convoy, but without his orders to do so. He regretted that Milne had not waited a few days longer, when the *Ariadne* would eventually have arrived.

On 8 October 1796 Milne, by now well out of the limits of the Leeward station, was approaching England when between Start Point and Portland Bill he captured prizes worth over £34,000. He arrived at Spithead the following day. The day after that he sent his account to the Admiralty to explain his return to England without orders from his commander-in-chief. Fortunately for Milne their lordships approved of his actions.[53]

Harvey claimed the flag-share of Milne's prizes, worth £4,261 4*s.* 8*d*, but Milne contested his claim. Harvey claimed that even after his departure from his orders, Milne remained under his command as commander-in-chief. As Grose J. pointed out, the real question was not whether Milne thought that he was acting wrong, or whether he acted in disobedience to the commands of his commander-in-chief, but whether he was acting under any orders at all. The court was not unsympathetic to Harvey. Le Blanc J. said that he 'should not have been sorry, on principles of public policy, if I could have found that [Harvey] was entitled to the flag-officer's share in this case, because it is not to be approved that an officer, however good his motives may have been, should derive any advantage from his disobedience of orders.' The court held, however, that the wording of the proclamation required a flag-officer to be 'directing' or 'assisting' in the capture and that that was not made out on the facts of the case. Harvey was not entitled to the flag-share.

Harvey could have argued that although Milne had no express orders to act as he did, he had implied authority to act as the exigencies of the situation required. Harvey's letter to the Admiralty confirming that Milne had sailed without orders posed a problem for that argument, but the fact that it was not raised at all is instructive. Even a flag-officer keen on obtaining £4,261 was not keen on arguing that his orders carried with them an implied authority to ignore them if the circumstances warranted it. The court had worried about giving a benefit to captains who disobeyed their orders, but the ruling provided a good reason for commanders to ensure that their captains always had up-to-date orders, and to draft their orders in such a way that they permitted useful activities that might lead to the taking of prizes.

Cases of captains sailing contrary to their orders were not as rare as may be supposed. Difficulties with communication frequently placed captains bound by their orders in difficult positions, needing to use their own initiative at their own risk. 'For the system of command to work effectively, to use initiative did not mean to do what a captain thought best, but to do what was expected of him by his commanding officer within a recognised and respected hierarchical structure and a framework of detailed doctrine.'[54] In 1779 the 24-gun frigate *Hyaena* was in the West

[53] Harvey v Cooke (1805) 6 East 220, 221.

[54] Sam Willis, *Fighting at Sea in the Eighteenth Century* (Woodbridge, 2008), p. 99.

Indies during the War of American Independence under Captain Edward Thompson when he too was pressed by worried merchants to convoy a rich fleet home contrary to his orders. He was convicted at a court-martial for his disobedience to his orders, but received only a formal reprimand as the court approved of his motive, being 'a desire of doing service to his country, by securing the trade, and not from any private motives'.[55] In 1781 Thompson and the *Hyaena* were back in the West Indies and Thompson was awaiting written orders to escort a convoy home again. Thompson had received a verbal message relayed by a lieutenant that Admiral Rodney intended him to escort the convoy and to take with him the admiral's despatches. Neither the written orders nor the despatches arrived, however, as Rodney, in ill health but buoyed by his plunder of St Eustatius, had already sailed for England. Thompson decided to sail with the convoy without orders and faced another court-martial for his trouble, but again his career emerged unscathed.[56]

The tribulations and trials of the Thompsons of the Royal Navy helped to set the limits of initiative, and the doctrine within which it operated. It did so without career-ending harm to able officers. Thompson died on the coast of Guinea in January 1796, after a successful career as a naval officer and poet despite his courts-martial.[57] The lieutenant who had brought the verbal message from Rodney was Lieutenant Home Riggs Popham, who had served as a midshipman under Thompson in 1779, at the time of Thompson's previous disobedience of orders. Thompson had become something of a father figure to young Popham, and the example of Captain Thompson may have contributed to a somewhat imaginative approach to compliance with orders on Popham's part, which was to fuel further litigation during a colourful career, as we have seen in Chapter 4 above, and will return to in Chapters 6 and 8 below. The temptation to sail without orders from the Cape to seek wealth and glory in the river Plate that Commodore George Johnstone had resisted in 1781 would prove too great for Popham, as we shall see below.

2nd Article: Size of the Flag-share

From 1793 to 1808 the share that went to flag-officers was one of the captain's three eighths. The flag-share had been one eighth since the proclamation

55 Jacqueline Reiter, *Quicksilver Captain: The Improbable Life of Sir Home Popham* (Warwick, 2024), p. 27.

56 Hugh Popham, *A Damned Cunning Fellow* (Tywardreath, 1991), p. 12.

57 Nicolas, *Dispatches*, vol. I, p. 62.

of 1744. If the captain was under direct Admiralty orders, or otherwise not under the command of a flag-officer, then the captain kept the full three eighths share. The most significant change in this arrangement came in 1808.[58] In that year the share received by captains and flag-officers was reduced, in order to distribute a greater share to the crew. After 1808 the captain's share was two eighths (i.e. a quarter), rather than three eighths. Where he had to account to a flag-officer or flag-officers, the captain still had to hand over one third of his share, but it was one third of his lower share. Thus, after 1808 the share going to flag-officers went down from an eighth to a twelfth, a one third reduction.

The 1808 changes to prize distribution are generally recognised as having redistributed prize money away from the commanding officers to the ship's company. Whilst that is true overall, the changes made were more subtle than that, as we will see in Chapter 7 below.

3rd Article: When does a new Flag-officer take over?

Before 1744 a flag-officer shared in all the prizes taken on a station from the moment he was appointed, even before he actually joined the station.[59] The June 1744 proclamation wording, repeated in 1793, changed that, so that a new commander-in-chief did not receive a share of prizes until after they came within the limits of their command. Once there, though, they were entitled to the flag-share of prizes from that time regardless of who had given the orders or sent the capturing ships out.

The 1803 proclamation attempted a further clarification requiring some act of command by the arriving flag-officer:

> a Flag-officer, sent to command on any station, shall have no Right to any Share of Prizes taken by Ships or Vessels employed there before he arrives within the limits of such station, and actually takes upon him the Command by communicating orders to the Flag-officer previously in command, save only that he shall be entitled to a share of prizes taken by those particular ships to which he shall actually have given some order and taken under his command within the limits of such station.[60]

A commander-in-chief could be reluctant to hand over to a new flag-officer sent by the Admiralty to take over. If the new flag-officer was junior

58 Royal Proclamation of 15 June 1808, *London Gazette*, 1808, No. 16155, p. 853.

59 Pigot v White, Easter 25 Geo. 3 B. R., noted in Johnstone v Margetson (1789) 1 H. Bl. 265n.

60 Proclamation of 7 July 1803, *London Gazette*, No. 15599, p. 801.

to his predecessor, then this could cause delay and tension, but it was not always the outgoing flag-officer who was reluctant to put the handover into effect. When Rear-Admiral Robert Digby arrived in New York to take over command of the North American station from Admiral Graves in 1781, the situation was so poor that Digby refused to take over until Graves had sorted some of the mess that he had created.[61] These conflicts presented the Admiralty with problems that they never really solved. If the Admiralty sent a new commander-in-chief to take over, then they intended that to happen, but respect for seniority was important in the service, so new wording adopted in 1808 came down in favour of deferring to seniority:

> a Flag-officer, sent to command on any station, shall have a Right to Share as Commander-in-chief Prizes taken by Ships or Vessels employed there from the time he arrives within the limits of such station, but if a junior Flag-officer be sent to relieve a senior, he shall not be entitled to share as Commander-in-chief in any prizes taken by the squadron until the command shall be resigned to him but shall share only as a junior Flag-officer until he assumes the Command.[62]

4th Article: Passage through the Station of Another

By 1803 the Admiralty thought it appropriate to include a specific provision to try and reduce the 'turf wars' caused by flag-officers passing through another flag-officer's station. On 14 September 1796 Vice-Admiral Sir Hyde Parker arrived at Barbados on the Leeward Island station. Although he was senior in rank to Admiral Harvey, the commander-in-chief of the Leeward Island station at the time, Hyde Parker had no orders appointing him to take command of that station, and nor did he. Hyde Parker waited in Barbados for Admiralty orders until 1 November 1796, when he sailed to Jamaica to take command there. Although he had simply been in transit through the station, Hyde Parker claimed that the commander-in-chief role had 'accidentally' devolved upon him as a senior officer happening to come within the station. When the claim came before Lord Ellenborough in 1805, he held that Hyde Parker's presence in transit gave him no right to the commander-in-chief's share of prizes taken by ships of the station while he was on the station.[63] The 1803 proclamation had in the meantime

61 Willis, *The Struggle for Sea Power*, p. 455.

62 Proclamation 15 June 1808, *London Gazette*, No. 16155, p. 853.

63 Referred to in the course of argument before Lord Ellenborough in *Harvey v Cooke* (1805) 6 East 220, 228.

provided expressly that a right of passage gave no right to prizes unless it included the right to take command of the station and that right was exercised:

> a Commander-in-Chief or other Flag-officer, appointed or belonging to any station and passing through or into any other station shall not be entitled to share in any prize taken out of the limits of the station to which he is appointed or belongs, by any ship or vessel under the command of a Flag-officer of any other station, or under Admiralty orders [unless such Commander-in-Chief or Flag-officer is expressly authorised by the Lords Commissioners of the Admiralty to take upon him the command in that station in which the prize is taken and shall actually have taken upon him such command, in Manner aforesaid].

The exception at the end of this wording in square brackets above for a flag-officer expressly authorised to take command was unnecessary as such an officer would not be 'passing through or into any other station' in any event. The wording therefore provided more confusion than clarity and was deleted in the 1808 proclamation.

5th Article: Junior Flag-officers Sent to Join a Station

Two issues arose when a junior flag-officer was sent out to join a superior flag-officer on a station. The first was when did he have to share the prizes he captured en-route with the superior flag-officer on the station? The second was when did that junior flag-officer become entitled to a share of the prizes being captured by the ships on that station?

The 1793 proclamation dealt with the first issue and stipulated that when a flag-officer was:

> sent out to reinforce a superior Flag-officer at Jamaica, or elsewhere, the superior Flag-officer shall have no right to any Share of Prizes taken by the inferior Flag-officer before the inferior Flag-officer shall arrive within the limits of the command of the superior Flag-officer, and actually receive some Order from him.[64]

[64] Proclamation 17 April 1793, *London Gazette*, No. 13521, p. 319.

The San Antonio

In the summer of 1801, the Admiralty sent Admiral Sir James Saumarez with a squadron of ships 'to invigorate the blockade of Cadiz', which the Mediterranean fleet was maintaining under Lord Keith. His orders required him to cooperate with the allied fleet of Portugal, but 'to put himself under Lord Keith's command'.[65] Saumarez was ordered to 'use his best endeavours to prevent the enemy's ships [in Cadiz] from putting to sea, or to take and destroy them should they sail', but he was also 'to keep a good look-out for any French squadron which may attempt either to join the Spanish ships at Cadiz, or pass through the straits; and to use his best endeavours to intercept, and to take or destroy it'.[66] On his arrival off Cadiz, Saumarez wrote to Keith telling him of his arrival and the vessels that he had taken under his command. Although he referred to his instructions from the Admiralty, Saumarez did not at that point send a copy of the instructions to Keith, nor did he expressly place himself under Keith's command.[67] At the same time Rear-Admiral de Linois had sailed with a small squadron of three French ships from Toulon, hoping to combine with five Spanish ships of the line at Cadiz and six ships of the line that Spain was transferring to France. He was also expecting to be joined by five French ships of the line from Rochefort, but in the event they did not sail. The intention was for the combined fleets to prey on British convoys bound for Egypt and then sail to join Rear-Admiral Ganteaume off Egypt to relieve the French army abandoned there by Bonaparte.[68]

Linois's fleet was spotted at Gibraltar by the 14-gun sloop *Calpe*, which sailed for Cadiz to warn the British blockading fleet. Linois took refuge at Algeciras, on the opposite side of the bay to Gibraltar, anchoring under the protection of Spanish shore batteries. Saumarez, with a squadron of six ships of the line, found Linois on 6 July 1801 and attacked. As he did so, however, the wind died, and the attack failed. One British ship, *Hannibal*, grounded under fire from shore guns and surrendered, while the others were beaten off and made their way across the bay to Gibraltar badly damaged.

[65] The San Antonio (1804) 5 Rob. Adm. Rep. 209.

[66] Sir John Ross (ed.), *Memoirs and Correspondence of Admiral Lord de Saumarez* (London, 1838), pp. 327–8.

[67] Letter 26 June 1801 Saumarez to Keith, Ross (ed.), *Correspondence of Saumarez*, p. 338.

[68] N. A. M. Rodger, *The Command of the Ocean* (London, 2004), p. 471; J. R. Dull, *The Age of the Ship of the Line* (Barnsley, 2009), p. 157; J. R. Musteen, *Nelson's Refuge* (Annapolis, 2011), pp. 31–51.

Keith had left Gibraltar before Saumarez's arrival, sailing into the Mediterranean with Abercrombie's forces bound for Egypt. He left orders at Gibraltar addressed to '*Sir Erasmus Gower, or any other flag-officer appointed to act on this station*', but Saumarez had not called at Gibraltar or seen the orders from Keith before the first encounter with Linois at Algeciras. Although he was provided with Keith's orders when he did arrive at Gibraltar, Saumarez later told the Admiralty Court that he had not read them and that he 'did not interfere with the Marine department', 'because he was otherwise employed'.[69] He was certainly busy. It is clear from his letters that Saumarez felt the failure of his attack deeply, although he accepted that 'Divine Providence' had decreed the lack of wind that was its downfall.[70] He was determined to get his ships ready to have another attempt to defeat Linois if he could, and regarded it as important to his personal honour that he should do so by his own responsibility and consistently with his Admiralty orders. It took feverish activity at Gibraltar to prepare the British ships for battle again. Hearing from Cadiz that support was being sent for Linois, Saumarez wrote again to Keith on 9 July 1801. He made no reference to Keith's orders, nor did he place himself under Keith's command, but sought help from Keith with his task of tackling Linois under, as he saw it, his orders from the Admiralty: 'I hope something may join me from your Lordship before they [the French] can put to sea.'[71] No such support arrived.

On 10 July Vice-Admiral Moreno arrived from Cadiz to escort Linois to safety. Had the combined Franco-Spanish allied fleet sailed for Cadiz that night then Saumarez would not have been ready to follow them. They did not sail, however, until the 12th, by which time Saumarez was just about ready. Fresh from their repairs, Saumarez and his squadron pursued the now larger allied fleet and attacked during the night. One French ship, the *San Antonio*, was captured and two Spanish ships blew up. Both sides claimed victory over the two encounters. By his efforts in Gibraltar, however, Saumarez had retrieved his reputation and inflicted a strategic blow to the alliance between France and Spain. Spain demanded its fleet back from Brest and relaxed its pressure on Britain's ally, Portugal. The battle contributed to the pressure for peace that led to the end of the war against revolutionary France with the Peace of Amiens signed in October 1801. The Battles of Algeciras were the last naval battles of that war.

[69] The San Antonio (1804) 5 Rob. Adm. Rep. 209, 217.

[70] Ross (ed.), *Correspondence of Saumarez*, p. 390.

[71] Ibid., pp. 387–8.

Saumarez wrote to Keith to tell him of his actions. Keith's response was to claim his share of the prize money for the capture of the *San Antonio* as the commander-in-chief on the Mediterranean station where Saumarez's activities had taken place. Keith's claim to the prize money was heard in the Admiralty Court by Sir William Scott, who gave judgment on 30 May 1804. Two issues arose: a) was Saumarez sent out 'to reinforce' Keith and b) had he actually received 'some order' from him?

Keith's fragile grasp on what had actually happened is illustrated by the fact that the submission made on his behalf suggested that Saumarez had arrived in Gibraltar 'in June, after having engaged the enemy's fleet in Algeciras Bay', a month before the action actually took place.[72] Scott, though, was unimpressed by Saumarez's evidence that he had not read Keith's orders. 'Certainly', he said, 'this Court can never admit an averment that the inferior officer had not read orders that were directed to him, and were delivered to him by his superior. Indeed I cannot but observe that Sir James Saumarez speaks with some uncertainty on this fact, which I am inclined to think did happen, though it may have escaped his recollection.' Scott considered that Saumarez's lack of interference with the Marine department (i.e. acting as Keith's subordinate in relation to the station as a whole) was because his other duties prevented him. It was not that Keith's orders did not apply to him, it was just that Saumarez had been too busy to attend to them.

Scott's analysis rather begged the question, since Saumarez's case was that he was not Keith's inferior officer because he was 'otherwise employed' under the direct orders of the Admiralty in attempting to intercept the enemy. Scott held though that it was not necessary that the Admiralty orders should use the word 'reinforce' in order to fall within the proclamation. It was enough if the inferior officer was directed to put himself under the command of his superior for the purposes of general cooperation. Saumarez's submission that he had been sent 'to perform a special and distinct service under the orders of the Admiralty' was rejected. He had received the order from Keith and was held to have read it but been too busy to remember having done so or to implement its terms.

In holding as he did, Scott was attempting to give effect to the Admiralty's intention that Saumarez would be under Keith's command. Saumarez could have said that he had read the orders but that they did not apply to him, so he ignored them as he was acting under direct Admiralty orders at the time, before placing himself under Keith's orders. He did not do so and that supported Scott's view that the Admiralty's orders were intended to

[72] The San Antonio (1804) 5 Rob. Adm. Rep. 209, 210. Keith was represented by the King's Advocate, Sir John Nicholl.

mean that by arriving on the station and receiving Keith's order Saumarez was placing himself under Keith's command.

That the capture was due to enormous effort on the part of Saumarez and his squadron, and none on the part of Keith, was irrelevant. Equity based on the effort applied did not enter into it. The court was simply determining the rights of the parties in accordance with the terms of the proclamation and the Admiralty orders. Although the judgment did not refer to it, the decision was consistent with Scott's decision the previous year that where the Admiralty had intended 'a distinct and separate service' the flag-officer in command of the station would not be entitled to a share of prize money.[73]

Although Saumarez had to share his prize money with Keith, he was rewarded by the Admiralty for his efforts. Already a baronet, he was made a knight of the Order of the Bath and awarded a pension of £1,200 p.a. by Parliament for his efforts.[74]

When war resumed, the 1803 wording provided that an inferior flag-officer joined a station when he was 'acting in execution of some Order issued by' the superior flag-officer. On its own this amendment makes little sense as a matter of drafting as it would be difficult to see how the inferior flag-officer would be 'acting in the execution of some Order' without actually receiving it. In the context of the then still ongoing dispute between Keith and Saumarez, it can be seen as an attempt to strengthen those in Saumarez's position in future, although the wording would not have removed the scope for dispute entirely. The 1808 wording attempted a further clarification of what was intended by stipulating that either the inferior flag-officer must have received some order 'directly' from the superior flag-officer or be 'acting in execution of some Order issued by him'.

The 1808 proclamation also dealt with the second issue, namely when did inferior flag-officers become entitled to a share of prizes captured by ships on the station they were joining, which had not been addressed in either the 1793 or 1803 proclamations. From 1808 inferior flag-officers were expressly entitled to their proportion of all captures made by the squadron they were joining from the time they arrived within the limits of command of the superior flag-officer.

Thus, the joining inferior flag-officer took the benefit of prizes captured by others as soon as he could show that he had reached the station but only

73 The Orion (1803) 4 Rob. Adm. Rep. 362, 372/3.

74 Annuity to Admiral Saumarez Act 1803, 43 Geo. 3 c. 37.

had to share his prizes once he had received orders from his new commanding officer either directly or indirectly.

6th Article: When did a Departing Commander-in-chief Lose his Right to a Share of Prizes?

This provision was one of the most controversial and disputed provisions of them all. The 1793 proclamation provided simply that 'a Chief Flag-officer returning Home from Jamaica, or elsewhere, shall have no Share of the Prizes taken by the Ships or Vessels left behind to act under another command.'

The provision had a history behind it. The 1740 proclamation referred simply to the well-worn, but flexible, phrase that a flag-officer should be 'actually on board, or directing and assisting in the Capture.' As disputes arose among flag-officers as to the meaning to be given to this wording, the 1744 proclamation introduced seven rules in the first edition of the Articles now being considered. The fourth rule was that 'a Chief Flag-officer returning home from Jamaica, or elsewhere, shall have no Share in Prizes taken by the ships left at Jamaica, or elsewhere, after he has left the limits of his Command.' This wording, however, was still considered to be 'always disputable and uncertain.'[75] It was not always possible to be certain when a ship passed a vague and hypothetical line at the edge of a station. For this reason, the wording used in the 1793 proclamation and extended by a proclamation of 25 January 1797 to Spanish prizes was adopted. When put to the test, however, even the 1793 and 1797 proclamations were found to be 'loosely, inaccurately, and ambiguously worded.'[76]

The St Anne

The 1793 wording was subjected to the scrutiny of the Admiralty Court in the case of The St Anne in 1800.[77] The *St Anne* was a prize taken by *HMS La Raison*, commanded by Captain John Beresford, on the Halifax station on 2 December 1796. Beresford was sailing under orders dated 5 November 1796 from Admiral George Murray as the only flag-officer on the Halifax station at the time and commander-in-chief of the ships on the station.[78] By the time the *St Anne* was captured, however, Murray had left the station.

75 Per Rooke J. Lord Nelson v Tucker (1802) 3 Bos. & Pull. 257 at 270.

76 Per Heath J. Lord Nelson v Tucker (1802) 3 Bos. & Pull. 257 at 272.

77 The St Anne (1800) 3 C. Rob. 60.

78 Not to be confused with Admiral Sir George Murray, a younger man who as a captain was chosen by Nelson as his captain of the fleet but narrowly missed out on being at Trafalgar.

When the orders were issued Murray was already suffering from the effects of a 'paralytic stroke', suffered on 22 October 1796. Although his condition had not stopped him carrying out his duties, he was clearly unwell. His own orders from the Admiralty permitted him to return home if he considered it necessary for his health and, accordingly, he resolved to return to England. He left the Halifax station on board *HMS Cleopatra* on 12 November 1796. Before doing so he gave orders to the senior captain on the station, Captain Henry Mowatt of *HMS Assistance*, to assume command during his absence. Although Murray intended only a temporary absence, he did not in fact return to the station. On 2 January 1797 he formally struck his flag, without having returned to the Halifax station, and died on 17 October 1797. A dispute then arose as to whether Murray was entitled to a flag-officer's share of the *St Anne*. The case came before Sir William Scott, who decided that the only question in the case was whether Murray had abdicated his command or not. He held that he had not and that his estate was entitled to the flag-share. Mowatt, who had assumed command of the fleet, was not a flag-officer, but that was not the basis of Scott's decision. Scott decided that Murray had not given up his command of the station as at the time of capture he still intended to return to the station, so he had not 'given up command' to anyone, be they a flag-officer or otherwise.

Nelson v Tucker

Scott's judgment in The St Anne featured prominently in a later dispute between Lord Nelson and the Earl St Vincent over the proceeds of two Spanish frigates loaded with treasure that were captured by ships of the Mediterranean fleet, including *HMS Alcmene* under Captain Henry Digby, off the coast of Spain in October 1799.

On 16 October 1799 two Spanish 36-gun frigates, *Santa Brigida* and *El Thetis*, were sailing off the coast of north-west Spain bound for any Spanish port they could safely reach. They had left Vera Cruz on the Gulf of Mexico on 21 August with cargoes of Spanish treasure. After 56 days at sea, they had evaded the Royal Navy and were nearly home. British frigates had seen strange sails over the preceding days and attempted to give chase, but lost contact. On 16 October, however, the Spanish ships were spotted by the British frigates *HMS Ethalion* (Captain James Young) and *HMS Naiad* (Captain William Pierrepoint), who gave chase. By midnight *Ethalion* and *Naiad* had discovered that the two ships were enemy ships and had identified each other by exchange of private signals. The two British frigates chased their Spanish quarry through the night. At daybreak on the 17th, they were joined in the pursuit by two more British frigates,

HMS Alcmene under Digby with *HMS Triton* under Captain John Gore fast bringing up the rear.

Alcmene had seen the sails of two ships to windward the previous day and given chase. According to Digby family history it was not mere chance that brought her the sighting, but supernatural prognostication. The tale is recorded in the biography of Digby's father-in-law, the agriculturalist, Thomas Coke of Norfolk.[79] Vouched for by the then Lord Digby and recorded as having been 'well known in the Navy', the tale is still recounted by the Digby family. While sailing south, Digby had tried to sleep but kept hearing a voice telling him to go northward. So realistic was the voice that twice he called the officer of the watch to ask whether anyone had entered his cabin. Both the officer and the sentry replied that no one had. After the second occasion Digby decided to heed the voice and turned north, ordering the officer to 'take another reef in your topsails, haul your wind, tack every hour till daybreak, and then call me'. The officer is said to have thought his captain was mad but obeyed and soon after seven that morning the vessels were sighted by the masthead lookout and the chase began. The captain's and master's logbooks for the ship confirm that the wind was in the north, so that if the ship was travelling south, she would have had to tack if she turned to the north. Otherwise, there is nothing in the log entries to support the tale, and the sighting is recorded at 6am, rather than soon after 7am. Coke's biographer, Anna Marie Stirling, was a great-niece of Digby's.[80] Her later works included *Ghosts Vivisected: An impartial Inquiry into their Manners, Habits, Mentality, Motives and Physical Construction* and her recording of the story may owe more to her interest in ghosts and the public interest in spiritualism at the time she was writing than any inherent credibility in the tale. The existence of the tale and the claim that it was 'well known in the Navy' is itself significant, however. It did a naval captain no harm to have a reputation among superstitious seamen for a supernatural ability to detect rich prizes.

Once the chase began, *Alcmene*'s crew knocked out the mast wedges and brought in their lee guns to improve her trim for extra speed. Only two days earlier they had carried away a mizzenmast shroud in a squall and had had to knot it to support the mast. There was a balance to be struck, therefore, between pushing the ship to catch the prizes and pushing her too hard and suffering disabling damage. The ships they were chasing were seen to hoist Spanish colours, but then they lost sight of the chase until coming up to them again with the other British ships. As the winds

79 A. M. W. Stirling, *Coke of Norfolk and His Friends* (London, 1908), vol. II, p. 57.

80 Mary Lovell, *A Scandalous Life* (Glasgow, 1998), p. 65.

went light, they pumped 18 tons of fresh water overboard from their water barrels to lighten the ship and get themselves up with the enemy ships.[81] They even resorted to the backbreaking use of sweeps, long oars used to provide propulsion in a calm.

By 7am on the 17th the Spanish frigates were steering different courses and *Naiad* signalled *Ethalion* to pass the rear Spanish ship, *Santa Brigida*, and pursue the foremost Spaniard, *El Thetis*. By 9am *Ethalion* was within range for a random shot at *El Thetis*, inducing her to alter course and separate even more from the *Santa Brigida*. *Ethalion* followed *El Thetis* and by 11.30am was within half the distance of a musket shot when *El Thetis* bore up athwart *Ethalion* and fired a broadside of her 12- and six-pounders to try and shake off her pursuer. In reply *Ethalion* fired two 'well directed' broadsides and a running battle ensued exchanging bow and stern chasers. Eventually they came within half the distance of a pistol shot and after an hour the captain of *El Thetis*, Don Juan de Mendoza, ordered her colours to be hauled down and surrendered. *El Thetis* had one killed and nine wounded among her 250 men. Her masts and yards were damaged in the battle and Lt Pym led a party of men from *Ethalion* to board and repair the prize. *Ethalion* had no dead or injured from the battle.

Naiad, *Alcmene* and *Triton*, meanwhile, pursued the *Santa Brigida*. Her captain, Don Antonio Pillou, made a determined push to the south, throwing boats, spars and other weight overboard, in order to try and reach the safety of a Spanish port. By the morning of the 18th, she had rounded Cape Finisterre and was sailing in towards the rocks of Monte Lora with *Triton* in close pursuit. Pillou obviously knew the waters well and trusted that he knew them better than the crew of the chasing *Triton* since at 5am he hove-to close to the rocks, leaving *Triton* to hit the rocks at seven knots. It is a considerable tribute to the rigging and hull of *Triton* that she survived the impact. Whilst she suffered some damage, she got off the rocks and started an animated fire on *Santa Brigida*, as did her companions.[82] Digby on *Alcmene* managed to block *Santa Brigida*'s path to Port de Vidre and at 8am the three attacking frigates closed with their prey among the rocks of Commarurto until she too hauled down her Spanish colours and surrendered. The four ships were by this time all in dangerous waters but fortunately for the captors an offshore breeze sprang up which blew the ships safely out to sea. *Santa Brigida* had two seamen killed and eight wounded, *Alcmene* one

81 Master's log Alcmene, TNA, ADM 52/2651, Captain's log Alcmene, TNA, ADM 51/1318. For the logs of the other Royal Navy frigates involved in the chase see TNA, 52/3241, 51/1291 and 51/1329.

82 Although described as 'little damage' in her log, she was 'very leaky' following the grounding: Triton Captain's log, TNA, ADM 51/1329.

seaman killed and one petty officer and eight seamen wounded. *Triton* had one seaman wounded. The crew of *Naiad* had avoided death or injury.

A lieutenant and 80 men from *Naiad* went to take charge of the prize, but as the captors began to shift their prisoners a Spanish squadron of four large ships appeared. The British ships readied themselves to meet the approaching Spanish squadron and defend their prize, but the Spanish squadron did not press on towards them, appearing instead to retreat to Vigo. A British privateer later claimed that she had been in sight of the capture of the *Santa Brigida* and had contributed to the capture by placing herself in a position where she might have been able to cut off a retreat by the *Santa Brigida* into a Spanish port. She was then driven off the coast by four Spanish vessels that came out from the Spanish coast. The claim for prize money was rejected by the Admiralty Court in April 1800 on the basis that the involvement was too remote from the action.[83] If the account is correct, and if they were the same Spanish squadron seen by the British frigates, then the privateer may well have played a role in distracting the Spanish squadron and preserving the prize.

Light and variable winds initially kept the frigates and their prize within sight of the Spanish coast, and within range of another Spanish squadron thought to be in Corunna, but they set course for Plymouth. The prize was distressed, with a sprung bowsprit and fore topmast, and was taken in tow by the *Naiad*. On 24 October 1799 they brought their prize into Plymouth, three days after *Ethalion* had arrived with the *El Thetis*.

Having arrived in Plymouth they reported the arrival of their prizes to Lord Bridport who, as commander-in-chief of the Channel fleet, was in Torbay. Bridport sent the letters on to the Secretary to the Admiralty, Evan Nepean, in London. Nepean endorsed Captain Young's letter[84] with the unsurprising sentiment 'Their Lordships have great satisfaction in this very valuable capture' and released the letters, with their accounts of the captures, to appear in the *London Gazette*.[85]

The Treasure

The letters gave the first news that *El Thetis* had a cargo of 1,411,526 dollars and a valuable quantity of cocoa and *Santa Brigida* had 1,400,000 dollars and a valuable cargo of goods on board. The Spanish coinage was loaded

[83] The Santa Brigada (1800) 3 C. Rob. 52 (whilst the name is misspelt, it is clearly the same action).

[84] TNA, ADM 1/814.

[85] *London Gazette* 1799, No. 15197, pp. 1093–5.

into 44 wagons and paraded under armed guard from Plymouth to London to be sold to the Bank of England for £661,286 13*s*. 9*d*.[86] At a time when the daily pay of even a full admiral was only £3 1*s*., this was a huge sum for the treasure alone.[87] Whilst a pragmatic step to take, the removal operation had not been approved by the Admiralty Court, which had exclusive jurisdiction to condemn the ships and their cargo as lawful prize, leading Sir William Scott, the Admiralty Court judge, to write a mild reminder to the Admiralty in November 1799, as recited in Chapter 2.[88]

The treasure, the other cargo, the ships themselves and their equipment were duly condemned as lawful prize by the Admiralty Court and, as a result of the sale of the treasure to the Bank of England, there was an unusually early pay-out in January 1800. Benjamin Tucker, St Vincent's secretary and prize agent, went on board *Alcmene* at Saltash on 6 January 1801 and paid out the shares of the prize money for the dollars sold to the Bank of England.[89] The share of the dollars alone for each sailor was £182 4*s*. 9¾*d*. It was a substantial sum representing over ten times the annual pay of an able seaman, which even after the post-1797 mutiny pay rises was still only about £18. The surgeon on board *Alcmene* was William Beatty. Like his captain, Beatty would later be at the Battle of Trafalgar, in his case as the surgeon on board *HMS Victory* and witness to the death of Nelson. Beatty's share of the dollars was the considerable sum of £2,468 10*s*. 9½*d*.

Digby's share was by any reckoning a fortune: £40,750 18*s*. 3¼*d*. Not only would the sum enhance his reputation as a supernatural prize-catcher, but it would admit him to an elite group of rich prize-takers. He could afford to be philosophical about the loss of prizes after Trafalgar, writing to his uncle from the Straits of Gibraltar, 'it has pleased God that the elements should destroy most perhaps to lessen the vanity of man after so great a victory.'[90] Having fought at Trafalgar as captain of the *Africa*, along with the dining furniture that he took from the *Santa Brigida*, he would marry the handsome Jane Coke, daughter of Thomas Coke, 1st Earl of Leicester, wealthy

86 Statement of Account, Digby family archive, Minterne House, Box 22a. According to the Digby family, a quantity of dollars was kept by Digby as 'mementos', most of which were later donated to the government during the Second World War for the purchase of arms from the US, where they were melted down.

87 Lavery, *Nelson's Navy*, p. 252.

88 Scott to Evan Nepean, TNA, ADM 1/3894. See page 39 above.

89 Muster Book *Alcmene*, TNA, ADM 36/12613; Statement of Account, Digby family archive, Minterne House, Box 22a; and Tucker's Account Book for 1800 in the Sim Comfort Collection. I am grateful to the Digby family and Sim Comfort for allowing me access to the account books.

90 Digby family archive, Minterne House, Box 22a.

agriculturalist and owner of the palatial Holkham Hall in Norfolk. Jane Coke was also the sister-in-law of Lord Anson, who had inherited his title from the Admiral Anson we met in the Introduction, who captured the *Nuestra Senora de Covadonga* and her 1.3 million pieces of eight in 1743.[91]

Digby's daughter Jane would in turn marry the son of Lord Ellenborough, the Lord Chief Justice who would finally determine the prize litigation about the commander-in-chief's share that arose out of Digby's captured treasure. That marriage ended in a scandalous divorce due to Jane's adultery with an Austrian prince. Jane's spirited nature and love of adventure would take her through a number of marriages and relationships through Europe and finally marriage to a Bedouin sheik in Damascus and Palmyra. Despite the calamitous events Digby's love for his daughter remained deep, but he also stayed on good terms with his former son-in-law, who enjoyed a successful political life, and after serving as Governor-General of India was elevated to an earldom.[92] Digby became an admiral.[93] On 4 August 1840 he hoisted his flag in *HMS Howe* as commander-in-chief at the Nore, in the presence of his daughter.[94] Digby died in 1842 at the age of 72, leaving his family a legacy of wealth and status. Four years later his former son-in-law became First Lord of the Admiralty.

The pay-out to the sailors, however, only marked the beginning of a dispute over who was entitled to the commander-in-chief's share that would end in High Court proceedings between two of the Navy's most prestigious admirals.

At the time of the capture Digby was sailing under orders issued by St Vincent as commander-in-chief of the Mediterranean station. By late 1798 St Vincent was exhausted and ill and requested permission to return to England for his health. The Admiralty granted permission by a letter of 2 November 1798, but only if St Vincent thought that the state of his health should absolutely require it. If he did return to England, he was to leave command of the fleet in the charge of the next most senior officer with such instructions as he might judge necessary. The Admiralty's task of managing St Vincent as commander-in-chief of the Mediterranean station was already proving difficult. It was St Vincent who had appointed Nelson to the command that led to the victory at the Battle of the Nile. The captains of

91 Lovell, *A Scandalous Life*, p. 3.

92 Ibid., pp. 58–9.

93 Rear-Admiral of the Blue 12 August 1819, Admiral of the Blue 23 November 1841: Commissions in the Digby family archive, Minterne House, Box 22a.

94 Lovell, *A Scandalous Life*, p. 121 (N.B. not '*HMS How*', nor was Digby Admiral of the Fleet). His appointment to the command at Sheerness was dated 27 July 1840: Digby family archive, Minterne House, Box 22a; he died on 19 August 1842.

Nelson's fleet at the Nile were his 'Band of Brothers' in that he did not have a great deal of seniority over them, unlike other flag-officers on the station. Nelson's victory at the Nile in August 1798 had been very welcome, but the appointment had been made at a cost. More senior officers on the Mediterranean station felt snubbed by St Vincent, and victory had done nothing to quell the disquiet. Sir John Orde had even demanded that St Vincent be court-martialled over his failure to treat him in a manner suitable to his rank. It was a request that the Admiralty declined, but without approving of St Vincent's decision to send Orde home, an outcome that upset both men.[95] There was every reason for the Admiralty to try and avoid upsetting St Vincent even further. They certainly did nothing to clarify whether St Vincent would still be the commander-in-chief of the station if and when he availed himself of the opportunity for sick leave.

St Vincent did not immediately avail himself of the permission to return home when it arrived. Instead, he wrote and declined until compelled to relinquish command by a return of his complaint. So, as commander-in-chief of the fleet, he continued to give his orders to the fleet and on 11 March 1799 ordered Digby to cruise off the north-west coast of Spain 'so long as his water and provisions should last, for the protection of the trade of his Majesty's subjects and allies'. The Court of Common Pleas found the cruise to be within the limits of St Vincent's Mediterranean command.[96]

By June 1799, however, St Vincent's complaint had returned, and on 16 June he wrote to Vice-Admiral Lord Keith, the next senior officer then within the Mediterranean station, directing him to take command:

> Desirous as I am of giving all possible effect and energy to his Majesty's service at a crisis which admits of no impediment, but, on the contrary, demands the fullest exercise of an efficient and uncontrolled authority, I have resolved, on maturely considering these important objects, and on contemplating your Lordship's zeal and persevering efforts in the attainment of them, to avail myself of the permission thus provisionally granted, and to leave the fleet serving upon this station under your command. Your Lordship is therefore hereby required and directed to take the several flag-officers and captains of the said fleet under your command accordingly.[97]

95 TNA, ADM 1/398, 10 October 1798 Nepean to Orde and ff.

96 (1802) 3 Bos. & Pull. 258.

97 Recited, Nelson v Tucker, King's Bench (1803) 4 East 238, 240.

Even then St Vincent remained on the station until 31 July 1799, when he went aboard *HMS Argo* at Gibraltar and sailed for England.[98] *Argo* arrived at Spithead on 16 August 1799.[99] Having returned to England, and unaware of Keith's whereabouts, St Vincent wrote to inform the Admiralty that he had 'been compelled, by the ill state of my Health, to transfer the command of His Majesty's fleet in the Mediterranean to Vice-Admiral Keith, and to avail myself of their Lordships' leave to return to England'.[100] Two days later, and with permission from the Admiralty, St Vincent left the quarantined *Argo*, remaining on her books as commander-in-chief of the Mediterranean, and went to Bath for his health. He remained in England until 26 November 1799 without having resigned or been superseded or replaced as commander-in-chief.

Two days before St Vincent left Gibraltar, Lord Keith had passed through the Straits of Gibraltar together with Admiral Sir William Parker, the officer next most senior to Keith on the station. They were sailing under St Vincent's orders with a detachment of the Mediterranean fleet in pursuit of a combined enemy fleet. On about 10 August 1799 they sailed past Cape Finisterre and out of the Mediterranean station. Having chased the enemy fleet into Brest, Lord Keith went to join Lord Bridport and the Channel fleet in Torbay, arriving on 16 August. By orders confirmed by the Admiralty on 19 August he placed himself and the flag-officers with him, Admirals Cotton, Collingwood and Hawkins-Whitshed, and 33 ships under the command of Lord Bridport, commander-in-chief of the Channel fleet.[101]

As St Vincent, Keith and Parker had all left the Mediterranean station, Nelson was the senior officer serving within the limits of the station, until after the capture of the treasure ships in October 1799. The Admiralty recognised that Nelson had been left in charge of operations by writing to him on 20 August 1799 but did not appoint him commander-in-chief of the Mediterranean fleet. Instead, the Admiralty informed Nelson that from the circumstance of St Vincent's return to England, and Keith and other flag-officers having quitted the Mediterranean station in pursuit of the enemy, he was the senior officer of His Majesty's ships in the Mediterranean. As a result, they informed him that he would have 'all the

98 With his secretary Benjamin Tucker and a 17-gun salute; *Argo* muster book, TNA, ADM 36/12823, captain's log, TNA, ADM 51/1295 and St Vincent's journal, TNA, ADM 50/93.

99 Having taken a prize en-route, the Spanish packet *Infanta Amelia* bound for Havana with dispatches; TNA, ADM 51/1295 and ADM 50/93.

100 TNA, ADM1/400/224, 16 August 1799 from St Vincent at Spithead to the Admiralty.

101 TNA, ADM 2/136/146 and 149.

important duties' of that station to attend to until the return of Keith or some other superior officer. The Admiralty letter observed that Keith would probably have left Nelson for his information and guidance such orders and instructions as he might have received from the Admiralty or St Vincent, but nevertheless they proceeded to point out the objects which required his particular attention and gave him directions respecting his services and the manner in which he was to employ the fleet. The unclear state of the command of the Mediterranean fleet was reflected in an order a week later from the Admiralty for *HMS Phaeton* to join the Mediterranean fleet, directed to 'St Vincent or the commanding officer for the time being of His Majesty's ships and vessels in the Mediterranean.'[102] Having assumed de facto command of the fleet by default, Nelson proceeded to issue orders to those parts of the fleet that he fell in with, but these did not include Captain Digby of the *Alcmene*.

St Vincent was at home in England when he heard the news of the treasure ship captures and acted immediately to take control of the treasure and claim the flag-officers' share. He sent his secretary and prize agent, Benjamin Tucker, down to Saltash to secure the prize. The very next day after the *Santa Brigida* was brought into Plymouth, St Vincent was writing a hasty note from Rochetts, his home in Essex, to Digby in Plymouth congratulating Digby and his colleagues 'most heartily on the well-earned fruits of your labours.' 'There can be no doubt,' he continued, 'of the pretensions of the flag-officers on the Mediterranean station, to shares in everything you have been concerned in the capture of, & Mr Tucker, who is at Saltash will explain any doubts upon this subject much better than I can.'[103]

Nelson realised he had a claim to a share of the prizes as soon as news of the captures made its way to him in Sicily. He immediately wrote to his agent Alexander Davison authorising him to lay claim to two thirds of the flag-share as commander-in-chief, with the remaining third to go to Sir John Thomas Duckworth as junior flag-officer. Even as a young captain, Nelson had had confidence in his abilities as a lawyer.[104] On this occasion he identified that *Ethalion* and *Alcmene* were attached to the Mediterranean station at the time of the capture and since all his superior officers had returned to England, he saw that he had a claim. Davison duly instructed

[102] TNA, ADM 2/136/174, 28 August 1799.

[103] Letter 25 October 1799, St Vincent to Digby, the Digby family archive, Minterne House, Box 22a.

[104] In construing the Navigation Acts; '*Well done, Lawyer, Nelson!*', Nelson to William Suckling, 14 November 1785, Nicolas, *Dispatches*, vol. I, pp. 144, 147.

Nelson's solicitors, Booth and Haslewood, to pursue it.[105] Nelson claimed that he had no idea when he made his claim to the prize money that St Vincent would attempt to lay claim as well, saying indeed that he considered it dishonourable of him when he did.[106]

Despite a veneer of mutual respect, both sets of advisors sought what they saw as a procedural advantage over the other. In January 1801 William Haslewood saw it as 'a desirable object' to bring an action directly against St Vincent rather than by the circuitous route of one of them suing Tucker. As a result, Davison called on Messrs Cooke and Halford, navy agents, to see if St Vincent himself had received any part of the prize money in the distribution, and so could be named as the defendant instead of Tucker. He reported to Nelson that in January and February 1801 St Vincent had received £14,000 on this account. Sharing his client's passion for taking a battle straight to the enemy, he wrote:

> I sincerely congratulate you having it in your power to try the question plainly with Lord St Vincent, without the embarrassment of any circuitous proceeding with Lord Keith or through Mr Tucker.[107]

Haslewood commenced an action against St Vincent, but the ensuing correspondence revealed that St Vincent had got in first and issued against Tucker. At this stage Davison was still trying to persuade Tucker and St Vincent to pay the flag-share to Nelson. He told Tucker that Nelson had obtained opinions from counsel on the matter and that they were 'clearly and decidedly in favour of Lord Nelson'. Thus, he wrote to Tucker:

> I have the greatest hope and expectation that the result has been or will be a persuasion that the claim of Lord Nelson must prevail ... on consulting with Lord St Vincent I hope you will remit to me the chief flag-officer's share of prizes in question, and of others which have been captured under similar circumstances.[108]

Davison's hope was in vain. On 8 January 1801 St Vincent's solicitor, Mr Kaye, of Winter and Kaye, Swithin's Lane, London, wrote to give notice of St Vincent's claim. He also said that he understood that Lord Keith and Admiral Duckworth made claim on the prize monies in addition to Lord

[105] Nelson to Davison, 19 December 1799 from Palermo; Nicolas, *Dispatches*, vol. VII, p. cxciii.

[106] Nelson to Davison, 9 May 1800, Nicolas, *Dispatches*, vol. IV, p. 233.

[107] Davison to Nelson, 15 January 1801, NMM CRK/3/125.

[108] January 1801, NMM CRK/3/125.

Nelson. Keith did indeed maintain a claim while the litigation continued, although he played no active part in it and accepted the result not just in his claim on these monies but in a similar dispute with Admiral Pringle.[109] Nelson acknowledged Duckworth's claim to a junior flag-officer's share of one third of the flag-share from the start and Duckworth did not involve himself in St Vincent's action against Tucker, but did have his own litigation with another claimant to the junior flag-officer's share, the Portuguese Admiral Marquis de Nisa.[110]

On 10 January 1801 Tucker replied to Davison that he too had had notice that St Vincent had commenced an action against him and asked whether Lord Nelson would defend the action. Two days later Tucker assured Davison that 'all that Lord St Vincent wishes is to have the facts and circumstances of the case fairly submitted to a court and jury.'[111]

Contrary to Davison's information that St Vincent had received £14,000, Kaye wrote to Haslewood on 14 January 1801 assuring him that St Vincent 'has not received one shilling.' Tucker maintained that he had received £13,015 4*s*, the sum in dispute in the proceedings.[112] Kaye warned Haslewood that if he proceeded directly against St Vincent in the name of Lord Nelson then the action would fail as St Vincent held none of the sums in dispute. More diplomatically he wrote: '… we believe it never was the wish of Lord St Vincent or Lord Nelson that their names should appear opposed to each other in a pecuniary contest in a court of Justice.'

Booth and Haslewood replied, equally diplomatically, that:

> It would be a matter of very serious concern to us to give offence to Lord St Vincent not merely on account of his Lordship's high rank and those eminent services which must endear him to all his countrymen but from motives of very high personal respect and regard.[113]

That same day Davison gave up trying to persuade Tucker to pay up, or to press the action by Nelson against St Vincent directly, and wrote to Tucker that: 'now it has gone to court the agents should make no further comment.'

Davison was glad to hear from Nelson that St Vincent made no mention of the dispute in his letters to him.[114] Davison assured Nelson that his solicitors:

[109] Keith v Pringle [1804] IV East 262.
[110] Duckworth v Tucker (1809) II Taunt. 7, Court of Common Pleas, see further below.
[111] January 1801, NMM CRK 3/125.
[112] Nelson v Tucker, Court of Common Pleas (1802) 3 Bos. & Pull. 261.
[113] January 1801, NMM CRK 3/125.
[114] Davison to Nelson, 27 January 1801, NMM CRK/3/127.

> at the same time that they are zealous for your interest will not be guilty of any professional chicane, or act with more hostility towards opponent than a vigilant attention to the success of your cause shall render absolutely necessary.[115]

Indeed, on 5 January 1801 Davison wrote to Tucker to reassure him that Nelson:

> would not without extreme reluctance adopt any measures which might lead to a public and unpleasant discussion of the matter or appear in any other light than as the warm friend of Lord St Vincent.[116]

The court, the reporters and the public were well aware, however, that the principal parties to the contest were Nelson and St Vincent, and the latter was far from happy with Davison's activities in the run-up to the litigation. On the same day that Davison noted the absence of comment from St Vincent to Nelson, St Vincent complained to Booth and Haslewood that:

> The whole conduct of Mr Davison and of those who have acted under his direction has been so offensive, and diametrically opposite to that which I have observed to him.[117]

Davison copied the letter to Nelson on 29 January 1801 with a bold defence of his actions:

> he means to insinuate censure on my conduct, is paying me the highest compliment, in an indirect way, by telling my solicitors that I have been more attentive to my friend's interest than that of the Great Earl's.[118]

For all Davison's bravado, Nelson did have cause to worry about his relations with St Vincent. Although, as he saw it, he was only seeking justice, the impact of the proceedings on St Vincent vexed him, as he complained to Lady Hamilton.[119] Davison was confident that Nelson's position with St Vincent was secure. On 4 April 1801 Davison was glad to hear from Nelson

115 January 1801, NMM CRK 3/125.
116 NMM CRK/3/125.
117 NMM CRK 3/128.
118 January 1801, NMM CRK 3/128.
119 February 1801, Nicolas, *Dispatches*, vol. IV, p. 285. St Vincent did not approve of the relationship with Lady Hamilton, which was part of the rift between the two men.

that St Vincent was writing warmly to him. 'The Earl,' he wrote to Nelson, 'will think twice – to cause a breach between you.'[120]

Davison was also convinced of Nelson's 'ultimate success' in the litigation. Nelson felt that he was entitled by the 'custom' of the navy. He claimed to Davison that when Lord Hood had gone home on leave Admiral Hotham had shared as commander-in-chief.[121] Nelson regarded this as a precedent. Pursuing this line Davison canvassed the opinions of a large number of senior naval figures as to the practice of the service.[122] He found no unanimity and some firm opposition. In the event, the naval opinions did not affect the outcome of the proceedings. Perhaps more significantly Davison also obtained positive counsel's opinions on the legal dispute.[123]

Writing to Davison, Nelson had asserted that 'No Admiral ever yet received Prize-money, going for the benefit of his health from a foreign station.'[124] His assertion had been disproved, however, only three days earlier when Scott had delivered his ruling in The St Anne in favour of the estate of Admiral Murray. On the basis of Scott's judgment in The St Anne, it could be expected that St Vincent remained entitled to the commander-in-chief's share of the prizes. If Murray had not resigned his command, then neither had St Vincent. At any rate, so it seemed.

The Court of Common Pleas

Nelson, St Vincent and indeed Keith all petitioned the king through the Privy Council hoping for some intervention in their favour, but the king and the Admiralty sensibly preferred to leave it to the courts of law rather than be drawn into the dispute.[125] With Nelson as a party to St Vincent's proceedings against Tucker, they came on for trial before Lord Alvanley,[126] the Chief Justice of the Court of Common Pleas, and a jury at the Guildhall

[120] April 1801, NMM CRK/3/129.

[121] Nelson to Davison, 19 December 1799, Nicolas, *Dispatches*, vol. VII, p. cxciii.

[122] BL Add MS 34918/325.

[123] Davison to Nelson, 15 January 1801, NMM CRK/3/125.

[124] May 1799, Nelson to Davison from Malta, Nicolas, *Dispatches*, vol. IV, p. 233.

[125] Per Serjeant Shepherd in submissions to Sir James Mansfield reported in *A Correct Account of The Trial at Large between Ross Donnelly, Esq. a Post Captain in His Majesty's Navy, Plaintiff and Sir Home Popham, Knt. Defendant* (London, 1807), pp. 92–3.

[126] *The Naval Chronicle* reported that the trial judge was Lord Kenyon, who at the time was Lord Chief Justice of England. The later law reports, however, state that the trial judge was Lord Alvanley, who was Chief Justice of the Court of Common Pleas, a different position next in superiority to the Lord Chief Justice. It seems likely, therefore, that the reporter for *The Naval Chronicle* heard that the judge was a Chief Justice and wrongly assumed that it was Lord Chief Justice Kenyon.

on 4 March 1801.[127] By that time St Vincent had been made First Lord of the Admiralty, but even that did not change Nelson's determination to fight for his share. As he wrote to Lady Hamilton on hearing of St Vincent's appointment, 'nothing will stop my Law Suit and I hope to cast him.'[128] The court heard evidence from Captain Digby to establish the fact of the capture and Alvanley, who lamented being called upon to give an opinion in a dispute between two such august naval officers, directed the jury to enter a formal verdict for St Vincent and sent the matter to be considered by a full court of four judges. The full court heard arguments from counsel for Nelson and St Vincent twice, from two separate sets of lawyers. Each team of lawyers in the Court of Common Pleas had to be led by at least one serjeant-at-law. They were members of an order of senior barristers, now abolished, who had exclusive rights of audience before the Court of Common Pleas. It was for this reason that Nelson's solicitor, William Haslewood, had had to tell Nelson that William Garrow (the real-life inspiration for the TV series *Garrow's Law*), who had previously been against them in an earlier matter, could not act for him in these proceedings.[129] Garrow and Nelson would cross paths again, however, in April 1803 when Garrow successfully (and somewhat surprisingly given the views of Heath J. that there was no defence) defended Nelson's colleague Captain Macnamara at the Old Bailey on a charge of manslaughter arising from a duel, with Nelson giving character evidence for the defendant.[130]

The Court of Common Pleas delivered its judgment on 26 November 1802.[131] Four careful and considered judgments were delivered, but they were split with two on each side. Alvanley and Rooke J. found for St Vincent on the basis of Scott's reasoning in The St Anne that St Vincent had not given up command of the station, even though he had left it with permission from the Admiralty for reasons of his health. Heath and Chambre JJ. found for Nelson on the basis that the rule was intended to deal with apportionment between flag-officers, and St Vincent was clearly returning home and had left the fleet under 'another command', namely the senior flag-officer present, Nelson. Heath J. asked what the word 'another' was referring to in the article. Looking at the antecedent articles, he considered

[127] The Middlesex Guildhall was on the site in Parliament Square, opposite the Houses of Parliament and alongside Westminster Abbey, that was subsequently occupied by the Middlesex Crown Court and is now occupied by the United Kingdom Supreme Court.

[128] Marianne Czisnik (ed.), *Nelson's Letters to Lady Hamilton and Related Documents*, NRS (Woodbridge, 2020), p. 147.

[129] BL Add MS 34918/233.

[130] Report of the trial of Captain Macnamara, BL GRC 06496a17.

[131] Lord Alvanley, Mr Justice Chambre, Mr Justice Rooke and Mr Justice Heath.

that it referred to 'another flag-officer'. Otherwise, the phrase would have no meaning as the fleet would always be under the command of someone when the commander-in-chief left the station. Nelson, he held, was another flag-officer, so St Vincent was not entitled. Murray had been entitled in The St Anne because he had not left his fleet under the command of another flag-officer.

To break the impasse the most junior member of the court, Heath J., who had been in favour of Nelson, withdrew his opinion. This allowed the court to enter a verdict for St Vincent and the case to go to appeal before the Court of King's Bench.

1803 Amendment

During the proceedings before the Court of Common Pleas, it was pointed out that there may be very good reasons why a commander-in-chief has to leave his station to come home where it would be unfair to deprive them of their share of prize money. It was expressed by Rooke J.:

> It is well known in point of fact, that officers have sent for home that Government might consult or advise with them – they may render the public as essential service by their return on such an account as if they had remained on their station. It would be hard that in such case they should lose the emolument of prize-money, which is a mere gratuity from the country, and disposable at the discretion of the Crown.[132]

To try and meet this concern the 1803 proclamation, applying to French and Batavian captures after the collapse of the Peace of Amiens, changed the wording of the article so that it provided:

> a chief flag-officer quitting a station either to return home, or to assume another command, or otherwise, except upon some particular urgent service, with the intention of returning to the station as soon as such service is performed, shall have no share of prizes taken by the ships or vessels left behind, after he shall have passed the limits of the station, or after he shall have surrendered the command to another flag-officer appointed by the Admiralty to be commander-in-chief upon such station.[133]

[132] Nelson v Tucker, Court of Common Pleas (1802) 3 Bos. & Pull. 261, 270.

[133] Proclamation 7 July 1803, *London Gazette*, No. 15599, p. 804.

A further proclamation on 31 January 1805 applied the same new wording to captures of Spanish, Italian and Ligurian prizes.[134] Although the 1803 proclamation came into force before final judgment in Nelson's case before the King's Bench, the revised proclamation wording was not retrospective and it was too late to assist in the dispute between St Vincent and Nelson.

The Court of King's Bench

The King's Bench heard arguments on appeal in the case of Lord Nelson v Tucker in the summer of 1803.[135] It was presided over by Lord Ellenborough, who had been appointed Lord Chief Justice in April 1802 after the death of Lord Kenyon a week earlier. Ellenborough was no stranger to the naval politics involved in the case. As Sir Edward Law, before his elevation to the bench and the peerage, he had served as Attorney General in Addington's administration, along with St Vincent as First Lord of the Admiralty, a post that St Vincent still held at the time the case was argued and decided.[136] Ellenborough was also married to the daughter of George Towry, a commissioner on the navy Victualling Board,[137] and would have been familiar not just with politics and the law, but also with the politics of naval administration. St Vincent certainly considered that Ellenborough would consult his father-in-law on naval matters.[138] Ellenborough had already heard a similar dispute involving the same issue of construction in an action concerning the command of the Indian Seas fleet in 1796 between Lord Keith and Admiral Pringle.[139] He had heard that case in Hilary Term in early 1803 in the Court of Common Pleas sitting again at Guildhall. Like Alvanley in the case of St Vincent/Nelson v Tucker, he had entered a verdict for the plaintiff, but subject to the issue of law being submitted for the opinion of a bench of judges. As Nelson's case was then pending in the list for argument

134 Proclamation 31 January 1805, *London Gazette*, No. 15777, p. 157.

135 Trinity Term; Nelson v Tucker, King's Bench (1803) 4 East 268 n.

136 St Vincent left the Board of Admiralty on 14 May 1804 when Pitt resumed the office of prime minister on the fall of Addington's administration. He took up command of the Channel fleet again from 9 November 1805. In 1806 Ellenborough controversially accepted a seat again in the 'cabinet of all talents' whilst remaining as Lord Chief Justice. Ellenborough was a near neighbour of Alexander Davison, but in 1808 sent him to prison for fraud.

137 Roger Knight, *Britain against Napoleon* (London, 2013), p. 40.

138 St Vincent to Captain John Markham, 2 December 1802, *Letters of Admiral Markham*, NRS (London, 1904), p. 7.

139 Keith v Pringle (1803) 4 East 262, also briefly reported in *The Naval Chronicle*, vol. X, p. 432.

before the King's Bench, he put off judgment in Keith's case until after the court had heard the arguments and given judgment in Nelson's case.

Ellenborough delivered a single judgment of the whole court on 14 November 1803. He agreed with Alvanley that the reason Murray had been held to be entitled to the flag-share in The St Anne was because Sir William Scott had found that Murray had not abdicated his command, rather than because Mowatt had not been another flag-officer and so was not 'another command' for the purposes of the proclamation. With all due deference, however, he disagreed with the decision. He considered that the construction of the proclamation could not depend on the intent with which a commander-in-chief returned home, but on the fact of the return home. Looking at the intent behind the proclamation as a whole, it was to encourage the active service of the navy, and that would not be achieved by granting prize shares to admirals who were not on active service. He thought that that approach followed the approach of the courts to other cases[140] apart from The St Anne, and accordingly he found for Nelson and overturned the judgment in favour of St Vincent.

It was an example of what today we would call a purposive approach to construction by the court. It is noteworthy that the Court of Common Pleas gave its verdict during the Peace of Amiens. By the time the King's Bench came to consider the matter, war had resumed and maybe the purpose of encouraging active naval officers such as Nelson seemed more pressing than during the Peace of Amiens. The potential unfairness to a flag-officer coming home in the interests of the nation had been addressed in the 1803 wording. Indeed, Nelson was to benefit from the 1803 (and 1805) wording as it justified the claims that Nelson's then secretary and prize agent, John Scott,[141] made to prizes taken during Nelson's absence to pursue Villeneuve across the Atlantic in 1805, when Admiral Sir Richard Bickerton was left in acting command of the Mediterranean station.[142] It has been suggested that Scott's claim put Nelson 'dangerously close' to St Vincent's position in the litigation arising from the 1799 captures.[143] Although Scott was not a trained lawyer, he had acted as a judge advocate at a court-martial, was experienced in handling prize claims and was as well qualified legally as

[140] Johnstone v Margetson 1 H. Blac. 261, Pigot v White 1 H. Blac. 265 n.

[141] Scott was killed at Trafalgar beside Nelson and therefore lost the opportunity to be prize agent for the Trafalgar prizes. For Scott's rivalry with Davison over Nelson's prize agency work see Downer, *Nelson's Purse*, pp. 239, 253–4, 275, 282–6, 316–17.

[142] John Sugden, *Nelson, the Sword of Albion* (London, 2013), p. 929, n. 4. The claims are cited by Sugden as examples of Scott's 'if in doubt, claim' approach.

[143] Sugden, *Nelson, the Sword of Albion*, p. 929, n. 4.

most undertaking such work.[144] The rules had changed since 1799, so while Nelson's position in 1805 may have been factually close to St Vincent's, under the rules then applicable it was legally quite different. There was no inconsistency between the claims made by Nelson in 1799 and 1805: the rules had changed.

Duncan v Mitchell

Even the decision in Nelson v Tucker did not put an end to claims by admirals departing on grounds of ill health. In 1799 Admiral Sir Andrew Mitchell was ordered to command an Anglo-Russian joint land and naval expedition in the Texel in Holland, then known as the Batavian Republic. The land forces were under the command of Sir Ralph Abercrombie.[145] Admiral Lord Duncan already had command of a fleet on that station, and Mitchell's orders required him to put himself and his fleet under the command of Duncan should it be necessary for the two fleets to cooperate. When Mitchell arrived off Holland, he placed himself under Duncan, who took command of the expedition, including drawing up a line of battle and sending a proposal to Admiral Story in command of the Batavian forces for their surrender. Before anything came of the preparations, however, Duncan sailed for home with his fleet as a result of his own ill health. After Duncan and his ships were out of sight and beyond the point where they could have seen signals of distress, heard the sound of guns or come to Mitchell's assistance, but before they reached England, Story, faced with mutiny in his own fleet, accepted Duncan's proposal and the Dutch fleet surrendered. Two days later and unaware of the surrender, Duncan wrote to Mitchell that he should not consider himself as having been under his command 'longer than from the 30th August' and that he had only been unable to notify him earlier due to his indisposition. The Dutch fleet agreed to surrender at about two o'clock on the 30th and struck their colours at about ten that night.

As the expedition was a joint land and naval expedition, the distribution of prize money arising from captures was determined by a warrant from the king dated 26 June 1800. It granted the proceeds of any captures to Abercrombie and Mitchell in trust to be paid by them to those in the army and navy as were entitled according to a plan of distribution set out in the

144 His certificate of this service was enclosed with the letter to Marsh and Creed of 11 August 1803, Maynard, *John Scott*, p. 41.

145 Law reports at the time frequently adopt this spelling of the name more generally referred to today as Abercromby.

warrant. The plan determined that the whole sum was divided into eighths, with one eighth to go to the commanders-in-chief and flag and general officers. Despite his departure, Duncan claimed the commander-in-chief's share of the Dutch prizes. Anticipating disputes, the warrant provided for 'any doubts' to be decided by the two commanders-in-chief and the flag and general officers, or such of them as could be conveniently assembled, or by such persons to whom they, or the majority of them, may agree to refer the issue. There being no other flag-officers than Duncan and Mitchell, four of the army generals who could be assembled referred Duncan's claim to three referees. The referees found for Duncan, but Mitchell objected that the clause did not cover a dispute as to who was commander-in-chief. Duncan died in 1804, but his executors pursued his claim, which only reached a hearing in 1814. Lord Ellenborough delivered the judgment of the court on 3 May 1815, rejecting Duncan's claim.[146] The court agreed that the dispute resolution clause in the warrant was not intended to cover the question of who was commander-in-chief, so the decision of the referees was not binding. The court decided, though, that as Duncan had sailed for home, he was no longer the commander-in-chief, and Mitchell was entitled to the commander-in-chief's share.

Departing Flag-officers after 1808

The 1808 proclamation sought to clarify the 1803 and 1805 wording even further, to make plain that there were two circumstances dictating when a departing commander-in-chief lost his right to share in prizes. The first was where another flag-officer had been appointed by the Admiralty to command the station, in which case he lost his right to prizes when he surrendered the command to his successor. The second was where he left his command without having been superseded, in which case he lost his right to prizes once he passed out of the limits of the station. In either case, the proviso reserving the right to share in prizes if the departure was temporary and upon some particular urgent service with the intent of returning to the station as soon as such service was performed still applied.

7th Article: Departing Junior Flag-officers

The 1803 and 1805 proclamations also introduced a provision relating to inferior flag-officers quitting a station. They had no right to a share of prizes taken by the ships remaining on station, but equally did not have to

[146] Duncan v Mitchell (1815) 4 M&S 105.

share the prizes taken by ships under their immediate command, once they had passed out of the limits of the station, unless they had been sent by the commander-in-chief for a special service with orders to return as soon as it was over. Thus, if Nelson had sent Bickerton to chase Villeneuve across the Atlantic and then return to the Mediterranean fleet, Bickerton would not have lost out on prizes taken in his absence but would have had to account for any prizes that he took. The wording of the proclamations, which was repeated in 1808, was that:

> an inferior Flag-officer quitting a station, except when detached by Orders from his Commander-in-Chief out of the limits thereof upon a special service, with orders to return to such station as soon as such service is performed, shall have no share in prizes taken by the ships and vessels remaining on the station, after he shall have passed the limits thereof; and in like manner the Flag-officers remaining on the station shall have no share in prizes taken by such inferior Flag-officer, or by any ships and vessels under his immediate command, after he shall have quitted the limits of the station, except when detached as aforesaid.

8th Article: Joint Captures with Ships from Other Stations

A long war revealed the intricate ways in which captures could be made by naval ships and the 1803 and 1805 proclamations dealt expressly for the first time with how captains of ships involved in joint captures with ships under a different command were to account for any flag-share. The provision, which again was repeated in 1808, was that:

> when vessels under the command of a Flag, which belong to separate Stations shall happen to be joint captors, the Captain of each ship shall pay one third of the share to which he is entitled to the Flag-officers of the station to which he belongs; but the captains of vessels under Admiralty Orders, being joint captors with other vessels under a Flag shall retain the Whole of their share.

9th Article: Captures Under Direct Admiralty Orders

The right of a captain involved in a joint capture but under direct Admiralty orders to keep the whole of his share, rather than share it with any flag-officers, was in line with longstanding provisions to that effect, even where a ship was sailing out of a port commanded by a flag-officer. If the captain was under direct Admiralty orders, the flag-officers had no right to a share of prizes taken by that captain.

The 1793 wording provided that:

> if a Flag-officer is sent to command in the Out-Ports of this Kingdom, he shall have no Share of the Prizes taken by Ships or Vessels which have sailed, or shall sail, from that Port by Order of the Admiralty

The wording was repeated in 1808, but thereafter the captain's share was reduced to two eighths in any event (see above). The provision was still of benefit, however, as at least the captain did not have to account to any flag-officers for a third of his remaining two eighths share if he was under direct Admiralty orders.

Confusion caused by a lack of clarity in orders issued by the Admiralty about whether a ship was sailing under Admiralty orders or the orders of a flag-officer at the time of a capture gave rise to numerous disputes.

In September 1796 the 32-gun frigate *HMS Unicorn* was sailing in the Channel when she met a number of large, valuable enemy Dutch ships sailing from Surinam bound for Amsterdam. Captain Sir Thomas Williams of the *Unicorn* was an aggressive frigate captain. He had just been knighted for his capture of the French frigate *Tribune* following a running fight of several hours and a half hour of close combat which left 37 Frenchmen killed and 14 wounded, but not a single casualty on the *Unicorn*.[147] Williams had intelligence that the ships had been loaded in Surinam and that, whatever they might pretend, they had indeed been loaded on Dutch account.[148] He swooped on his prey and captured the *Eliza* on 22 September 1796, the *Orion* on the 23rd and the *Christian VII* on the 24th. Williams sent the prizes into Portsmouth with prize crews aboard and then fell in with some English merchant ships and transports, which had become separated from the British homeward-bound Leeward Island convoy in a heavy gale a few days earlier. Williams saw the ships safely into the Channel against an easterly wind and then escorted them up the Channel once the wind changed in their favour. En-route he captured two more of the Surinam fleet, the *Wilhemsberg* on 1 October and the *Frieheden* on the 4th.

On 5 October he anchored at Spithead to put his Dutch prisoners ashore and recover his prize crews and officers. The captures were condemned as

[147] ODNB/29552, J. K. Laughton, rev. Andrew Lambert (accessed 6 June 2016).

[148] Letter, Williams to Admiralty after the captures, recited at The Orion (1803) 4 Rob. Adm. Rep. 362, 377n.

prizes, but a question arose as to whether Williams was sailing at the time under Admiralty orders or the orders of Admiral Kingsmill, the commander-in-chief of the Irish station.

The Irish station had been created at the beginning of the French Revolutionary War as a new, independent station. There was concern that Ireland could be a backdoor means for the French to mount an invasion of England, so a fleet based in Ireland could patrol for French activities supporting any possible landing of troops, as well as guarding British shipping in and out of the Channel.[149] The limits of the station were poorly defined at the outset, however, and remained so in 1796. Indeed, in 1797 ships of the Irish station recaptured two large Portuguese ships, the *Galatea* and the *Doris*, south of Ushant, which prompted the Admiralty to write to Kingsmill congratulating his officers on the recaptures, but directing Kingsmill to 'in future confine the limits of the stations of cruising ships under your orders to the northward of Ushant, that they may be at hand, in case their service should be required on the coast of Ireland.'[150] *Unicorn* was attached to the Irish station when it captured the *Tribune* in June 1796, but was then sent by Kingsmill to Portsmouth to refit. Kingsmill's orders were that Williams should tell the Admiralty of his arrival in Portsmouth, lose no time in refitting, and then return to Cork for further orders.[151] When Williams informed the Admiralty of his arrival at Portsmouth, their acknowledgement required him to 'take in stores, &tc. and having so done to continue to follow the orders of Admiral Kingsmill for his farther proceedings.'[152] Before Williams returned to Cork, however, the Admiralty gave him a number of direct orders, but without telling Kingsmill that they were detaching the *Unicorn* from his command, which they usually, but not invariably, would do if that was the case.[153] Some of the orders were frustrated by events, but the last ones, dated 8 September 1796, were effective, material to the dispute over the Surinam captures.

The first part of the Admiralty order to Williams of 8 September 1796 was to carry £20,000 from Portsmouth to Plymouth. This relatively simple task would have earned Williams the sum of £200 in freight money, which he would not have had to share with his officers or crew, or with his flag-officer

[149] As an example of the alarm such worries caused see W. G. Perrin, 'Pellew and the Departure of the Bantry Bay Expedition, December 1796,' *MM* 6:6 (1920), 178–83.

[150] Evan Nepean to Kingsmill, 4 August 1797, recited at The Orion (1803) 4 Rob. Adm. Rep. 362, 374n.

[151] Orders 20 June 1796, recited at The Orion (1803) 4 Rob. Adm. Rep. 362, 368.

[152] June 1796, recited at The Orion (1803) 4 Rob. Adm. Rep. 362, 368.

[153] 'certified by several officers of distinction, and by clerks of long experience in the business of the Admiralty,' The Orion (1803) 4 Rob. Adm. Rep. 362, 367.

as the order came from the Admiralty.[154] Once he had delivered the money, Williams was 'to proceed in the *Unicorn* to Cork agreeable to former orders, taking a short range on your way thither, so as to enable you to fall in with any homeward-bound ships coming into the Channel, to which you are to afford any protection in your power they may stand in need of'. It was while undertaking these orders that the *Unicorn* made the captures of the Surinam ships. It so happened that the area within which the *Unicorn* was to range under the Admiralty orders was none other than the area that ships from the Irish station were frequently sent to cruise by their flag-officer, but the only order that Williams had from Kingsmill was to return to Cork, not to undertake a cruise. Kingsmill argued that the return route to Cork would, or could, have taken the *Unicorn* through the same waters and led to the captures, and that as Williams' actions were reconcilable with his orders from Kingsmill, then he as flag-officer was entitled to his share.

The action was heard by Sir William Scott, the Admiralty Court judge, on 12 August 1803. He concluded that the question was whether anything had been done to supersede or suspend Kingsmill's command as flag-officer. It was enough, he held, 'if another competent authority, and still more if a paramount authority (i.e. the Admiralty), had employed him on a clear, distinct and separate service, although that service might, in its own nature, be very short, and a party be directed immediately after the performance of it to return to his former relation of subjection'.[155] Scott held that the Admiralty order was inconsistent with the order from Kingsmill to return to Cork, as the instruction to afford protection to the homeward trade contained the prospect that the *Unicorn* would not return straight to Cork, as in fact happened. He held, therefore, that the Admiralty orders constituted a 'separate and distinct' service from any orders that Kingsmill had given and that the flag-officer therefore had no share in the prizes.

Williams had just distinguished himself in ship-to-ship battle at a time when the nation stood in need of good news. His knighthood brought no financial reward but raised expensive social expectations. A payment of freight money for a simple voyage from Portsmouth to Plymouth and the provision of 'intelligence' that there were ships due back from Surinam, with instructions that could lead to their capture without giving the game away, would both be ways to reward an enterprising frigate captain in a more material way. Although not expressly identified in the law report, it is entirely consistent with the idea that the Admiralty intended a 'separate

[154] See chapter 8.

[155] The Orion (1803) 4 Rob. Adm. Rep. 362, 372/3.

and distinct' service for Williams for his benefit, rather than that of Admiral Kingsmill, who was already milking the Irish station.

The Admiralty had to be careful, however, not to offend the captain's flag-officer. That would explain why, contrary to the usual practice, the Admiralty never wrote to Kingsmill to tell him in express terms what they were doing. As with the instructions concerning St Vincent's sick leave from the Mediterranean station in 1799 considered above, the Admiralty could leave matters somewhat vague and let the courts sort out their dirty washing in due course at a time conveniently far into the future.

Scott's judgment in The Orion was affirmed on appeal to the Privy Council. Lord Ellenborough, the Lord Chief Justice, and Sir William Wynne, the Master of the Rolls, sat on the appeal. It was a high-powered court sitting at 'the Cockpit', the site of the old cockpit theatre off Whitehall in Downing Street that was used as a judicial chamber by the Privy Council. Ellenborough later recalled that the decision on appeal was that:

> there was a new departure as it were from Captain Williams' original command by the special and paramount order of the Admiralty, appointing a certain deviation from his original orders, after which he was to return again under the command of Admiral Kingsmill: and the prize happened to be taken during that deviation.[156]

Both judgments were in line with the law of deviation from voyage instructions that had developed in the field of marine insurance during the eighteenth century, and in which both courts were imbued.[157] Even if the courts in The Orion were attempting to give effect to the wishes of the Admiralty, they were applying a legal test of general and proven use. The Admiralty could leave the law to take its course.

10th Article: More Than One Flag-officer

Where there was more than one flag-officer on a station they shared the 'Flag-eighth' between them. Thus, although Nelson had claimed the commander-in-chief's share of prizes taken by ships of the Mediterranean fleet after St Vincent's departure in 1799, he recognised the right of Sir John Thomas Duckworth to a share as the other flag-officer remaining on the station.

[156] Per Lord Ellenborough during argument in Harvey v Cooke (1805) 6 East 220, 232.

[157] E.g. Lavabre v Wilson (1779) 1 Doug. P. 284; Parker v James (1814) 4 Campb. 112 per Lord Ellenborough; Marsden v Reid (1803) 3 East 572, 577; Lawrence v Sydenham (1805) 6 East 45; Parr v Anderson (1805) 6 East 202.

The size of the share depended on the number of flag-officers involved, but the commander-in-chief always took a larger share. Where there were two flag-officers, the commander-in-chief took two thirds of the flag-share, and the inferior flag-officer took the remaining third. If there were more than two flag-officers entitled to share, the commander-in-chief took half of the flag-share, and the remainder was split equally between the other flag-officers irrespective of seniority.

Allied Fleets and their Flag-officers

Combined actions of the Royal Navy with allied squadrons in the Mediterranean raised the issue of whether a flag-officer of an allied squadron attached to a British fleet was entitled to share as a flag-officer on the station for the purposes of prize money.

Duckworth v Tucker

The officer who eventually brought the issue before an English court of law was Admiral Marquis de Niza.[158] De Niza commanded a Portuguese squadron attached to St Vincent's British Mediterranean fleet. His squadron of four Portuguese ships led by his flagship *Principe Real* had been attached to the British fleet since May 1798. Initially, Nelson doubted the contribution that the Portuguese ships could make, even though the other three ships, *Rheine de Portugal* (74 guns, Captain Thomas Stone), *Alfonso d'Albuquerque* (74 guns, Captain Donald Campbell) and *St Sebastian* (64 guns, Captain Sampson Mitchell), were captained by British trained officers.[159] De Niza and his ships played a significant role, however, on the Italian coast and in the taking of Malta after the Battle of the Nile.[160]

Where allied ships were jointly involved in the actual capture of prize ships, they could claim a share of the prize money as joint captors. St Vincent recognised the rights of the Portuguese ships in such captures when de Niza was under his command, on the basis of his own anecdotal understanding

[158] Don Domingos Xavier de Lima was the Marquis Consort de Nisa, having married Eugénia Maria Teles de Castro da Gama (1776–1839), 11th Countess of Vidigueira, 7th Marchioness of Nisa and 7th Countess of Unhão, a descendant of Vasco da Gama, to whose family the de Nisa title had been granted by King John IV of Portugal in 1646. Niza and Nisa were alternative spellings that were both used at the time.

[159] Sugden, *Nelson, the Sword of Albion*, p. 120.

[160] Ibid., p. 150.

of precedent.[161] His understanding was that the Dutch squadron serving with the British fleet in 1745 had shared in the fleet's prize money and he and Lord Hotham had shared in a similar way with the Neapolitan squadron that had served with them in the Mediterranean. His view was confirmed by others, including Sir Philip Stephens.[162] The 1803 proclamation dealt expressly with captures that the Royal Navy made with the ships of allied countries. It provided that a share of such prizes equal to that which the allied ships would have been entitled to if they had been HM ships would be set apart and be at the king's disposal. Even in such cases, however, disputes could arise, and the Prize Act 1807 made express provision for Sicilian ships acting in conjunction with British ships under Admiral Keith at the surrender of Genoa and Savona to share in prize money.[163] To avoid getting involved in disputes among the Sicilian officers, their share was to be paid to the Sicilian envoy in London to be distributed as the Sicilian king might direct. The provisions of the 1807 Act were extended the following year to include all other joint captures, including the joint capture of Malta in which de Niza was involved.[164]

What de Niza claimed, however, was not limited to a share of the captures where he was actually involved. He sought a flag-officer's share of captures made by the fleet even where he was not directly involved.

On 17 June 1799, while St Vincent was commander-in-chief of the Mediterranean station, a French frigate squadron under Rear-Admiral Perree was spotted by a British fleet of 30 ships under Lord Keith near Toulon. Three ships of the line and two frigates under the command of Captain Markham of *HMS Centaur* were detached by Keith to give chase. After a lengthy running battle Perree and his ships surrendered to Markham. By October 1799 both St Vincent and Keith had left the Mediterranean station, leaving Nelson in command of the fleet, including de Niza, when the Spanish treasure ships that gave rise to Nelson's dispute with St Vincent were captured.

De Niza claimed a share of both the French and the Spanish prizes as a junior flag-officer attached to the British Mediterranean fleet. The claim to the Spanish ships in particular presented something of a diplomatic problem. Both Britain and Portugal were at war with France. Britain was at war with Spain, but Portugal was not. The treaties of alliance between Britain

[161] St Vincent to Viscount Duncan, 18 January 1802, D. Bonner Smith (ed.), *Letters of Lord St Vincent*, NRS (London, 1921), vol. 1, p. 299.

[162] A member of the Board of Admiralty who had previously been the longstanding First Secretary to the Admiralty.

[163] Geo. III c. 47.

[164] Geo. III c. 100.

and Portugal provided for their navies to act together, and specifically that the officer of either contracting power who commanded the smaller number of ships should be subordinate to the commanding officer of the larger portion of the joint fleet regardless of their respective rank.[165] Thus de Niza was subordinate to St Vincent at the time of the French captures and to Nelson when the Spanish treasure ships were captured. By an agreement between the British and Portuguese governments, however, the Portuguese ships were not to act against Spain or be employed in any manner likely to give offence to that power. If the French and Spanish combined their fleets in the Mediterranean and tried to pass through the Straits of Gibraltar, then Portugal would consider itself threatened by Spain and the Portuguese ships could then be used against the combined enemy fleet, but not otherwise. Both St Vincent and de Niza were aware of the terms that their governments had agreed. Thus, de Niza could not himself have taken the Spanish treasure ships as prizes, and neither St Vincent nor Nelson could have ordered him to do so. Nevertheless, the Portuguese ships did contribute to the captures as their activities off the coasts of Italy and Malta freed British ships to capture Spanish ships off the coast of Spain.

Neither St Vincent, Nelson nor Duckworth recognised de Niza's claim to a share of any of these prizes. None of them had been directly involved in the captures and any entitlement depended on the terms of the 1793 proclamation, or that of 25 January 1797, which applied the terms of the 1793 proclamation to Spanish prizes.[166] Even after Nelson had won his litigation against St Vincent, however, de Niza's claim grumbled on. Tucker insisted on keeping a retention to meet any possible claim by de Niza despite being pressed by Nelson's lawyer, William Haslewood, to pay over the monies.[167] If de Niza was entitled to a share, then Nelson's share would reduce from two thirds to one half of the flag-share and Duckworth's share would reduce from one third to a quarter. De Niza, who had received legal advice from the experienced Admiralty Court lawyer Sir John Nicholl, pressed on with his claim.[168] His representatives used the admiral's absence from London as a reason for delay, but there may also have been good diplomatic reasons to keep the claim by a Portuguese admiral to Spanish prizes quiet. Nelson was killed before the issue was resolved, and those who survived him had to wait until 1809, when judgment was given in an action that Duckworth

165 Duckworth v Tucker (1809) 2 Taunt. 7.

166 If de Niza had actually assisted, he would have had to make his claim as a joint captor in the Admiralty Court proceedings leading to condemnation of the prizes in favour of the captors, per Mansfield C. J. Duckworth v Tucker (1809) 2 Taunt. 7, 34.

167 Haslewood to Tucker, 15 March 1804, NMM CRK/6/139.

168 De Niza's London representative to Tucker 1804, NMM CRK/6/141.

had brought against Tucker for payment of the disputed share.[169] By 1809 the diplomatic niceties had become less pressing as war had come to the Iberian Peninsula. In November 1807 the entire Portuguese Braganza court, including the queen and prince regent, escaped to Brazil on board the *Principe Real* under the protection of the Royal Navy.[170] By 1809 the British had begun the military action that became the Peninsula War and there was no need to keep the dispute quiet.

In June 1809 the Court of Common Pleas held that the proclamation only applied to officers in the pay of the king, and that Portuguese officers were therefore not entitled to claim a share.[171] Despite a later attempt by the Portuguese ambassador to persuade the court that the matter should be reconsidered, the judgment prevailed.[172]

The size of the claims for flag-shares led to extensive litigation, which has left a trail of evidence that assists in understanding the dynamics of the changes that were introduced. The Admiralty was concerned to try and reduce friction between officers and reduce the scope for disputes to improve the operational strength of the Royal Navy. Notably, however, the Admiralty was happy to leave the resolution of disputes to the courts, rather than intervene itself. An area of particular dispute involved the final two articles of the proclamations dealing with flag-share rights enjoyed by captains despite their not having reached permanent flag status. The next chapter deals with those circumstances, and the acrimonious litigation they led to.

[169] Duckworth v Tucker (1809) 2 Taunt. 7.

[170] The mental incapacity of Queen Maria I of Portugal had led to the regency under Prince Regent Joao.

[171] Mansfield C. J. (Chief Justice of Court of Common Pleas), Heath J., Lawrence J. and Chambre J.

[172] Duckworth v Tucker (1809) 2 Taunt. 7, 37.

6.

Who Got What: Problems with Commodores

11th Article: Commodores as Flag-officers

In the Georgian navy an Admiralty appointment of a captain as a commodore was a temporary position, rather than a permanent rank. A commodore flew a broad pennant and could exercise the powers of a flag-officer, but without the permanent elevation to flag-rank. Once his appointment as a commodore came to an end he reverted to his rank of captain. A commodore could be ordered to take charge of a squadron of ships as their commander-in-chief or could serve with a fleet as a junior flag-officer. Thus, Commodore Horatio Nelson fought at the Battle of St Vincent under the command of Admiral Sir John Jervis.[1]

There were two forms of appointment as a commodore. A captain could be appointed as a commodore either with or without a captain serving under him. A captain appointed commodore with a captain serving under him had a captain appointed to command his flagship, leaving him free to deal with command of the squadron. He was entitled to the pay and allowances of a rear-admiral. He also ranked as a flag-officer for prize money purposes. A captain appointed without a captain under him was expected to captain his own flagship in addition to commanding the squadron and was entitled to the less generous allowance of an extra ten shillings per day. Known dismissively as 'ten-shilling commodores', they were not entitled to a flag-share of prize money. Going into the Battle of St Vincent on *HMS Captain*, Nelson had a captain under him, Ralph Miller. On that basis, he would have been entitled to a flag-share of prize money and was not a mere ten-shilling commodore.[2] The distinction led to problems, and litigation.

1 R. J. B. Knight, *The Pursuit of Victory: The Life and Achievement of Horatio Nelson* (London, 2005), p. 220.

2 Cf. John Sugden, *Nelson: A Dream of Glory* (London, 2005), p. 594.

In 1805 Captain Sir Home Popham was appointed to command a squadron being sent to recapture the Cape from the Dutch, to whom the Cape had been returned as part of the peace treaty negotiated in Amiens in 1802. When hostilities resumed in 1803 the Cape remained in Dutch hands, and available for use by French ships. Although the British had a base at St Helena en-route to the Indian Ocean, the Dutch base at the Cape threatened the economically important British trade with India, including the vital trade in Indian saltpetre, which was needed by Britain as an ingredient for gunpowder. In June 1805 Popham received intelligence from a dragoon captain who had been at the Cape as a prisoner of war that the Cape was preparing for use as a base for a French fleet.[3] Although opinions differed on the value of the Cape, the thought of it being a base for the French was too much. Eager to intervene, Popham shared his news with the prime minister, William Pitt, and the Admiralty, then under Lord Barham, an experienced naval administrator, as its First Lord.[4] An expedition to retake the Cape would need a man who could exercise considerable discretion to react according to the circumstances on arrival without having to rely on instructions from London. Popham was an intelligent, imaginative officer, who displayed a scientific bent in his career, introducing innovations such as an improved method of signalling. He had something of a chequered reputation, however. During a period of leave of absence from the navy after the American War of Independence, Popham, like Pitt's family before him, had tried his hand at earning a fortune in the East Indies. His mercantile activities had drawn allegations that he was prepared to play fast and loose with the law and that he had engaged in unlawful trading, embezzlement and smuggling. Fifteen years of litigation ensued. The dispute took on a political flavour, as Popham was associated, through his connections with Lord Melville, the disgraced former First Lord of the Admiralty, with Pitt's faction in Parliament.[5] A biography of Popham published in 1991 by a distant descendant took a contemporary description of him as its title: *A Damned Cunning Fellow*.[6] A later biography by historian Jacqueline Reiter is entitled *Quicksilver Captain: The Improbable Life of Sir Home Popham*, which captures both the dangerous and unpredictable nature of the man, as well as his thirst for making a quick fortune.[7]

3 J. D. Grainger, *British Campaigns in the South Atlantic, 1805–1807* (Barnsley, 2015), pp. 2–3.

4 As Sir Charles Middleton, Barham had served as a reforming comptroller of the navy.

5 Grainger, *British Campaigns*, p. 2; Hansard, HC 31 May 1808, vol. 2, cc 721–63.

6 Popham, *A Damned Cunning Fellow*.

7 Reiter, *Quicksilver Captain*, p. xi.

Barham has gone down in history for making an inspired appointment of a singular naval leader when in 1805 he appointed Nelson to deal with the French and Spanish fleets in what became the Battle of Trafalgar. The same year, Barham appointed Popham to take a military force to secure the Cape with land forces commanded by Lieutenant-General Sir David Baird, who was to act as governor of the Cape once the occupation was complete. Popham had experience in combined amphibious operations and had previously worked well with Baird. Like Nelson, Popham was an imaginative and enterprising officer, and it was understandable that Barham appointed him to command an operation that called for a large land force to be put on a distant shore on the initiative of the commander on the scene. As seen in Chapter 5, however, Popham also had experience of serving with Captain Thompson, whose decisions to act in breach of his orders had been condoned by the Admiralty.

The Cape was not the only destination that Popham had his eye on. South America and the Spanish colonies were of great interest to Popham, who held himself out as an expert on the area, even though he had never been there. Pitt had been lobbied by a Venezuelan nationalist adventurer, Francisco de Miranda, to support the independence cause against Spain, and in 1803 Popham proposed a plan to the Admiralty for attacking Spanish colonies in South America to support an uprising. Miranda was not alone. His journey to London was followed by over 70 South American independence era leaders, including Bernando O'Higgins, Simon Bolivar and Jose de San Martin.[8] Popham was not the only one to see the potential advantages from trade with South America. In response to the economic warfare of the Continental System in Europe, 'British exports to North America and particularly the untapped territories in South America grew dramatically in the years after 1806, and proved a crucial supplement to the trade lost on the Continent.'[9] In November 1806, John Fordyce, a member of the Commission of Naval Revision convinced of the need to maintain a dominant navy, wrote to Barham:

[8] Karen Racine, '"This England and This Now": British Cultural and Intellectual Influence in the Spanish American Independence Era', *Hispanic American Historical Review* 90:3 (2010), 423–54; Colley, *The Gun, the Ship & the Pen*, pp. 219–43.

[9] James Davey, 'Economic Warfare and the Defeat of the Continental System: The Royal Navy in the Baltic 1808–1811', *Trafalgar Chronicle* 25 (2015), 29, at p. 42.

> This country must not end the war without preserving the connection with South America which affords the best chance of enabling us to afford the expense of such a navy and of providing a nursery of seamen superior to that of other nations.[10]

Popham's proposal was not universally welcomed, however. Nelson's prescient view was that:

> A blow struck in Europe would do more towards making us respected, and of course facilitate a Peace, than the possession of Mexico or Peru; in both of which, I am sure, we are perfectly ignorant of the disposition of the inhabitants; and above all, I hope that we shall have no buccaneering expeditions.[11]

The Admiralty abandoned the South American expedition, but not Popham. He later claimed that Pitt shared his interest in South America and had tacitly approved the actions that he would take, but Pitt was dead by the time the consequences had to be dealt with, and Popham's orders made no reference to a conquest in South America.

Popham's orders, dated 31 July 1805, directed that when he left Madeira for the Cape, he was to hoist a broad pennant as commodore on board his ship, *HMS Diadem*, and authorised him to wear the flag in the absence of a flag-officer until given further orders. No mention was made of his being entitled to have a captain under him, and no such appointment was made by the Admiralty. Two years later Barham, by then out of office, wrote to the Admiralty that he had 'no hesitation in declaring' that when he directed Popham to hoist a broad pennant it was his intention that he should have a captain to serve under him and that the order authorised him to appoint a captain to *Diadem* to serve under him.[12] The form of orders used by the Admiralty for the two different appointments as commodore was clear, however, and Popham's order did not contain the wording that he was

10 Roger Morriss, *The Royal Dockyards during the Revolutionary and Napoleonic Wars* (Leicester, 1983), pp. 203–4.

11 Undated letter to Lord Moira 1804/5, recited from Clarke and M'Arthur, vol. ii, p. 398, in Nicolas, *Dispatches*, vol. vi, p. 310.

12 June 1807 Barham to Admiralty, Papers relating to Property captured at Buenos Ayres, HC Miscellaneous Accounts and Papers vol. X, 1812, p. 382.

appointed to have a captain under him.[13] Barham explained the omission in his letter to the Admiralty as rebounding to Popham's credit:

> Sir Home's disinterestedness was such that he never introduced any subject to me which had for its object his own private or personal interest, but always confined himself to the more essential details of the service on which he was to be employed and if I had conceived it possible for any doubt to have arisen on the construction of his authority, or that my intentions towards him should, by any accident or interpretation have been defeated, a Commodore's Commission should certainly have accompanied him; and I meant to have sent one after him, but, owing to the hurry of business, it escaped my memory at the moment, nor did it occur to me on leaving the Admiralty, or a Commission should have been ante-dated and transmitted afterwards.

Barham had other matters on his mind at the time when he dispatched Popham to the Cape. Villeneuve had put to sea with the Toulon fleet and Nelson was chasing him out and back across the Atlantic. Britain was in danger of invasion, and it was Barham's job to prevent it. The fact remains, however, that Barham's 1807 letter was written after the event, amid the controversy that had arisen in the meantime, with the benefit of hindsight and when he was already out of office. The order to Popham made no provision for him to appoint a captain under him, as it would, or should, have done had that been intended.

When Popham left Madeira he raised his commodore's flag, but he went further and appointed a captain under him. Before Madeira, Popham had been captain of *HMS Diadem* (64 guns) with William King as his first lieutenant. Captain Hugh Downman had been captain of *HMS Diomede* (50 guns) and Captain Joseph Edwards captain of the smaller brig-sloop *HMS Espoir*.[14] In order to appoint a captain under him, Popham gave King command of *Espoir* and moved Edwards into *Diomede* and Downman into *Diadem*. The 32-gun frigate, *HMS Narcissus*, remained under the command of Captain Ross Donnelly.

The captains of Popham's squadron thus appointed then turned their minds to the distribution of prize money, and agreed to share all prize money from prizes taken by any of their number regardless of who was actually present at the time of capture.[15] Confident in the right of Popham

[13] Anon., *A Correct Account of The Trial at Large between Ross Donnelly, Esq. a Post Captain in His Majesty's Navy, Plaintiff and Sir Home Popham, Knt. Defendant* (1807).

[14] *Espoir* is sometimes referred to by her original French name of *L'Espoir*.

[15] HC Papers Vol. X, p. 385.

to the flag-share as they all were, their agreements made no provision for Popham as his flag-share was assumed as a given.

Cape Captured: An Expedition to the Rio Plata, 1806

By January 1806 the Cape had been recaptured, but there remained anxiety about the security of the Cape. A French squadron under Rear-Admiral Linois was thought to be still in the area posing a real threat and Popham prepared to defend the Cape. By March, however, Popham correctly assessed that a French attack was unlikely. On 28 March an American merchantman arrived at the Cape from Buenos Aires. Her captain, Thomas Waine, brought news that Buenos Aires was defenceless and that a British force would be welcomed. Given the tensions between Spain and her distant colonies, that was a credible, if simplistic, claim, and it was welcome news to Popham. It would not be the last time that an invading force made the same error.

Popham's orders provided for him to send some of his force on to India and to return his transports to England. He also had an order to send a ship to cruise the waters off South America. His orders did not provide for him to strip the Cape of its defences and set off with all that he could muster for an invasion of the Rio Plata. That, however, is what he did in April 1806. Just before the fleet set off from Table Bay for South America, the captains renewed their prize money agreement, once again evincing no need to mention Popham's share on the basis that he was the commander-in-chief entitled to his flag-share.[16]

On 2 July 1806 Buenos Aires capitulated to the forces landed by Popham and under the command of Brigadier-General Beresford. The British, however, were not welcomed by the local civil or military powers. Regarded as invaders rather than liberators, their position was untenable without urgent reinforcement. So enthusiastic was Popham about his new conquest, however, that he wrote directly to merchants in Britain's mercantile centres encouraging them to trade with the Rio Plata. Amongst the Spanish treasure seized by the British forces was a considerable sum in Spanish dollars. Popham decided to send £275,000-worth of dollars back to Britain, retaining the balance for use in the campaign. The only suitable ship available to take the enormously valuable cargo of dollars to Britain was the *Narcissus*, under Captain Ross Donnelly. It was usual at that time for

[16] April 1806, Memorandum of agreement between Josiah Rowley, Raisonable, Ross Donnelly, Narcissus, Joseph Edmonds, Diomede, and William King, Diadem, *Correct Account*, Appendix 12.

the Treasury to pay a percentage of the value of public specie carried by Royal Navy ships as freight to the captain of the ship entrusted with the carriage. On this occasion a payment of 2 per cent was granted, amounting to £5,500. Whilst the distribution of prize money was governed by royal proclamations in force under the Prize Act, no such provision existed for freight money. Nevertheless, it was at that time the custom and usage in the Royal Navy for captains to pay a flag-share of freight money to their flag-officer as if the money had been received as prize money.[17] Accordingly, when Donnelly's agents received his freight money they accounted to Popham's agent, Thomas Collier, for a flag-share.

By that time Popham was still in Buenos Aires. Donnelly, appointed as captain of *HMS Ardent*, had also sailed back to Buenos Aires, but questions had already been raised about Popham's entitlement to a flag-share, with suggestions that he was a mere 'ten-shilling commodore'. Accordingly, Donnelly's agents took the precaution of obtaining a conditional receipt from Thomas Collier in the following terms:

> Received of Ross Donelly, Esq, Late Captain of HMS Narcissus, by the hands of his Agents, Messrs J.J. and R. Mangles and Thomas Goode, Six Hundred and Eighty-seven Pounds Ten Shillings, for the use of Lady Popham, being one-eighth of 5,500l freight money, for the bullion and specie brought in that ship from Buenos Aires to England. Some doubts having arisen, whether Sir Home Popham is entitled to share as a flag-officer, it is hereby acknowledged, that the payment thereof, is made and received by me, as not tending to prejudice the interest of Captain Donnelly, or as an admission of Sir Home's claim, and is to be repaid, should Sir Home be declared not entitled thereto by any suit at law.[18]

Donnelly carried with him on *Ardent* a letter to Popham from William Marsden, the secretary to the Board of Admiralty, containing elements of both disapprobation and approbation:

> I have received their Lordship's commands to acquaint you, that although they have judged it necessary to mark their disapprobation

[17] See Chapter 8.

[18] Recited in the Court of Common Pleas by Donnelly's counsel, Serjeant Shepherd, per *Correct Account*, p. 28.

> of a measure of such importance being undertaken without the sanction of the Government and of your having left the station which it was your duty to guard, without any naval defences, they are nevertheless pleased to express their entire approbation of the judicious able and spirited conduct manifested by yourself the officers, seamen and marines employed under your orders on the above occasion.[19]

Popham took on board the comments of approbation rather than those of disapprobation and cited the letter in his defence at his court-martial.

Popham was replaced as commander-in-chief by a reinforcing fleet under the command of Rear-Admiral Charles Stirling. By that time Popham's invasion had been repulsed, leaving prisoners in the hands of the local forces. Another invasion was undertaken, which was also ultimately defeated, but by then Popham and Donnelly had returned to Britain. When they arrived back, they discovered that the payment made to Popham's agent for the 'flag-share' had been one eighth of the monies received, rather than one third, which was the custom, as captains accounted to their flag-officer for one third of the money that they received. Donnelly then prompted his agent to pay the balance to Popham. On this occasion no conditional receipt was obtained, but the payment was treated in court as having been made on the same basis as the original, conditional, payment.[20]

The Court-Martial of Sir Home Popham, 1807

On his return Popham found that the government had changed. Pitt had died in January 1806. Pitt's Tories had been replaced in government by a Whig 'Ministry of All the Talents' and Barham was no longer at the Admiralty. The new Admiralty Board under Charles Grey was unimpressed by Popham's South American adventures but constrained by the popular enthusiasm his publicity for his 'victories' had engendered. To the new Admiralty Board, the letter Marsden had to send to Popham in September 1806 contained more disapprobation than approbation. The result was a court-martial on board *HMS Gladiator* in March 1807. Popham defended himself with his customary confidence. His written defence is held in the National Archives at Kew and is a joy to read.[21] He rattled off a number of events that he regarded as ample precedent for his glorious conduct. It

19 Letter dated 23 September 1806, cited Popham Court-Martial Defence ADM 1/5378, pp. 8–9.

20 *Correct Account*, p. 29.

21 Popham Court-Martial Defence, TNA, ADM 1/5378.

reads as though he had been a collector of examples of glorious breaches of orders. He included Rooke's seizure of Gibraltar under Queen Anne, Sir Peter Parker's expedition against the Spanish settlement of Omoa in the American war, Hood's capture and surrender of Toulon and Corsica, St Vincent sending Nelson to attack Tenerife in 1796 and Sir Sidney Smith's Treaty of El Arish in Egypt, which allowed the French army to return to France. He prayed in aid Nelson's pursuit of the French fleet across the Atlantic in 1805 without orders, claiming that Nelson had left the Mediterranean station without a single ship. This was a classic Popham exaggeration as Nelson had in fact left ships to guard the station under Sir Richard Bickerton. Popham also referred to his own experience of the conduct of Captain Thompson as seen in Chapter 5, convoying merchant ships home without authority.

Popham not only relied on what he saw as the letter of approbation from the Admiralty in September 1806, but reiterated his claim that he had originally been planning a strike on South America with Melville and Pitt when the opportunity to strike at the Cape arose, and that as a result of his conversations with Pitt (now dead) he expected to be involved in a strike on Spanish South America once the political situation in Europe allowed, which he thought was the case once he heard of the success at Trafalgar and the defeat at Austerlitz.

Popham's confident performance did not prevent him from being convicted by the court-martial and sentenced to a severe reprimand. According to *The Morning Chronicle*, the reprimand restrained the king from promoting Sir Home Popham from a knight of Malta to a baronet of the United Kingdom.[22] In a masterstroke of spin, however, *The Star* newspaper of 11 March 1807 declared that Popham had been 'Honourably Acquitted', which represented Popham's view of the affair, rather than what had actually occurred.[23] Reiter has concluded that Popham was his own worst enemy, but he was politically astute and useful to people who mattered and as a result the sentence had little effect on Popham's naval career.[24] It merely added to an already maverick reputation: 'A Damned Cunning Fellow'. *The Morning Chronicle* also suggested that despite the loss of a baronetcy, Popham 'will have the consolation of prize-money'. The extent of that consolation, however, had already come under scrutiny.

22 *The Morning Chronicle*, 16 November 1807, issue 12013.

23 Reiter, *Quicksilver Captain*, p. viii.

24 Ibid., p. xi.

A Ten-Shilling Commodore?

Having got through the court-martial, Popham sought to deal with the doubt that had arisen in his absence about his status as a commodore. On 14 April 1807 he wrote to the Admiralty requesting to be paid the pay of a rear-admiral in full for his time as a commodore from when he raised his flag at Madeira until he was relieved on the Rio Plata. Popham prayed in aid the example of Captain George Losack, who had been captain of *HMS Jupiter* at the Cape in November 1798. The British had first taken the Cape from the Dutch in the summer of 1795. They correctly feared that there might be an attempt to regain the territory and in 1796 a fleet under Admiral Lucas was sent to recapture the Cape. Lucas' fleet was discovered in Saldanha Bay, near the Cape, by a fleet under Vice-Admiral Sir George Elphinstone and forced to capitulate.[25] Elphinstone sailed home to be made Lord Keith for his efforts, but unlike Popham he left a fleet protecting the Cape against the chance of another attempt at recapture. In 1798 Losack and *Jupiter* were part of that protective British fleet under Rear-Admiral Sir Hugh Christian, when Christian died in service. Losack as the senior officer in the fleet took it upon himself to hoist a broad pennant as commander-in-chief of the fleet. Although Losack had no express or written authority from the Admiralty to act as he did, he exercised his discretion as senior captain as he considered the situation demanded. On 30 November 1798 he wrote to the Admiralty to tell them what he had done. The circumstances of the station required the commander-in-chief to reside at Cape Town and on 31 January 1799 Losack appointed Captain Granger to act as captain of *Jupiter*, while he stayed on shore. By a letter dated 1 February 1804 the Admiralty wrote approving of what Losack had done and authorising him to be paid the daily ten-shilling commodore's allowance from when he hoisted his flag on the death of Christian.[26] From 1 February 1799, following Losack's appointment of Granger to the *Jupiter*, however, the Admiralty authorised the full flag-pay of a rear-admiral, including the daily allowance for servants. On 16 October 1799 a more senior officer, Captain Valentine Edwards, arrived on the station and Losack was not paid the full rate from that time for nearly a month until Edwards also died, on 6 November 1799. Thereafter Losack was paid the full rate until the arrival of Sir Roger Curtis as a replacement for Christian. Thus, so Popham argued, there was a precedent for a commodore having authority to appoint a captain under him and to benefit from the full rate of pay in consequence, even where the

[25] K. D. McCranie, *Admiral Lord Keith and the Naval War against Napoleon* (Gainesville, 2006), p. 52.

[26] Letter 1 February 1804, *Correct Account*, App. 14.

appointment of neither the commodore nor the captain had been expressly authorised by the Admiralty. If Popham thought that a precedent of that sort would be automatically followed, he was soon disappointed. The following day William Marsden replied peremptorily that his assuming the rank of a commodore with a captain under him having not been approved by the Admiralty Board, they could not comply with his request.[27]

In April 1807 Donnelly was living at 34 Welbeck Street, London, only one street away from where Popham was living, in Wimpole Street. Towards the end of that month Donnelly and Popham met in Wimpole Street and Donnelly raised Popham's entitlement to a flag-share. Popham, despite his rebuff by the Admiralty, told Donnelly that he had not been a mere ten-shilling commodore and was entitled to the flag-share. This seems not to have laid Donnelly's doubts to rest as a fortnight or so later, on Friday 8 May 1807, Donnelly asked Popham for an interview to discuss his authority as a commodore. By the following Tuesday he had not received a response so Donnelly wrote to Popham saying that if Popham could prove explicitly that he had been legally authorised to bear a captain under him then he would give 'no further trouble', but that Popham could not feel hurt if he endeavoured 'to assert my rights openly and legally, which I mean to do.' He again requested an interview, now asking for it to be in the presence of some other naval officers of 'rank and honour, who are well acquainted with the customs of the service, for the purpose of elucidating subjects which may be generally spoken by both parties, under the impression of bearing different interpretations, if not explained candidly.'[28] Popham replied the same evening raising no objection to such a meeting, but stating that 'I am not aware of the misrepresentations you refer to in your letter, or any misconstructions of the facts appertaining to the subject in question.'[29] Donnelly received the reply the next morning, but it satisfied neither Donnelly nor the 'friends' to whom he showed the letters. On Saturday 16 May 1807 Donnelly wrote to Popham that 'as you are not aware of the necessity of the explanation desired in my letter', the affair should be settled by their solicitors.[30] Within a week, on Friday 22 May 1807, Donnelly's solicitors, Parker, Young and Hughes of Essex Street, on the Strand, London, had written to Popham demanding repayment of the sum of £2,004 17*s.* 2*d.* paid to his

[27] Letter 15 April, William Marsden to Captain Popham, ibid., App. 15. The request was denied even though the 'Ministry of All Talents' had collapsed, and Lord Mulgrave had taken over as First Lord of the Admiralty in March 1807 with the return of the Pittites under Lord Portland.

[28] Letter 12 May 1807, Donnelly to Popham, *Correct Account*, App. 6.

[29] Letter 12 May 1807, Popham to Donnelly, ibid., App. 7.

[30] Letter 16 May 1807, Donnelly to Popham, ibid., App. 8.

agent 'under the misconception of your being entitled to receive the same as a Flag-officer, with orders to bear a Captain under you, and which he now understands not to be the case'.[31] As Popham did not intend to back down and matters appeared to be going to law, Popham instructed his solicitors, Crowder, Lavie and Garth, to act for him in the coming proceedings.

The Trial of Donnelly v Popham, 1807

In a display of remarkable alacrity, the dispute came on for hearing at Westminster Hall before Sir James Mansfield, Chief Justice of the Court of Common Pleas, and a jury on Saturday 27 June 1807, only a month after the letter before action.[32] Neither side stinted on instructing counsel. Donnelly instructed two serjeants-at-law, Serjeant Shepherd and Serjeant Best.[33] Even when Serjeant Best was indisposed for the trial, a replacement, Serjeant Onslow, was asked to 'hold his brief'. They appeared at the trial with the assistance of Charles Abbott of counsel. Abbott was considered an excellent, if dull, lawyer and would rise to be Lord Chief Justice in succession to Lord Ellenborough. Popham instructed Serjeant Bayley with Robert Dallas KC and William Harrison of counsel.[34]

Popham had not accepted his rebuff by the Admiralty but had petitioned the Privy Council for the redress that he felt entitled to. Indeed, when the case was called on for trial his counsel applied to adjourn the matter to await a decision of the Privy Council. Mansfield refused the adjournment on the basis that a decision of the Privy Council could not retrospectively determine the rights of the parties, which were for the court of law to determine. In the short time between the letter before action and the

31 Letter 22 May 1807, Parker, Young, and Hughes to Popham, ibid., App. 9. The sum included the share of the freight money plus some additional head money for ships captured by Donnelly.

32 Sir James Mansfield was no relation to the more famous (and senior) Lord Mansfield, Lord Chief Justice, 1756–88, though they did both appear in the famous slavery case of Somerset v Stewart (1772) 98 ER 499, the former as counsel, the latter as judge.

33 The serjeants-at-law were, like Sir James Mansfield, 'Brothers' of Serjeants' Inn, an order of senior barristers, now abolished. Serjeants-at-law had exclusive rights of audience before the Court of Common Pleas, though, as appears in this case, they could appear with the assistance of other counsel.

34 Robert Dallas had at this time been appointed King's Counsel. Although he was not a member of Serjeants' Inn at this time, he did go on to become Chief Justice of the Court of Common Pleas in 1818. He succeeded Charles Abbott, Donnelly's junior counsel, who had been made Chief Justice of the Court of Common Pleas in 1816, having turned down an offer of the post in 1808, and was promoted to the more senior role of Lord Chief Justice in 1818, succeeding Lord Ellenborough.

case coming on for trial Donnelly had gathered a stellar line-up of senior naval officers prepared to give evidence on his behalf. They must have been part of the group of interested 'friends' that Donnelly had referred to in his correspondence with Popham. The court heard from Admirals Sir John Borlase Warren, Peter Rainier, Lord Hotham, Sir Samuel Hood and Commodore (later Admiral) Richard Goodwin Keats. Admiral Montagu was also at court. A curious footnote in the published account of the trial indicates that his evidence 'would only go to conversations' and was not called as it was objected to by Popham's counsel.[35]

Donnelly's distinguished naval witnesses all testified that they had acted at various times as a commodore, that the order appointing them had indicated whether they were to have a captain under them or not and that they had only had a flag-share of prizes if they had been appointed with a captain under them. Although there were attempts at cross-examination, Dallas ended up accepting on behalf of Popham that a commodore who did not in fact have a captain under him was not entitled to share. Popham's case was that as commander-in-chief he had implied authority to appoint a captain under him and that he had done so. Although the appointment was subject to approval by the Admiralty, at the time it had been effective, so he was in fact a commodore with a captain under him at the material time. Thus, so it was argued, he was entitled to a flag-share under the terms of the royal proclamation.

Popham called Captain King as a witness. From being Popham's first lieutenant on *Diadem*, Willam King had been appointed to command of *Espoir* by Popham when they left Madeira bound for the Cape. He had then gone ashore and seen action alongside the army, commanding a brigade of seamen and marines ashore in Buenos Aires. King gave evidence of Popham's promotions within the fleet and of the prize money agreement that the newly appointed captains had entered into on the basis that Popham was a flag-officer. King had to accept, however, that his appointment to *Espoir* had not been confirmed by the Admiralty and that he had been forced to appeal to the Privy Council against their refusal to accept his appointment, an appeal that had yet to receive a response. A footnote to the published account of the trial suggests that the Admiralty had informed Popham of their disapproval of his appointments as early as a letter dated 12 April 1806, shortly after the departure of Lord Barham from the Admiralty following the death of William Pitt.[36] The footnote also suggests that Popham had received the letter whilst still in the river Plate, carried out to

35 *Correct Account*, p. 48.

36 Ibid., p. 91.

him by Captain Bouverie of *HMS Medusa*, but that Popham had neither told the captains under his command about that letter, nor told Donnelly about the letters he received from the Admiralty.

Popham then called evidence that he had been treated as a flag-officer for the distributions that resulted from the seizures of treasure on land by the joint operations with the army, although that was not covered by the royal proclamation under the Prize Act. Although the king, in the Privy Council, determined matters of conjunct prizes, the Privy Council did not decide matters of naval prize law. As Serjeant Shepherd for Donnelly reminded the court, Lords Keith, Nelson and St Vincent had tried to involve the Privy Council in their dispute over prize money but had been told to go to the courts of law.[37]

The case turned on whether Popham had authority to appoint a captain under him, when the written terms of his appointment did not provide for him to do so. As in his letter to the Admiralty, Popham relied heavily on the precedent that he saw in Losack's conduct after the death of Christian at the Cape. The evidence called about this did not, however, help his cause. The written instructions given to commanders-in-chief on foreign service under which Losack had appointed himself a flag-officer to fill the vacancy due to Christian's death provided that, in the case of a death of any officer, they were empowered to fill the vacancy, and in the event of the commander-in-chief being unable to act for any reason then the instructions passed to the next senior officer.[38] Losack, therefore, had power to act as he did. There had been no vacancy in Popham's case, and he had no power to do what he did. Had Barham been called to give evidence in accordance with his letter to the Admiralty about his intention that Popham should be able to appoint a captain under him, that may have turned the case. Equally, Mansfield may have ruled that whatever Barham said now about his intentions, the form of order actually issued was what mattered, and later evidence about intention could not alter that. In any event, Barham was not called.[39] On the evidence, Popham was not appointed as a commodore with a captain under him and he could not make himself into such a commodore without authority. Mansfield, having made his views plain during the course of the hearing, summed the case up to the jury in these terms and the jury immediately found for Donnelly without troubling to retire to consider their verdict.[40]

37 Ibid., p. 92; Nelson v Tucker (1802) 3 Bos. & Pull. 257 and Keith v Pringle (1803) 4 East 262.

38 *Correct Account*, App. 13.

39 Barham's letter to the Privy Council dated 14 June 1807.

40 *Correct Account*, p. 107.

Popham did not give up in the face of the jury's verdict. On 11 November 1807 Serjeant Bayley addressed the Court of King's Bench on Popham's behalf to try and overturn the verdict of the Court of Common Pleas. Mansfield was again presiding, but this time he sat with Mr Justice Heath and Mr Justice Chambre. Still there was no reference to Barham's letter. Bayley argued that although the Privy Council had still not reached any determination there was reason to believe that it may do so and thus establish the validity of Popham's appointments and his entitlement to the flag-share. The court held unanimously that even if the Privy Council did confirm the appointments Popham had made, it would not signify that he had at the time been a commodore with a captain legitimately under him and so it would be to no avail on the issue of a flag-officer's share. The judgment in favour of Donnelly stood.[41] If ratification of the appointments by those with the power to do so would not have helped Popham, then evidence from Barham, who was no longer in office, would not have assisted either if all it amounted to was an attempt at ratifying something after the event.

Petitions to the King in Council

Meanwhile things were hotting up before the Privy Council. Beresford's agent had written to the Privy Council suggesting that he alone should take the commanding officers' share of 'the booty captured at the Cape of Good Hope, and at Buenos Ayres, in the year 1806, by conjunct Expeditions of your Majesty's sea and land forces.' Popham, he submitted, should only be entitled as a senior captain present at the capture, and not as a commanding officer.[42] Beresford's claim was rejected, but the treasure that had been seized was up for grabs.

On 28 November 1807, only 17 days after Popham's application to set aside the judgment had been dismissed by the Court of King's Bench, Donnelly wrote to the Privy Council about the distribution of the joint booty. Applying the logic of his success before the courts Donnelly submitted that King should be considered only as a lieutenant when it came to sharing such booty. This astonished and horrified King. He had a wife and six small children and had need of the money that he had expected to receive. He had after all been appointed to command by his commanding officer and was not in a position to question the powers of his commander-in-chief. Indeed, it would materially affect the discipline of the navy if such questioning were

41 Donnelly v Popham (1807) 1 Taunt. 1.

42 HC Papers, vol. x, p. 383.

to be encouraged.[43] He had worked hard for the booty both at sea and on land and everyone, including Donnelly, had conducted themselves on the basis that he was entitled to a share as a captain.

William King, with his wife and six children, was finally awarded his pay as a captain in January 1808. Popham had to wait another year, but in January 1809 he was awarded the full pay and allowances of a rear-admiral from 5 October 1805 to 7 December 1806, the date when he was superseded by Admiral Stirling in the river Plate. Then, in October 1809, the Admiralty were even more generous and awarded him the full pay and allowances up until the end of his court-martial on 11 March 1807.[44]

The right of a flag-officer to a share of freight money paid by the Treasury to a captain for the carriage of public treasure was not challenged in the case of Donnelly v Popham. If there was no right to a share then the argument that was considered, as to Popham's status as a flag-officer, would have been an unnecessary one so far as the freight money claim was concerned. That argument would arise later, as we will see in Chapter 8.

12th Article: Captains of the Fleet as Flag-officers

Commodores with captains under them were not the only captains with additional responsibilities who were granted a flag-share. Certain 'flag captains', i.e. captains of ships carrying a flag-officer, were granted a junior flag-share themselves where they were captain to the commander-in-chief of a fleet. Senior captains in such positions took on the role of chief of staff for their commander-in-chief, with the additional responsibilities that that involved. They were sometimes referred to as captain-of-the-fleet, but that was an ambiguous term, as where there were junior flag-officers in the fleet the captain-of-the-fleet, chief of staff, role could be filled by a rear-admiral with that title. Where the role was filled by a captain, however, then they ranked above all other captains in the fleet and could issue fleet orders in their own name to be obeyed by the fleet as if given by the commander-in-chief, in addition to the temporary privileges of a rear-admiral, including a junior flag-share of prize money.[45]

The captains benefiting from this flag-share status were, from 1793:

43 Ibid., pp. 369–71.

44 Ibid., pp. 387–8.

45 Lavery, *Nelson's Navy*, p. 252.

a) The First Captain to the Admiral and Commander-in-Chief of a fleet,

b) the First Captain to a Flag-officer appointed to command a Fleet or Squadron of Twenty Ships of the Line of Battle, whether they be made up of British or British and allied ships,

c) the First Captain to a Flag-officer appointed to command a Fleet or Squadron of Fifteen Ships of the Line of Battle where all the ships are British ships.[46]

From 1803 the size of any junior flag-officer's fleet or squadron to qualify the flag captain as entitled to a flag-officer's share was reduced to ten, whether they were made up of all British ships or a mixture of British and allied ships, and that position continued after 1808.

The previous chapters show that the rules for distribution of prize money to the Royal Navy were a dynamic system that reacted to the pressures of war and were supervised by the courts applying English law. As has been seen in the last three chapters, there were significant changes in the distribution of prize money in 1808. The next chapter considers the reasons behind those changes, and what they tell us about the Royal Navy at the time.

[46] Proclamation 7 July 1803, *London Gazette*, 15599, p. 805.

7.
1808: The Year of Revolution?

Like a lot of wars, the French Revolutionary and Napoleonic wars coincided with, and propelled, a period of social change. Britain had been shaken by its loss of American colonies, and there followed a period of soul-searching. The British economy, however, was doing well. Between 1783 and 1802 it grew at a faster rate than at any time during the previous century, an annual rate of nearly 6 per cent.[1] Britain's industrial and commercial development was pulling ahead of the rest of Europe. The government machinery to deal with this growth, however, was creaking. In 1780 Lord North established a committee for examining the public accounts. Over the next seven years it produced reports which were welcomed by the new prime minister, William Pitt, as giving 'light to parliament on subjects hitherto involved in the most inscrutable obscurity'.[2] The investigation into the public accounts revealed widespread sinecures held by public officials and disturbing levels of inefficiency.[3] The committee proposed a new principle. Those holding government posts should be there to serve the public and should not exploit their official positions for personal profit. To implement this principle, Pitt appointed a further Commission on Fees in 1785.[4]

Perquisites to Salaries

The new commission found a baffling array of inefficient, bureaucratic bodies whose officials received small official salaries and relied on the receipt of a range of 'Fees, Gratuities, Perquisites and Emoluments' paid by contractors, subordinates seeking to retain or improve their position or other interested parties seeking an advantage. Between 1786 and 1788

1 Knight, *Britain against Napoleon*, p. 21.
2 John R. Breihan, 'William Pitt and the Commission on Fees 1785–1801', *The Historical Journal* 27:1 (March 1984), 59–81.
3 Knight, *Britain against Napoleon*, p. 25.
4 By Act of Parliament 25 Geo. III cc. 19, 47 and 52.

the three commissioners reported not just on the Treasury, but on the Admiralty, the Treasurer of the Navy, the navy commissioners, the royal dockyards, the Sick and Hurt Office, the Victualling Office, the Naval and Victualling Departments abroad as well as the Post Office.[5] They recommended that the sinecures and private charges supplementing public pay should be done away with and replaced with adequate salaries, funded where possible by taking the payments previously paid to the officials into the public purse and under proper public control. This change did not occur overnight, but the ideas began to take root. The eventual reforms have earned Pitt a reputation as a new broom who swept clean the public finances, but as important as his actual reforming achievements in office was the legacy of administrative goals that he left to his successors.[6]

Pitt had a reforming ally in Charles Middleton, the comptroller of the navy.[7] Despite complaints both that he was reforming too much and too little, Middleton encouraged significant changes to the administration and resources of the navy. Some naval officers (then and throughout the navy's history) shared the view that their lords and masters were a penny-pinching 'farthing-candle admiralty'.[8] However, impressive levels of investment prior to 1793 led to significant developments in the royal dockyards and elsewhere. It was in no small part the result of Middleton's reforms that the navy was ready in 1805 for the task of taking on the French fleet when Middleton, as Lord Barham, the First Lord of the Admiralty, appointed Nelson to command the fleet that would bring the Franco-Spanish fleet to battle. The credit for Trafalgar is owed as much to him as to his commander-in-chief on *Victory*. Yet despite the vigour of these reforms the payment of prize money remained untouched and accepted. Between 1793 and 1815 there were at least 14 Acts of Parliament whose provisions touched and concerned the payment of prize money. Over ten royal proclamations decreed the distribution of prize money. Numerous court cases highlighted the gains being made by officers, normally senior officers, fortunate enough to be able to argue about their share of prize money. That all this activity took place in the public eye in a country with a parliamentary system indicates that the principle of prize money remained fundamentally secure from attack, and those in government felt able to risk adjustments without bringing the underlying system into question. Pitt's First Lord of the Admiralty during the French

5 Knight, *Britain against Napoleon*, pp. 26, 506.

6 Breihan, 'William Pitt and the Commission on Fees 1785–1801', p. 81.

7 Knight, *Britain against Napoleon*, p. 29.

8 Letter, Capt. Macbride to Charles Middleton, 18 August 1787; Sir John Knox Laughton (ed.), *Letters of Lord Barham* (NRS, 1909), vol. II, p. 257.

Revolutionary War was the conscientious and caring Lord Spencer.[9] Though reform-minded, he was wary of taking on his senior admirals, as we have seen in Chapter 5 with the tensions between St Vincent, Nelson and Orde. Despite demands for change he would not redistribute prize money to the lower decks.

Mutinies

In 1797, four years into the war with revolutionary France, the Royal Navy was shaken by unprecedented mutinies by its seamen at Spithead, the naval anchorage off Portsmouth, and at the Nore, the naval anchorage off Sheerness at the mouth of the Thames and Medway rivers. With the country under threat of invasion the sailors refused to weigh anchor and set sail. Their demands appeared in petitions to the Admiralty.[10] They also became public in petitions to Parliament, printed in the press. The petition of the Spithead delegates in *The Times* on 22 April 1797, like the others, sought a pay increase to reflect the fact that inflation had undermined seamen's pay, which no longer reflected either the pay available to merchant seamen or the pay increases that had been granted elsewhere in the military. It also sought full meat allowances without deductions, more vegetables, shore leave for the sailors when in harbour and improvements in welfare provision for the sick and wounded.[11] It did not include a demand for fairer prize distribution. By the time the demands found support on the east coast, however, the mutinous tone had changed to one of greater overt radicalism, and the demands now included fairer distribution of prize money.[12] Unable to achieve the publicity and public support that had been achieved at Spithead and facing a harder line from the Admiralty, the later Nore mutiny failed. The different nature of the two mutinies called forth different responses from the government. A peaceful end was found to the Spithead outbreak, but with the government placing blame on Fox and the Whig opposition for encouraging revolutionary ideas, 29 Nore mutineers were hanged.[13] Whilst the Admiralty gave way on the demanded increase in sea-

9 Charles Spencer, *The Spencer Family* (London, 1999), p. 235.

10 TNA, ADM 1/5125.

11 'Ship News', *The Times*, 22 April 1797.

12 Cf. P. MacDougall and A. V. Coats (eds), *The Naval Mutinies of 1797* (Woodbridge, 2011), p. 253; Ellen Gill, *Naval Families, War and Duty in Britain, 1740–1820* (Woodbridge, 2016), pp. 217–22; TNA, ADM1/727, 12 June 1797, paper no. 25.

13 James Davey, 'Mutiny and Insecurity', in Quintin Colville (ed.), *Nelson, Navy and Nation: The Royal Navy and the British People 1688–1815* (London, 2013), pp. 141–3; James Davey, *Tempest* (Yale, 2023), pp. 199–234.

men's pay, did away with the hated right of pursers to deduct an eighth of their food allowance to cover wastage, increased provision for care and pay of sick and injured seamen and even removed 113 particularly detested officers from their ships, they did not alter the distribution of prize shares.[14]

It was not just the sailors who saw the justice of their demands. Admiral Adam Duncan, commanding the North Sea fleet facing the Batavian threat from Holland, favoured a number of the demands, including a redistribution of prize money to give more to the lower decks, and told the Admiralty so.[15] His pleas fell on deaf ears, and when the Admiralty was eventually forced by the mutiny to give ground, the distribution of prize money as between officers and men remained unaltered.

In response to the mutiny the government sent a magistrate, Aaron Graham, to investigate. Graham was a good choice. A former midshipman and admiral's secretary, he was a self-taught lawyer who had served as chief magistrate of the bleak Newfoundland station and defended Peter Haywood, a young midshipman charged with mutiny against Bligh on the *Bounty*.[16] Graham, recognising the inherent loyalty of the sailors striking to improve their lot, recommended in May 1797 that a more 'reasonable Distribution of Prize-money' be introduced.[17] Specifically he suggested that captains should give over one of their three eighths to their ships' companies. He did so even though reform of prize distribution had 'never much been insisted upon'. He thought that in time the demand would arise and be claimed as a right. A claim to equal distribution of prize money 'without even the exception of the captains or commander-in-chief' would, he thought, be 'encouraged by landlords and common women at the sea ports whose interests and inclination no doubt is to get the seamen as much as possible'. If such calls were pre-empted and reform of prize distribution was 'granted as a boon' then it 'would tend much to the purposes of a prompt reconciliation' after the mutinies. The recommendation from a man who understood the navy and its men was ignored. The next royal proclamation dealing with prize shares following the mutinies was three years later to deal with prizes taken from the Italian states that had been overrun by the

14 MacDougall and Coats (eds), *The Naval Mutinies of 1797*, p. 27.

15 Richard Blake, *Evangelicals in the Royal Navy, 1775–1815* (Woodbridge, 2008), p. 134; Duncan Papers, NMM: DUN/19 Public and Private Correspondence, 2 vols; DUN/31 Memorandum Book of Captain Adam Duncan; P. Le Fevre and R. Harding, *British Admirals of the Napoleonic Wars* (London, 2005), p. 54.

16 *Annual Biography and Obituary*, vol. 4, 1820, p. 402; G. Aldous, 'Mutiny: The Trial of William Muspratt of the Bounty', *Inner Temple Yearbook* (2015), p. 18.; Caroline Alexander, *The Bounty: The True Story of the Mutiny on the Bounty* (London, 2004), pp. 205–6, 380.

17 BL Add. MS 37, 877, Windham Papers, vol. 36, folio 73, May 1797.

French. It contained no material change from the proclamations of 1793 and 1797 against France and Spain respectively, which themselves also remained unchanged. Three eighths of the prize money still went to the captains and flag-officers.

The demand for a more equal distribution of prize money fits with both of the two main underlying explanations offered for the mutinies: the injustice suffered by oppressed and underpaid seamen boiling over, and an outbreak of Jacobin revolutionary zeal against the hierarchy of the navy. The more immediate explanation for the mutinies was that perfectly polite and reasonable, if worryingly organised, petitions had seemingly been ignored by the Admiralty. The French Revolution adopted the language of liberty, but instilled a fear of revolution in Britain, aggravated by the agitating activities of 'societies' in Britain, such as the London Corresponding Society. Even if they were intending to encourage peaceful reform, the societies were seen as dangerously close to the Jacobin clubs in Paris.[18] The British government's response included the Police Act, passed by Parliament in 1792 and leading to the creation of a new police force, and a network of counter-revolutionary agents organised by William Wickham. There was intellectual and popular opposition to unrestrained Crown authority, but 'it is striking the degree to which reformism and anti-revolutionary fervour merged in endorsing stronger top-down power and a sharper vision of hierarchical order'.[19] The execution of Louis XVI in January 1793 did nothing to assuage the concern. Instead, it led to war, and increased suspicion. Internal political factionalism, Irish insurrection, fears of invasion, the reign of terror across the Channel and failed harvests did nothing to encourage liberalisation. Suspensions of habeas corpus in relation to 'high treason, suspicion of high treason or treasonable practices' and laws against seditious practices and assemblies followed. So too did informal penalties for liberal views, on the streets and in the corridors of public life.[20] As is often the case, the fear of revolution acted as a brake on moderate reform rather than an encouragement. The result was that even after the 1797 mutinies the distribution of prize money was not reformed. Despite the support they had received, the sailors' demands for changes to prize distribution went unmet.

[18] Elizabeth Sparrow, *Secret Service: British Agents in France, 1792–1815* (Woodbridge, 1999), p. 7; Davey, *Tempest*, pp. 216–17.

[19] L. Benton and L. Ford, *Rage for Order* (Cambridge, Mass., 2016), p. 11.

[20] Clive Emsley, 'Repression, "terror" and the rule of law in England during the decade of the French Revolution', *English Historical Review* 100:357 (1985), 801–25; Halliday, *Habeas Corpus*, p. 134; Mark Philp, *Reforming Ideas in Britain: Politics and Language in the Shadow of the French Revolution, 1789–1815* (Cambridge, 2017), pp. 102–32.

War Against Napoleon

St Vincent's Commission on Frauds, reporting at the resumption of war in 1803, led to only limited prize reform, mainly aimed at tightening up abuses by agents of the funds they were holding.[21] The practice of taking prize agency commissions while farming the real work out to others was forbidden, agents were required to lodge a sizable bond of £5,000 as a surety for their good faith and the sending in of prize lists of those entitled to a share of prize money was tightened up. The court was given power to order that proceeds of prizes be invested for the benefit of the captors and/or paid into court pending an appeal, to prevent appeals being used to delay payment in order to leave monies in the hands of agents. Once time for any appeal had elapsed, payment then had to be made within three months. If the balance of proceeds was not distributed after four months, the residue was to be sent to the Royal Hospital at Greenwich. Perhaps most significantly, the agents' commission was to be calculated on the net proceeds rather than the gross award.[22]

None of these changes affected the distribution of prize shares. They were as much to do with ensuring that the captains and flag-officers obtained their lion's share of the prize money as ensuring that ordinary seamen were fairly treated. An uncharitable observer might have dismissed them with St Vincent's own criticism of Middleton's reforms as 'scraps of Tape & Buckram'. For all his abhorrence of greed and corruption in others, St Vincent was very keen on amassing the flag-share of prize money and he did not seek to redistribute it to the lower decks. Nor did his successor, Lord Melville. Melville had previously held the post of Treasurer to the Navy and had the knowledge and aptitude to introduce reforms. His one year in office as First Lord of the Admiralty from May 1804 to May 1805 ended, however, under a cloud of allegations of misappropriation of public monies in his time as treasurer.

The major change in the distribution of shares in prize money came eventually in 1808. As has been seen above, the fundamental shift was to take one of the three eighths that had previously gone to the captains and flag-officers and redistribute it to the lower ranks. It is easy to see this as a victory for ordinary tars after years of pressure. The reality, however, is rather different. The change did not come about through pressure for a more equitable system, and the real beneficiaries of the change were the 'middle classes' on board, the skilled and experienced men who were much

21 1803 45 Geo. III c. 72, see Chapter 2 above.

22 Hill, *The Prizes of War*, p. 145.

in demand, and without whom the navy could not function. Whilst some had already been treated more favourably than the ordinary seamen before 1808, they were to take the main share of the extra money that trickled down from above. To understand how and why this was so it is important to understand the context in which change finally arrived in 1808.

Trafalgar had not ended the war at sea in 1805. Another ten years of war provided plenty of work for the navy, for a large navy, even if it was not to fight such a glorious battle again. Although Napoleon had turned his army away from the Channel and marched it to Austria before the battle off Cape Trafalgar, the threat of invasion still troubled the British government and public until at least 1810. Further, when Britain was ready to go on the offensive on mainland Europe, the navy was essential to its success.[23] The French and Spanish allies lost most of their main battle fleets at Trafalgar or its associated actions, but Napoleon responded by embarking on a major shipbuilding programme, intending to build 150 new ships of the line against the British equivalent of 113, and seeking access to the other navies of Europe. Between 1806 and 1809 naval action ensured that 99 ships of the line were destroyed or otherwise kept from Napoleon's grasp.[24]

Both the British and the French could build ships. Manning them was another matter. France struggled to man its fleet, but so too did Britain. The Royal Navy's manpower needs increased considerably during the wars. Having had 16,613 men on its books in 1792, the figure rose to 69,868 with the outbreak of war the following year. By 1805 it had risen to 109,205, but by 1808 it had increased to 140,822 and would peak over the next two years at over 142,000.[25] The position was aggravated by the changing nature of naval war. From essentially seasonal expeditions from home waters earlier in the eighteenth century, the navy had now spread its reach, maintaining fleets at sea year-round both in home waters and on foreign stations. As the need for men after 1805 increased, the shortage of skilled men became a serious problem.[26] The navy could not use the ships that it had for lack of men, and it needed to attract and keep skilled men. Between May 1804 and June 1805, 12,302 men deserted, mostly to merchant ships, but occasionally to other Royal Navy ships.[27] When men did desert, they tended to do it

23 Davey, *In Nelson's Wake*, p. 292.

24 Ibid., pp. 10–11.

25 Roger Morriss, *The Foundations of British Maritime Ascendancy* (Cambridge, 2014), p. 227.

26 Lambert, *The Challenge*, pp. 243, 258–9.

27 Davey, *In Nelson's Wake*, p. 26.

early on in their service on a ship.[28] Once they had accrued a right to some prize money they had a stake in remaining on board in order to collect it. If they deserted, they lost the right to claim their money.

The popular view of the Royal Navy in this period is that it filled its ships by impressment of innocent landsmen seized by unscrupulous press gangs. Rodger recognised that 'it is extremely difficult to say with certainty what proportion of the men of the Navy were volunteers'.[29] Lewis put the figure as high as 75 per cent serving under compulsion with only 25 per cent true volunteers in 1812.[30] A centralised Impress Service had been created during the Seven Years' War and both this administrative branch of the Royal Navy and the press gangs sent out by individual captains continued to operate during the revolutionary and Napoleonic wars, particularly in times of high demand. Recent research has suggested, however, that most of the men on the lower decks were volunteers, rather than pressed men. J. Ross Dancy has suggested that impressment accounted for no more than 20 per cent of the men on the lower decks.[31] In coming to this figure Dancy attempted to adjust his assessment of the number of men shown in muster books as pressed, in particular for those coming through the Impress Service. Horizontal analysis of muster book records has revealed additional practices that need to be allowed for.[32] Men pressed direct into ships by their own press gangs might well be entered initially as pressed men in a ship's supernumerary muster but then transferred to the ship's company as 'volunteered' so as to earn the bounty payable to volunteers.[33] That bounty, as with prize money, was payable after a delayed period and so provided a new 'recruit' with an incentive to make the most of his lot and serve 'willingly'. Slope's estimation was that some 31 per cent of men were pressed, although a precise calculation is as impossible as with the calculation of prize money.[34] Either way, however, the evidence of such research reveals that the Royal Navy had a significant dependence on real,

28 Nick Slope, 'Discipline, Desertion and Death: HMS *Trent* 1796–1803', in MacDougall and Coats (eds), *The Naval Mutinies of 1797*, p. 234.

29 Rodger, *The Wooden World*, p. 153.

30 Lewis, *A Social History of the Navy 1793–1815*, p. 139.

31 Jeremiah R. Dancy, *The Myth of the Press Gang: Volunteers, Impressment and the Naval Manpower Problem in the Late Eighteenth Century* (Woodbridge, 2015), p. 187.

32 N. Slope, doctoral thesis, 'Serving in Nelson's Navy: a Social History of Three Amazon Class Frigates Utilizing Database Technology (1795–1811)', published posthumously as *Nelson's Navy: Recruitment, Promotion, Discipline and Death* (London, 2019).

33 Nick Slope, 'Review of Dancy's *Myth of the Press Gang*', *The Nelson Dispatch* 12:5 (2016), p. 314.

34 Summary of Slope's work in Michael Duffy's obituary for Nick Slope, 'How Nick Slope became a naval historian', *The Nelson Dispatch* 12:9 (Winter 2017), p. 537.

as opposed to pretend, volunteers as well as impressed men. Research such as this, based on state archives, has been criticised as downplaying both the social impact of impressment as shown in contemporary discourse, and the greater willingness to resort to impressment after 1803.[35] Neither the debate about the figures, nor the success of the navy that the press gangs manned, should disguise the horrors of a brutal and often unfair method of manning the fleet. As Brunsman has put it: 'we do not have to deny the injustice of impressment or sailor resistance to recognise the extraordinary achievements of British seamen in the eighteenth century.'[36] Impressment caused problems for the Admiralty before the courts, as has been seen in Chapter 1. It also gave rise to social unrest and resistance on the streets.[37] Such concerns, however, merely enforce the idea that there were good reasons to find inducements for skilled seafarers to volunteer for the Royal Navy, and to remain there once on board, however willingly they may have arrived.

In the mutinies at Spithead and the Nore the men on the lower decks had found a voice and although the prize money proclamations had not been altered, the relationships between the men and their masters had.[38] The pay of seamen increased in 1797 as a result of the mutinies, but the navy still had to compete with others who wanted the same manpower. Other branches of the military wanted men, both for armies abroad and militias at home. Merchant ships needed skilled men to keep the lifeblood of the nation's commerce flowing and paying for the war. Navies and merchant ships abroad offered opportunities to British seamen, for example in Russia and the US, whose use of British sailors would help bring about a conflict between the two nations in 1812.[39] The prospect of the US using sorely needed British sailors to profit from the difficulties that Britain was experiencing in the war against Napoleon on behalf of the whole free world was galling for the British.

35 E.g. Q. Colville and J. Davey (eds), *A New Naval History* (Manchester, 2019), p.7; Isaac Land, 'New Scholarship on the Press Gang Part 1', *Port Towns & Urban Cultures*, 2015, porttowns.port.ac.uk/press-gang-1/; Isaac Land, 'New Scholarship on the Press Gang Part 2', *Port Towns & Urban Cultures*, 2015, porttowns.port.ac.uk/press-gang2/; Gill, *Naval Families*, pp. 184–7.

36 Brunsman, *The Evil Necessity*, p. 139.

37 E.g. Nicholas Rogers, *The Press Gang: Naval Impressment and Its Opponents in Georgian Britain* (London, 2007), pp. 37–58.

38 J. Davey, 'Mutiny and Insecurity', in Q. Colville (ed.), *Nelson, Navy & Nation* (London, 2013), pp. 143–4.

39 Davey, *In Nelson's Wake*, p. 24; Lambert, *The Challenge*, p. 7.

Honour and Duty

It was not just the men on the lower decks who had changed. The lure of prize money had been an undeniable influence on naval officers, but so had concepts of honour and duty traditionally associated with the aristocratic classes. The increasingly technical demands of seamanship had put the conventional social categories under considerable strain. Yet, as N. A. M. Rodger has put it, 'the sea officer still needed the status of a gentleman, not only because society expected it, but because his condition required it. The code of honour was an essential psychological support on the day of battle.'[40] Prize money helped to sustain the status of a gentleman. The cost of such status applied not just on shore but also at sea, where captains and flag-officers were expected to keep up a level of entertainment not covered by the Admiralty allowances alone.[41] As Rodger has concluded, however: 'towards the end of the eighteenth century, the old idea of honour was infiltrated by the new ideal of duty. Personal, interested, egotistical service of one's king and one's honour were gradually replaced by disinterested duty to God, the Crown, and the good of the Service.' Indeed, in Rodger's view, 'The Navy was uniquely well-placed to exemplify if not to lead this movement, because in many ways it was already half-way there. It had always been a professional, quasi-bourgeois organisation, with a strong unaristocratic, if not anti-aristocratic, tradition in which honour and duty co-existed.'[42]

Patronage played a significant role in the eighteenth-century navy, as it did in all public and professional life.[43] It is easy to misunderstand the nature of this patronage looking back from the twenty-first century, even though it remains a force today. Eighteenth-century patronage has been described as 'a system of exchanging or trading interest and influence, rather than a corrupt distribution of favours.'[44] There is no doubt that patronage did play a part in promotion and deployment of officers in the navy. Blatant nepotism can be seen in Pellew's promotion of his sons under his own command and through his friends, and he was not alone. Family ties, and influence, were strong in the navy, and regarded by the service with pride.

40 N. A. M. Rodger, 'Honour and Duty at Sea, 1660–1815,' *Historical Research* 75:190 (November 2002), 425–47, at p. 430.

41 Rodger, *The Command of the Ocean*, p. 524.

42 Rodger, 'Honour and Duty,' pp. 446–7; Evan Wilson, *A Social History of British Naval Officers 1775–1815* (Woodbridge, 2017), pp. 200–2.

43 Tom Wareham, *The Star Captains* (London, 2001), p. 110.

44 Davey, *In Nelson's Wake*, p. 28, citing Moira Bracknall, 'Lord Spencer, Patronage and Commissioned Officers' Careers, 1794–1801' (PhD thesis, University of Exeter, 2008), pp. 274–5.

Contemporary accounts are full of the supposed effects of 'interest' in gaining both promotion and lucrative opportunities in naval service. Even fictional accounts by the likes of Jane Austen have been treated as evidence of a system depending on interest.[45] They need, however, to be treated with some caution.

In *Mansfield Park* a key part of the drama is provided by the emotional hold that the unscrupulous Henry Crawford gains over the heroine, Fanny Price, by claiming to have gained a naval commission for her brother William through the influence of his uncle, the beastly, but unseen, Admiral Crawford. This is held out as evidence of interest at work in the navy. It certainly was in the interests of the many who sought to use their connections to obtain favours for others to claim that they had succeeded. Equally those who were asked for favours had an interest in claiming that they had obliged, thus appearing to be paying off previous obligations or laying down return obligations for the future. Yet why take the word of the likes of Henry Crawford for such success? Fanny Price may have done so, but that does not mean that we should. Austen's novel reveals William Price as 'a young man of an open, pleasant countenance, and frank, unstudied, but feeling and respectful manners' who demonstrates 'proof of good principles, professional knowledge, energy, courage and cheerfulness – everything that could deserve and promise well'. Crawford envies William because, unlike himself, William is 'distinguishing himself and working his way to fortune'.[46] In short, William is just the sort of person to attract promotion on his own merits regardless of the 'interest' of others. Just because it suited someone to claim the credit for his promotion does not mean that the claim was justified. In the later 'naval' novel, *Persuasion*, Jane Austen's hero who wins the hand of the heroine, Anne Elliot, is Captain Wentworth of the Royal Navy. This naval hero is a man of 'no connections' to secure his rise in the navy.[47] He is, however, a man described as possessing 'intelligence, spirit and brilliancy', whose 'genius and ardour' set him on the 'prosperous path' to prize money.[48] This is emphasised in the text, perhaps in part to gloss over the fact that he moved in circles where his sister married a man who by the time of the story was a rear-admiral of the white. Ultimately, the drama unfolds as merit is promoted and Wentworth wins the heroine.

45 Brian Southam, *Jane Austen and the Navy* (London, 2000), p. 10, instancing historians Arthur Bryant, C. Northcote Parkinson and Daniel Baugh.

46 Jane Austen, *Mansfield Park*, 1814, ed. Kathryn Sutherland (London, 2014), vol. II, Ch. VI, pp. 217–19.

47 Jane Austen, *Persuasion*, 1818, ed. Margaret Drabble (London, 1989), Ch. 3, p. 23.

48 566 *Ibid., Ch. 4, pp. 27–8.*

Jane Austen's understanding of the navy came through her brothers, Francis and Charles, who both served in the wartime navy and rose to high office. They petitioned for, and called on the influence of connections to try and gain, plum positions including the lucrative command of frigates that might be able to seize valuable prizes. Francis, in particular, felt aggrieved that promises made through these approaches went unfulfilled.[49] Instead he was assigned to convoy duties, crucially, yet laboriously, shepherding merchant fleets. Not chasing prizes, but a crucial task that matched his skill set. Even Austen family anecdotes cast Francis as 'a sea officer conscientious, correct and finicky to the last degree'.[50] 'Interest', it seems, was not an automatic route to preferment in the Royal Navy, but part of a system of communication based on ink and paper and word of mouth rather than emails or online human resources assessments. Sailors did not become dashing and successful frigate captains because they were given command of a frigate. They were given such commands because they were dashing and successful or showed the potential to be so. Life and fiction mirror each other in that claims of influence were often made but may be too readily accepted.

Attitudes towards the use of powers of patronage for private gain were changing by the time the navy was plunged into new wars against France at the end of the eighteenth century, leading to, and encouraged by, the Commission on Fees and its aftermath. Unlike the army, it was not possible simply to buy a commission in the navy. Those wishing to become officers had to serve at sea and 'pass for Lieutenant' by being examined on their seamanship skills by panels of senior officers.[51] Those wishing to exercise patronage not only had to comply with the requirement for qualification but also had to persuade the Admiralty that their recommendations could be relied upon. Patronage therefore had to be used to promote merit and not otherwise.[52] Men promoted without merit were side-lined and though they may have enjoyed rank, they did not necessarily achieve command. An unemployed officer enjoyed half-pay, so long as he remained available for service, but not the income from prizes that an officer given command could achieve.[53] Meritocracy could, and can, be an unforgiving system.

Hand-in-hand with the changing attitudes towards private gain from public office and the changes in naval attitudes towards honour and duty came a new sense of respect and public recognition. The effect of the public adulation for the likes of Admiral Vernon after the taking of Porto Bello in

49 Southam, *Jane Austen and the Navy*, pp. 93–4.
50 Ibid., p. 217.
51 Lavery, *Nelson's Navy*, p. 93.
52 Rodger, *The Wooden World*, p. 277.
53 Lavery, *Nelson's Navy*, p. 99.

1740 through to Nelson rubbed off on the service as a whole.[54] As a result the vast majority of naval officers came from 'the ambitious middle classes, for whom a naval career offered affordability, a degree of gentlemanliness, and the possibility of social advancement'.[55] By 1808, therefore, attitudes to the wealth enjoyed by those at the top of the naval tree were changing and there was a desperate need for skilled men, seamen and petty officers.

Trafalgar to 'All Talents'

When Barham, who succeeded Melville as First Lord of the Admiralty in 1805, had been comptroller of the navy at the end of the American Revolutionary War in the 1780s he had enforced a comprehensive overhaul of the standing orders for the royal dockyards. In 1783 he oversaw 255 revised standing orders issued to the dockyards, with a further 96 the following year.[56] Despite being First Lord of the Admiralty from May 1805 to February 1806, he did not change the distribution of prize money, even though it was a task well suited to his talent for regulatory reform. Admittedly he had his hands full with operational matters during his brief period in office, but it would take a fresh approach to the war and to the Admiralty before reform was carried out. Barham left office following Pitt's death in 1806 and the ironically named 'Ministry of All the Talents' followed, with a period lacking in decisive leadership of the war effort.[57] Charles Grey, despite his affair with Georgina, Duchess of Devonshire, took over at the Admiralty. His father, General Charles Grey, had filled the family coffers through the plunder of the Caribbean for prize and booty along with Sir John Jervis.[58] General Grey was given an earldom in April 1806, upon which his son at the Admiralty became Lord Howick, inheriting the earldom on his father's death and giving his name to Earl Grey tea. Grey did not move any of the flag-share to the lower decks.

For the last six months of the Ministry of All the Talents the prime minister, Lord Grenville, appointed his brother Thomas to the Admiralty upon Howick's appointment as foreign secretary on the death of Charles James Fox.[59] Though diffident about his own talents, Thomas Grenville worked

54 Kathleen Wilson, 'Patriotism, Trade and Empire', in Colville (ed.), *Nelson, Navy & Nation*, p. 46.

55 Davey, *In Nelson's Wake*, p. 31.

56 Knight, *Britain against Napoleon*, p. 29.

57 Ibid., p. 237.

58 Duffy, *Soldiers, Sugar, and Seapower*, pp. 106–14.

59 Knight, *Britain against Napoleon*, p. 234.

hard to make something of his short period in public office, the last he would choose to undertake. One of the last acts of his period of office, along with Lord Henry Petty at the Treasury, was to restore Treasury payments to Royal Navy captains for the carriage of public bullion in their ships. This was not so much an act of generosity, however, as a grudging submission to the claims of captains who had taken to deducting what they considered their entitlement before discharging their treasured cargoes.[60] Beset by numerous demands for his attention, the amiable and popular Grenville did not take away any of the share of prize money from captains or flag-officers for the benefit of the lower decks.

Change at Last

By April 1807 the Talents were spent, replaced by a new government in the spirit of the late prime minister, William Pitt. Although riven by personality differences, especially those between Canning as foreign secretary and Castlereagh as secretary of state for war, which ended in a duel, the administration brought a new energy and realism to the war effort. The new administration understood that Britain was fighting a war for national survival and was accordingly prepared to bring greater organisation and drive to the fight.[61]

Henry Phipps, Lord Mulgrave, took over from Grenville as First Lord of the Admiralty in April 1807.[62] Mulgrave's background was in the army before entering politics and it did not make him an instinctive reformer of naval matters when he first took office at the Admiralty. He took some persuading to follow up the recommendations of the Commission of Naval Reform that finished its business as he came to office, but he would eventually carry through reforms in the name of efficiency.[63] Just as significant was the arrival of a new treasurer to the navy in the form of George Rose, who had been injured while serving as a young midshipman in the navy. Coming ashore, he had risen as a follower of Pitt and become very well connected as clerk of the House of Lords, and on friendly terms with George III, who stayed at Rose's Hampshire home, Cuffnells, in 1789 when travelling from Weymouth to London. By 1804 Rose counted the Lord Chancellor, Lord Eldon, as a confidante, along with Eldon's brother

60 See Chapter 8.

61 Davey, *In Nelson's Wake*, p. 151.

62 The king appointed the new Admiralty Board on 4 April 1808, *The Naval Chronicle*, vol. 17, p. 351.

63 Knight, *Britain against Napoleon*, pp. 329, 343.

Sir William Scott, the Admiralty judge and expert on prize law.[64] In that year Rose became joint paymaster to the forces, a role previously held by Mulgrave's elder brother, Constantine. Rose was also a friend of Nelson, who invited him to dine on board *HMS Victory* at anchor in the St Helens anchorage off Portsmouth before he sailed for Trafalgar.[65] On 6 October 1805, after arriving off Cadiz, Nelson wrote to Rose thanking him for his efforts on behalf of his family and telling him that 'I verily believe the Country will soon be put to some expense for my account, either a Monument, or a new Pension and Honours; for I have not the very smallest doubt but that a very few days, almost hours, will put us in Battle', and acknowledging that in his view it was 'annihilation that the country wants, and not merely a splendid Victory'.[66]

Although Rose was denounced as a sinecurist by the playwright Richard Brinsley Sheridan, who had briefly preceded him in the office of treasurer to the navy, he was hard-working and serious in his approach to his duties.[67] Those duties included supervision of the navy Pay Office, which had been responsible for the former Prize Office before 1708, and Rose took an active interest in reforming the administration of prize money, including keeping a central register of prize captures.[68] He was always deferential to the Board of Admiralty in matters of reform, but his efforts included initiating an investigation of prize accounts by Samuel Hancock at the public expense and steps to ensure that deductions wrongly made from prize funds were distributed to the captors, and proceeds were invested for the benefit of the captors until payment.[69]

Mulgrave was very conscious of the tax burden of funding the war and the need to keep public opinion on side by exercising 'very rigid economy', even in the face of support for loosening the public purse-strings from both the foreign secretary, George Canning, and George Rose.[70] Whilst refusing demands for a pay increase for the Navy Board, Mulgrave nevertheless increased salaries for navy office clerks in order to keep up the standard of applicants.[71] Reform of warrant officers' pay leading to increases in 1802

64 George Rose, *The Diaries and Correspondence of the Right Honourable George Rose* (London, 1860), vol. 2, p. 78.

65 Nicolas, *Dispatches*, vol. vii, p. 35.

66 Ibid., p. 80.

67 ODNB George Rose, by Roland Thorne, 3 October 2013.

68 Gutteridge, 'Aspects of Naval Prize Agency 1793–1815', p. 50.

69 TNA, ADM 15/1 Rose's letterbook 1807–10. Papers Relating to Proceedings of The Treasurer to the Navy on Prize Matters, 13 June 1811, HC (234), xi, 1811.

70 Rose, *Diaries and Correspondence*, vol. 2, pp. 336–8.

71 Knight, *Britain against Napoleon*, p. 343.

and 1807 had not cured problems with manpower.[72] With the realisation that Britain was in for a long economic war, the outcome of which would depend on an effective and well-manned navy, a solution to the need to motivate petty officers without further increasing the burden on the public purse by increasing pay was just the sort of proposal to attract itself to this military man, even if it did involve sacrifice by senior naval officers.

As we have seen, the period before 1808 had been one of profound political and cultural change, with mounting, but unanswered, pressures for a change to the distribution of prize money. By 1808 the language of the conflict had changed, however. It was less of a conflict with revolution, or even France. The enemy had been reinvented in the 'bogey-man' persona of Napoleon.[73] Further, by 1808 Napoleon's Continental Blockade had reached a peak of effectiveness.[74] It was naval and economic realities that finally brought the pressure for reform to the point of change. The precious, skilled middle ranks of the Royal Navy were the ones to reap the benefit when Mulgrave and Rose implemented the long-delayed change, combining it with continued vigilance to try and ensure that prize money was paid when due.[75]

The 1808 changes to prize distribution are generally recognised as having redistributed prize money away from the commanding officers to the ship's company.[76] Whilst that is true overall, the changes made were more subtle than that. A more detailed analysis of the changes reveals that the change was not made out of a desire for equity, but as a practical measure to encourage the skilled men that were needed to serve in the navy.

The last royal proclamation concerning the distribution of prize money before 1808 had been as recent as 23 December 1807.[77] The Treaty of Tilsit between Russia and Napoleon's France the previous July had brought Russia into the war as Napoleon's ally. In response the British ordered reprisals against the ships, goods and subjects of Alexander I of Russia by an order-in-council of 18 December 1807. Five days later a further order-in-council provided for the distribution of prizes seized under the reprisals. This hastily introduced proclamation maintained the pre-existing flag-share of one of the captain's three eighths.

[72] Evan Wilson, *A Social History of British Naval Officers 1775–1815*, p. 138.

[73] Mark Philp (ed.), *Resisting Napoleon: The British Response to the Threat of Invasion, 1797–1815* (Aldershot, 2006), p. 8.

[74] Katherine Aaslestad, *Revisiting Napoleon's Continental System* (Basingstoke, 2014), p. 8.

[75] Knight, *Britain against Napoleon*, p. 348.

[76] E.g. Lewis, *A Social History of the Navy 1793–1815*, p. 318; Lavery, *Nelson's Navy*, p. 131; MacDougall and Coats (eds), *The Naval Mutinies of 1797*, p. 14.

[77] *London Gazette*, No. 16105, January 1808, p. 21.

In contrast, the 1808 proclamation of 15 June was not prompted by any further order for reprisals against a new enemy.[78] It was a deliberate attempt to reform the distribution of prize money, introduced to change the division of the spoils for prizes taken from the enemy states that were already subject to reprisals, and where there were already existing proclamations dealing with distribution of prizes from all the hostile states. Its revised terms indicate that considerable thought had been given to the changes. Thought had even been given to a transitional provision to allow for the practical implementation of the change. All previous proclamations distributing naval prize money were revoked, but the new provisions were expressly stated not to affect any prizes taken before the date of the proclamation, nor any prizes that were condemned in any of the British prize courts abroad, the Vice-Admiralty courts, before they had notice of the proclamation. In such cases the old rules still applied. The effect of the transitional provisions was to create a ripple effect as notice of the change was carried through the fleets and to the Vice-Admiralty courts on foreign stations.

The headline change was to remove one of the three eighths that went to the captains and flag-officers and redistribute it to the lower categories serving on board. As we have seen in Chapter 4, however, the redistribution was carefully targeted amidst a more up-to-date categorisation of those on board. The reason, according to the proclamation itself, was:

> Whereas it has been represented to Us by our Commissioners for executing the Office of the Lord High Admiral, that it will be productive of beneficial Effects to the Service, if instead of the Three Eighth Parts of the neat Produce of Prizes, which have hitherto been granted to the Captains and Flag-Officers serving in Our Fleet, Two Eighth Parts only shall be allocated to them, and the remaining Eighth Part distributed amongst the Petty Officers, Seamen, and Marines, in addition to their present shares.[79]

Petty officers and below now had one half of the total proceeds to divide between them, rather than the three eighths they had previously enjoyed. Thus, they had the extra eighth that had been taken away from the captain and flag-officers. The way it was distributed, however, benefited the petty officers rather than those below them. Petty officers first class each had four and a half shares of the available half of the prize money. Petty officers second class each had three shares. All the remaining specified ratings, including able and ordinary seamen, had one and a half shares each.

[78] Ibid., No. 16155, June 1808, p. 853.

[79] Proclamation 15 June 1808, *London Gazette*, No. 16155, p. 853.

Landsmen, admiral's domestics, any unspecified ratings and all passengers and other persons carried as supernumeraries and doing duty and assisting on board had one share each. The lowly young gentlemen volunteers and boys of every description received only a half share each.

The impact of these changes was thus different for the different categories of men on board. The precise redistribution depended on the particular ships on which they served, but an overall picture of the effect can be seen. It is clear that the captain and flag-officers were not the only ones to lose out. The readily replaceable landsmen, the men who had not had enough sea experience to be rated even as ordinary seamen, and the untrained boys lost out as a result of the changes. Commissioned and warrant officers still enjoyed the same quarter share that they had previously had. Seamen and petty officers first class enjoyed a limited increase in the share they received, about 50 per cent and 25 per cent respectively. Petty officers second class, however, received an increase in their share to nearly three times their previous entitlement.[80]

The Naval Chronicle welcomed the change with a letter from its regular contributor on matters of naval discipline:

> I must congratulate my naval readers, and the country in general, on the spirit of the liberal justice which appears in the new distribution of prize-money. It gives me most sincere satisfaction; and I trust that this truly wise, because truly just amendment, will be followed up by some regulations, respecting liberty for the seamen to go ashore, and to visit their friends on board other ships.[81]

The Morning Chronicle initially reported the change without comment but later covered the protests of those captains and flag-officers who were unwilling to accept the change without complaint.[82] Over 400 of them were reported to have petitioned the Admiralty against the change. One petition signed by a number of naval captains was sent to the Admiralty through Admiral Sir George Montagu, the Port Admiral at Portsmouth. The response was that the captains would have to be satisfied with a daily increase in pay of two shillings that had been allowed to them at the same time as the change. Montagu was not satisfied and submitted a further

80 Daniel K. Benjamin, 'Golden Harvest: The British Naval Prize System, 1793–1815'.

81 *The Naval Chronicle*, vol. 20 (1808), p. 26.

82 *The Morning Chronicle*, 20 June 1808, issue 12199.

petition, drawing the response that he should not suffer himself to be made the channel of such communications. An incensed Montagu declared that he considered it part of his bounden duty, and from which he would not shrink, to forward to the Admiralty Board the letters and memorials of the brave men under his command, and struck his flag amidst the acclaim of his captains, but he never served again.[83]

The detailed nature of the redistribution provisions suggests that their effect had been thought through. The changes do not have the somewhat random appearance of previous amendments. Shortage of manpower was a real problem in the navy at this time. The need to encourage the very people it in fact benefited suggests that the effect of the reform was indeed intended. That the redistribution of prize money away from captains and flag-officers was a wartime move to deal with the shortage of petty officers, rather than a long-term plan for liberalisation, is confirmed by what happened when the war ended. Although the two classes of petty officer were retained, the Admiralty reverted to the three eighths share for captains and flag-officers where prizes were captured in the course of peacetime operations against smugglers, pirates and slave-traders.[84] The practices of the prize court were seen by abolitionists as a model for the enforcement of British laws abolishing the slave trade, and prize money remained an important incentive to enforce the abolition of the trade in practice, not just in law.[85] Prize money from captured smugglers, Barbary pirates and slave ships remained a valuable source of both income and power of patronage for flag-officers into the nineteenth century, without the need to leave the senior officers' additional eighth in the hands of the lower decks.[86] The need by then was to induce those in command to accept the risks of often unhealthy postings in areas such as the west coast of Africa.[87] Manning the ships without the problems of a major naval war was less of an issue. The immediate reversion back to the previous distributions indicates that the 1808 change was a temporary reaction to circumstances, not part of the updating modernisation that can be seen in the division of petty officers into two distinct classes, nor an indication of any particular desire for greater long-term equity.

83 Ibid., 10 February 1809, issue 12403.

84 *London Gazette*, No. 17189, 9 November 1816, p. 2109.

85 Burton, 'British Evangelicals, Economic Warfare and the Abolition of the Atlantic Slave Trade, 1794–1810'.

86 Roger Morriss, *Cockburn and the British Navy in Transition: Admiral Sir George Cockburn, 1772–1853* (Columbia, 1997), p. 213.

87 For the Royal Navy's campaign against the slave trade see Peter Grindal, *Opposing the Slavers* (London, 2016).

Prize money was not the only method by which private profit could be made, and patronage exercised, during service in the Royal Navy in the eighteenth century. The next chapter considers other financial bounties as incentives for such public service

8.

Freight Money, Head Money and Booty

Freight Money

Captains of vessels in the Georgian Royal Navy were allowed to earn freight money by carrying gold, silver and jewels both for the government and for private individuals. Unlike prize money, the arrangements for such freight payments were not governed by statute, but were a matter of perceived custom and usage, as emerges from the disputes that found their way to court and into the contemporary law reports.

Article 17 of the Admiralty Articles of War prevented Royal Navy officers from carrying any goods or merchandise other than for the sole use of the ship, to save them from a shipwreck, or under express orders from the Admiralty. The purpose of the Article was to prevent Royal Navy ships from being used for private trade at public expense. The temptation to save on wages by remunerating officers through allowing them to use voyages for trade had proved detrimental to the development of fighting navies in the past.[1] Gold, silver and jewels, however, were exempt from the prohibition.[2] In common parlance such items were variously referred to as treasure or specie. Thus, not only did the Admiralty give orders for Royal Navy ships to carry bullion and specie on behalf of the government at the request of the Treasury, but there existed a custom of captains agreeing to carry bullion and specie for merchants in return for a payment of freight. For those captains lucky enough to have opportunities to gain prize money, freight money may have been a relatively minor addition to their income.

1 See the example of the Portuguese navy, C. B. Boxer, 'Admiral Joao Pereira Corte-Real and the Construction of Portuguese East-Indiamen in the Early Seventeenth Century', *MM* 26:4 (1940), 388–406.

2 A similar provision governed the US navy, see Article 23 of 'An Act for the better government of the Navy of the United States', 6th Congress: 1st sess., ch. 33, 2 U.S. Stat. 45, 3 March 800, Benjamin Homans, *Laws of the United States, in Relation to the Navy and Marine Corps* (Washington, 1841), p. 62. See further, Chapter 9.

For those less fortunate, particularly those assigned to convoy duties with more opportunities for freight than prizes, it could provide a significant boost to their pay, along with any additional sums paid by bodies such as the East India Company in recognition of particular convoy services.[3]

Whereas prize money was governed by statute and royal proclamations made by order-in-council at the outbreak of each war, payment of freight was not governed by such provisions until 1819. Freight for public cargoes was determined by Treasury decisions as a payment of a bounty, and freight for private cargoes was by private arrangement. Unlike prize money, none of the freight money went to the officers and crew. Before 1801 it was the custom of the Treasury to pay one per cent freight money for the carriage of bullion in Royal Navy ships. It was also the custom and usage in the navy before 1801 that if a captain received freight for carriage of either private or public specie, they paid one third of the sum received to the commander-in-chief under whose orders they sailed.[4] Where there was more than one flag-officer on a station, the junior flag-officers took a share of the monies in the same proportions as if it was prize money. While commander-in-chief of the American station, in charge of the Leeward Island fleet undertaking combined operations with the army under Sir Charles Grey, Admiral Sir John Jervis had tried to deny a share to his junior flag-officers of freight money received by him from his captains. The dispute joined the plethora of disputes and litigation that arose from that campaign.[5] It came to a head in court in 1801 in an action brought by Rear-Admiral Sir William Parker against Jervis' secretary and agent, Benjamin Tucker. Jervis had by then become the Earl of St Vincent, after the battle of that name in which both he and Parker had fought. Many admirals were called to give evidence in support of the universal practice of sharing freight money with junior flag-officers back to the time of Sir George Rooke and the War of Spanish Succession. Parker recovered his share and established the right for the other junior flag-officers. The right of a commander-in-chief to be paid the one third flag-share by the captain was not in dispute in that case since everyone's claim depended on its existence.[6]

3 E.g. Francis Austen, see Southam, *Jane Austen and the Navy*, p. 136.

4 Montagu v Janvarin (1813) 3 Taunt. 442, 445.

5 Duffy, *Soldiers, Sugar, and Seapower*, pp. 106–114; J. M. Fewster, 'Prize-money and the British Expedition to the West Indies of 1793–4', *Journal of Imperial and Commonwealth History* 12 (1983), 1–28.

6 Montagu v Janvarin (1813) 3 Taunt. 442, 452. The account there recited was from Serjeant Shepherd, who had appeared as counsel in the case of Parker v Tucker in 1801.

In 1801, however, the government stopped paying freight to captains of Royal Navy ships for carrying public bullion. The public was, after all, already paying for the services of the ship and her captain. By March 1802 a fragile peace had been negotiated at Amiens, but when war resumed in May 1803 the payment of freight did not resume with it. It was not until March 1807 that the Treasury gave in to pressure to resume the payment of freight. On 5 March 1807 the Treasury wrote to the Admiralty saying that it was prepared to pay a half per cent of the value of bullion cargoes as freight. The change of heart came about as captains were refusing to give a receipt for the amount of bullion taken on board and were withholding 'their' freight money from the cargo when they discharged it 'under the pretence of a right founded upon ancient usage, to a charge, in the nature of a poundage on the sum shipped, for their care and trouble during the time that such specie was on board'.[7] By this time Benjamin Tucker had been appointed Second Secretary to the Admiralty by St Vincent and it was in that role that he replied to the Treasury on 10 March 1807. He recognised that naval officers had no right or claim to demand payment for the freight of any public items put on board their ships and that it was the duty of every naval officer to execute his orders without any claim of freight, and accepted the payment of a half per cent as a bounty rather than a right. Thereafter payment of a half per cent freight for public bullion resumed.

With the resumption of payments of freight came the resumption of demands by flag-officers for their one third share. One of those who claimed a flag-share was Captain Home Popham, claiming as commodore of an expedition to capture the Cape in 1805, and thereafter to conquer the river Plate. Commodores counted as flag-officers for the purposes of prize money if they were entitled to a captain under them on their flagship.[8] Popham had appointed a captain of his flagship under him assuming that he had a right to do so. On the assumption that he was entitled to a one third share of any prize money earned by each captain under his command, Popham also claimed a one third share of freight money that Captain Ross Donnelly earned for bringing back captured treasure that Popham consigned to his care. In fact Popham's orders did not contain any authority to appoint a captain under him and in 1807 the Court of Common Pleas held that as he had appointed his captain under him without authority to do so he was not entitled to share as a flag-officer.[9] Donnelly was repre-

7 Recited in Montagu v Janvarin (1813) 3 Taunt. 442, 446.

8 See Chapter 8.

9 Anon., *A Correct Account of The Trial at Large between Ross Donnelly, Esq. a Post Captain in His Majesty's Navy, Plaintiff and Sir Home Popham, Knt. Defendant*. See also Donnelly v Popham (1807) 1 Taunt. 1.

sented in his action against Popham by an experienced team of counsel, Serjeants Shepherd and Best, with the future Lord Chief Justice Charles Abbott as their junior. None of them argued that a flag-officer was not, in any event, entitled to a share of freight money in the way that he was entitled to a share of prize money. It mattered not to the outcome in that case, as Donnelly won on the alternative argument that Popham was not a flag-officer for prize purposes. The argument would be raised, however, in a later claim by Admiral Sir George Montagu against Richard Janvarin, commander of *HMS Pluto*. On this occasion, Shepherd and Best were on opposite sides. Shepherd was for the admiral claiming a customary admiral's share of freight money but was met with an argument advanced by Best that there was no right to such a share, flag-officer or not. Although the point had not been argued in Donnelly v Popham, it was open to be argued now, and if successful could deprive Montagu of his claim. On 16 July 1808, as a result of an order from the Admiralty the previous day, Montagu ordered Janvarin to carry 500,000 dollars from Spithead to Gijon in Spain to be delivered to the British agent. Amounting to some £300,000 in value, the dollars were intended for use to encourage Spanish provinces in revolt against the French.[10] Janvarin was chosen by Montagu for the lucrative task as the vessel specified by the Admiralty order, *HMS Solebay*, was no longer at Spithead. Having delivered the money safely, Janvarin was paid the sum of £548 9*s*. as freight by the Treasury. Montagu claimed his one third, the sum of £182 18*s*. 4*d*. At a trial in the Court of Common Pleas held at Guildhall before Chief Justice Sir James Mansfield and a jury in 1810, judgment was given for Montagu but with permission to apply to the full court of judges of the King's Bench to overturn the judgment. The matter came before the King's Bench, presided over by Mansfield, in the autumn of 1810, with judgment handed down in May 1811. In a judgment given by Mansfield the court held that there could be no custom to divide money given by way of a bounty and that the Admiralty had intended the half per cent to be given to the commander of the ship that carried the bullion. Thus, the court held, Montagu and other admirals who gave effect to Admiralty orders for the carriage of bullion were not entitled to a share.[11] Payment of freight by merchants for the carriage of private bullion was not affected by the changes in arrangements for carriage of public specie. That, as Mansfield observed in Montagu v Janvarin, was governed by the contractual terms negotiated with the merchant and between captains and their commanders-in-chief.

10 *The Morning Chronicle*, 20 June 1808, issue 12199.

11 Montagu v Janvarin (1813) 3 Taunt. 442, 455.

The decision in Montagu v Janvarin caused consternation among those captains who had paid over a share of their freight money to their commanders-in-chief, and they tried to obtain repayment. One such captain was Sir Charles Brisbane. In April 1808 Brisbane had been serving under Admiral Dacres in Jamaica as captain of the 38-gun frigate *HMS Arethusa.* This was the same James Richard Dacres who had been at the capture of the Spanish treasure ship *Hermione* in 1762, as described in the Introduction. Dacres ordered Brisbane to carry 700,000 dollars of public money to Portsmouth. Brisbane also took on board 1,530,000 dollars belonging to private individuals for delivery to the Bank of England.[12] In November 1808 Brisbane received £7,438 18*s.* 5*d.* from the Bank of England as agents for the private individuals as payment of freight for the carriage of their dollars. In March 1809 Brisbane received £850 from the Treasury as payment of freight on the public monies that he had carried.[13] Under the belief that Dacres was entitled to one third of each of the payments, Brisbane paid £2,500 to his admiral. By the time the judgment was given in Montagu v Janvarin, Brisbane was governor of St Vincent in the Caribbean, a post he remained in until his death in 1829. When Brisbane discovered what had happened in Montagu v Janvarin he instructed Serjeant Best, who had acted as counsel for Richard Janvarin in the successful defence of Montagu's claim, to try and recover the money he had paid over.

Dacres had died by this time, so Brisbane brought his action in the Court of Common Pleas against Dacres' widow and executrix, Eleanor, seeking repayment out of Dacres' estate. Dacres' eldest son, Barrington, had died in Bath in 1806 after his own successful, but short-lived, naval career. At the time of Dacres' death in 1810, however, his younger son, also James Richard, was a naval captain in England on half pay who could have acted as executor of his father's estate.[14] There were also a number of other naval officers in the family who could have dealt with the estate. As was seen in Chapter 5 with Susanna, Lady Gardner, however, it was Eleanor as Dacres' widow who was executrix of her late husband's estate. In her case she was named in her husband's will as the sole executor of his estate.[15] Thus it was she who was named in the proceedings. When judgment was given by the full court in July 1813 Brisbane was disappointed.[16] The executrix won and held on to the money for the estate. The court held that it was illegal for a commander

12 The total value being carried at today's values was therefore over £32 million.

13 Payment having been authorised by the Treasury five months earlier on 15 November 1808.

14 Obituary, *Gentleman's Magazine* (1854), vol. XLI, p. 202.

15 TNA, PROB 11/1507/351.

16 Brisbane v Dacres (1815) 5 Taunt. 143.

of a Royal Navy ship to carry private bullion without an order from the Admiralty or one of his commanding officers to do so. As such, it held, the private freight was tainted by illegality, and the court would not assist in its recovery. The effect of this judgment was to hand back considerable power to admirals in command of a station. As Mansfield had foreseen in his judgment in Montagu v Janvarin, where an admiral had a financial interest in selecting the captain for carriage of bullion it left that captain open to abuse and could lead commanding officers into the temptation to dispatch ships away from their station in pursuit of private bullion to carry. In Montagu v Janvarin the court heard evidence about such a practice, Mansfield describing it as 'very dangerous'. That was not all the bad news for Brisbane, however. The court also held that as Brisbane had authorised the payment of the money to Dacres in full knowledge of the facts, his mistake as to the law and as to Dacres' entitlement to the money did not mean that it was recoverable. Accordingly, Brisbane recovered none of the money that he had paid to Dacres as a share of the freight money that he had received.

The history of this legal finding since 1813 has a lesson for those who may be tempted to feel that with modern sensibilities these arguments about private profit resulting from taking liberties with public money in public service are a scandalous historical anachronism. The principle identified in Brisbane v Dacres, that a mistake of law did not render a transaction void and lead to repayment of sums paid under the mistake, remained good law until overturned by the House of Lords in 1998. In Kleinwort Benson v Lincoln City Council, the House of Lords allowed recovery of sums paid as a result of 'swap' agreements entered into by local authorities with merchant banks involving public monies.[17] The agreements had previously been thought to be legal, but had been held to be ultra vires and illegal in Hazell v Hammersmith and Fulham LBC.[18] The principles of law established in the eighteenth century, far from being maverick decisions of their time, formed the basis of our commercial law today and even where they have been altered recently it has only been after having been accepted as good law for many a year.

Britain's Need for Cash

The encouragement and protection of private trade, whilst important in itself, was not the only reason for allowing Royal Navy ships to carry private wealth. Nor was it simply a matter of finding ways to enrich and encourage

[17] [1998] 2 A. C. 349.

[18] [1992] 2 A. C. 1.

commanders of vessels to do their duty. Britain needed the cash. As the war secretary Henry Dundas, later Lord Melville, expressed it to the prime minister, William Pitt, at the outbreak of war: 'All modern Wars are a Contention of Purse.'[19] Such were the government's demands for gold that in 1797 the Bank of England was forced to suspend convertibility of its own notes into gold at its offices in Threadneedle Street, and to issue £1 and £2 notes for the first time. This step was pilloried by James Gillray in a cartoon showing Pitt attempting to ravish an old lady in an attempt to get at the chest of gold on which she is seated. The old lady is wearing a dress made from the new £1 notes and represents the Bank of England. It was this cartoon that gave rise to the bank's colloquial name as 'the old lady of Threadneedle Street.'

The total cost to Britain of the wars between 1793 and 1815 was around £830 million, of which some £59 million was paid in cash subsidies to keep Britain's various coalition partners in the field against France.[20] War in the Iberian Peninsula meant that cash was required to keep British forces in the field, with Wellington complaining to the prime minister that he would have to withdraw from the field for want of cash.[21] The British had even become involved in operations to smuggle cash around the world to provide money where it was required.[22] Thus there were good economic and military reasons to encourage merchants to repatriate specie in the relative security of His Majesty's ships.

Insurance

Prudent merchants insured their treasure in transit even if it was being carried on board a Royal Navy ship. It was not an idle precaution. In 1799 the Bank of England was trying to bolster the merchants of Hamburg who had used their reserves to support Britain during a run on the pound in 1797. Admiral Lord Duncan, commander-in-chief of the North Sea fleet, was ordered to make a vessel available to transport consignments of cash from London, to be loaded at Gravesend, to the Elbe. The first vessel that he sent, the armed cutter *Nile*, set sail with cash received from the house of Messrs Goldsmid and Co. Although she got through, she had left before the considerable sums from other merchants arrived. Duncan therefore dispatched a second vessel, the 32-gun frigate *HMS Lutine*. She set off with

19 Updating Cicero's maxim 'nervos belli, pecuniam infinitam', Niall Ferguson, *The House of Rothschild* (London, 1998), p. 83.

20 Ibid., p. 84.

21 Ibid., p. 83.

22 Ibid., p. 87.

over £1,000,000 on board. As she approached the Dutch coast she was driven onto a bank near Vlieland by a gale and destroyed by the tide. The single survivor died on the way back to Britain and all the gold was lost. Lloyds famously paid the insurance on the lost bullion in full. The *Lutine*'s bell was salvaged with some of the gold in 1859 and still hangs in the underwriters' room at Lloyds. It was traditionally rung to draw the attention of underwriters to market sensitive news, once for a loss and twice for a safe arrival, so that they all heard it at once. The advent of alternative means of communication and a crack in the bell have rendered its role ceremonial, but it is still rung on special occasions.[23]

'A Dreadful Responsibility'

During submissions on behalf of Janvarin in 1810, Mansfield C.J. said to Serjeant Best that 'If the captain takes on board merchants' bullion, he signs a bill of lading for it, like the captain of a merchant ship, by which he incurs a dreadful responsibility, and is therefore entitled to freight from the merchant.'[24] Best and his new client, Thomas Foulerton, were about to discover what that responsibility meant in practice.

When *HMS Cheerly* sailed for home from the river Plate in October 1809 there were good reasons for her commander, Lieutenant Thomas Foulerton, to be satisfied. His ship was one of the workhorse gun brigs of the Royal Navy, built in 1804 in Bridport as part of the urgent re-arming of the navy following the short-lived Peace of Amiens. Not renowned as a great sailor, and only 177 tons with 14 guns, she nevertheless provided the opportunity for independent command. Her complement of 50 men had suffered some losses from desertion in Buenos Aires, but the losses had been mitigated by the signing on of volunteers seeking to sail home to Britain. He had even recruited one 'volunteer' in Montevideo, on his way down the river from Buenos Aires to the open sea.[25] William Wilson, the 26-year-old Montevideo recruit originally from Epping in Essex, turned out to be a deserter from *HMS Apollo* and was handed over to naval justice on arrival at Portsmouth. Another seaman, Henry Bergen, had tried to desert in Montevideo, but had been captured and given 24 lashes as *Cheerly* left Montevideo in a light breeze.

The crew had been fairly idle before departure. Foulerton exercised them at striking and raising the upper masts, and sails had been repaired. Both

23 Geoffrey L. Green, *The Royal Navy & Anglo-Jewry 1740–1820* (London, 1989), pp. 75–6.

24 Montagu v Janvarin (1813) 3 Taunt. 442, 450.

25 *HMS Cheerly* Muster Book, TNA, ADM 37/2302.

his and the master's log show that the crew had on many occasions been put to 'making up junk'.[26] The undemanding task of picking the fibres out of old rope to make material for caulking the seams between the wooden planks of the ship was often undertaken by prisoners, but had been used to fill the time in the close heat of the Rio Plata. Despite the lack of action, Foulerton had not needed to resort to the lash to keep discipline. When Bergen's sentence for desertion was carried out on leaving Montevideo it had been six weeks since the lash had been used on board. The crew had also had the task of stowing items brought on board before departure. Twenty-one sheep were taken on board at Montevideo to provide fresh meat for the crew. This supplemented 312 lbs of raisins, 212 gallons of brandy, four casks of beef, five barrels of pork, 5,200 lbs of bread, 258 lbs of flour and four sail needles that had been taken on board in Buenos Aires. It was not these provisions, however, that gave Thomas Foulerton such particular cause for satisfaction.

The year 1809 was an interesting time for a Royal Navy ship to be in the river Plate. The river now forms the border between Argentina and Uruguay and houses on its banks Buenos Aires and Montevideo, the respective capitals of each. In 1809 it was nominally a key part of the Spanish Vice-royalty of Peru. When Napoleon forced the abdication of the Spanish royal family and put his brother Joseph uneasily on the Spanish throne in 1808, however, Spanish authority in South America was loosened rather than strengthened. The local civic authorities had been emboldened by their success in repelling the British invasions of the Rio de la Plata in 1806–7.[27] The failure of the invasions was a setback for British merchants who had received Popham's appeals to support his military action, but it did not put an end to British trade in the area. Whether out of loyalty to the deposed Bourbon royal family or, more likely, to their own interests the locals had engaged in trade with the British despite the continuing war in Europe, as the story of the *Cheerly* confirms.[28]

Among those who had made use of the opportunity to trade in South America created by the political vacuum that existed there was the South Sea Company. The company had been granted a monopoly of the trade with South America by Queen Anne in 1711 during the negotiations with France to end the War of Spanish Succession that led to the Treaty of Utrecht in

[26] TNA, ADM 51/2170, ADM 52/4441.

[27] Popham, *A Damned Cunning Fellow*, pp. 144–65; Grainger, *British Campaigns in the South Atlantic, 1805–1807*, pp. 69ff.

[28] Alberto Spektorowski, *Nations and Nationalism: A Global Historical Overview* (California, 2008), p. 269.

1713.[29] While Spain had controlled much of the South American trade the monopoly had served little purpose, apart from fuelling the well-known bubble. A scam involving the use of insider information about the national debt to ramp up the value of shares in the company, the scandal had ruined many and brought the company under government control. With renewed interest in trade in the South Sea, as the trading area of South America was called, the company granted a licence to a Mr Hodgson and his ship the *Braganza*, to 'sail, trade, navigate, and adventure to all and every port or ports within the company's limits' for 18 months from February 1809.[30] The voyage proved profitable for on the sale of the outward cargo the *Braganza* had the enormous sum of nearly £15,000 in Spanish dollars to remit home.[31] To get them home safely they were loaded in 21 casks on board the *Cheerly* and entrusted to the care of Thomas Foulerton. In return it was agreed that Foulerton would receive 'the usual' commission of 2½ per cent, a sum of nearly £369.[32]

While his men were picking fibres from old rope, Foulerton had been arranging to make some serious money. He certainly had a reason to be satisfied. He may well have thought, in the words of Patrick O'Brian, that:

> freight money, that charming unlooked-for, unlaborious, almost unearned shower of gold, fell only on those fortunate captains of men-of-war who carried treasure for Government or for the owners of bullion or specie who did not choose to trust their concentrated wealth to any conveyance less sure; it amounted to two or three per cent of the value carried, and very welcome it was. Although it was far rarer than prize-money (the sea officer's other road to a decent competence) it was surer; it had no possible legal difficulties attached, and no man had to risk his ship, his life or his career in getting it.[33]

Foulerton was no stranger to profiting legitimately from service in His Britannic Majesty's navy. In June 1801, whilst first lieutenant of the sloop *HMS Kangaroo*, he had led a cutting out expedition at Oropeso in the Mediterranean during a joint enterprise with Captain Thomas Cochrane and his crew from *HMS Speedy*. Though slightly injured, Foulerton had taken as prizes three brigs loaded with wine, rice and bread, as well as destroying

29 Statute of 1711, 9 Ann. C. 21, S. 49.

30 Hodgson v Fullerton (1813) 4 Taunt. 787. Foulerton's name is misspelled in the law report.

31 Worth nearly £1 million today, Gregory Clark, *The Annual RPI and Average Earnings for Britain, 1209 to Present (New Series)*, www.MeasuringWorth.com.

32 About £24,000 today, ibid.

33 Patrick O'Brian, *HMS Surprise* (London, 1973), p. 334.

other ships from a Spanish convoy.[34] In addition to prize money, Foulerton earned a mention in dispatches by Captain Pullings of the *Kangaroo*, and an association with the legend of the great prize-taker Lord Cochrane. Now, as commander of his own ship, here was an opportunity for reward without risk. Or so he may have thought.

Cheerly arrived at Spithead in March 1810. Having made her number to the guard ship at South Yarmouth she took a pilot, unloaded her powder and entered Portsmouth harbour.[35] The strong gales that had brought her in subsided to moderate, but squally, breezes. Foulerton borrowed a flat-bottomed boat from *HMS Gladiator* which his crew used to discharge the dollars they had carried from Buenos Aires. On 12 March they landed 30 packages of dollars and the following day they landed a further 49. Foulerton could look forward to receiving his freight money.

Unfortunately, when the dollars were counted it was found that two of the 21 casks were unaccounted for and 5,865 dollars, valued at £1,407 6*s*. 4*d*., were missing. Hodgson sued, and Foulerton turned to Serjeant Best and his colleague Serjeant Vaughan to find a defence. The sum claimed was the full £1,407, nearly four times the value of the freight that Foulerton was to get for his trouble. The claim came before Mansfield C.J. in the autumn of 1812. He heard the evidence and gave judgment for the plaintiff, Hodgson, but reserved the legal argument to the judges of the King's Bench.[36] They heard arguments the following term in early 1813 before giving judgment in May 1813. Best argued that, as the licence to trade had been given by the South Sea Company to the *Braganza*, the use of *Cheerly* to remit the dollars amounted to a breach of that licence and of the company's monopoly. Thus, he argued, the transaction was illegal and Hodgson could not recover the value of the missing dollars as the loss resulted from an illegal transaction. The court was having none of it. Parliament had guarded against a literal construction of the Act of Queen Anne by outlawing acts 'contrary to the true meaning of this act'. The court held that sending the proceeds of licenced trading back by a Royal Navy ship was no breach of the monopoly on trade, and the transaction was lawful. Foulerton was liable for the failure to deliver the missing dollars.[37] He had learned the hard way that there is no such thing as easy money at sea.

34 *The Naval Chronicle* (1801), vol. 6, p. 320. The enterprise was part of a prize-taking spree of 33 prizes taken by Cochrane while in the *Speedy*.

35 TNA, ADM 51/2170.

36 In this instance Heath, Chambre and Gibbs JJ.

37 Hodgson v Fullarton (1813) 4 Taunt. 787.

Statute Intervenes

In 1819 Parliament finally brought freight payments under the control of royal proclamations by the Freight for Treasure Act 1819.[38] Proclamations under the Act applied lower rates of commission to carriage of Crown treasure than to treasure of other parties, and a higher rate of commission was paid for non-Crown treasure in war than in peace. In all cases, the further the carriage the higher the rate payable. From July 1819 the rates ranged from ¾ per cent to 1 per cent for Crown treasure and 1½ per cent to 3 per cent for private treasure.[39] The stipulated terms for the bill of lading limited any liability to three quarters of any loss or damage. Any other arrangements were decreed to be void. The captain of a ship took three quarters of the freight where there was no flag-officer. The remaining quarter went to the Greenwich Hospital. Where the ship was under the command of a flag-officer, they received a quarter of the freight so long as they signed a written engagement in their own ship's order book undertaking to share the risk of an order for payment for loss or damage. Where there were two flag-officers on station, they shared the flag-quarter two thirds/one third in favour of the commanding officer. If there were more flag-officers, the commander took one half of the quarter, and the others shared the remaining sum equally. If the cargo was transhipped between two or more vessels during the voyage, the freight was apportioned between them.

By 1914 the government had finally had enough of paying both for the Royal Navy and for its officers to carry treasure in their ships. An order-in-council of 26 October 1914 did away with payments of freight to officers. Although the Royal Navy received £1,753,150 in freight during the 1914–18 war, none of it was paid to the officers involved. The Greenwich Hospital received £15,500 and the remainder went to pay for the Royal Navy.[40] The Freight for Treasure Act 1819 was finally abolished entirely by the Naval Discipline Act 1957.

Gun and Head Money

In addition to prize money, the officers and crew of Royal Navy ships of war and privateers were paid head money where they captured, sunk, burnt or

[38] Geo. III c. 25.

[39] Order-in-council 12 July 1819, *London Gazette*, 3 August 1819, issue 17500, pp. 1358–60.

[40] Hansard, 3 March 1920.

otherwise destroyed enemy state ships of war or privateers. The payments were made by the treasurer of the navy under statute and were calculated by the number of men living on board any destroyed ship at the beginning of the attack or engagement. Before head money was introduced, gun money was paid on the number of guns carried by ships destroyed in combat under provisions introduced during the interregnum as part of the reforms to professionalise the navy and bind it to the commonwealth cause.[41] Gun money had been introduced first as a hasty reform and then followed up with a more considered provision. 'An Act for the encouragement of Officers and Mariners' passed by the Rump Parliament on 22 February 1649, under a month after the execution of Charles I, provided for payment of gun money by the Treasury where commonwealth ships 'shall sink, fire, or in any other ways or means destroy' the admiral, vice-admiral or rear-admiral of 'the Revolted Ships, or other Fleet in hostility against this Commonwealth' at a rate of £20, £16 and £12 respectively for each piece of ordinance.[42] Two days later, having realised that provision had only been made for the destruction of flagships, a further Act provided for gun money at the rate of £10 'for each piece of ordnance above Minion'[43] in each non-flagship destroyed.[44] These and other temporary arrangements were then confirmed in a consolidating Act of 17 April 1649.[45] Gun money was distributed to the captains, officers and mariners of ships acting in the destruction of the enemy ships. Gun money was not paid under these Acts for the capture of ships, which was rewarded by prize money alone. The payment of gun money continued after the interregnum but was extended to include captured ships. The Trade with France Act of William and Mary in 1692[46] provided a bounty of £10 for each gun on the taking or destroying of any enemy man of war, whether naval or privateer.

Queen Anne's Cruizers and Convoys Act of 1708 did away with gun money, but awarded the whole proceeds of prizes to the captors and introduced head money for captured ships, but not those destroyed, at a rate of £5 per head for every man living on board the captured ship at the beginning of the engagement.[47] Referred to sometimes rather floridly as 'blood money', the bounty was paid whether the enemy sailors were killed, injured

41 Capp, *Cromwell's Navy*, p. 57.

42 Firth and Rait (eds), *Acts and Ordinances of the Interregnum 1642–1660*, vol. II, p. 10.

43 A small cannon of 3-inch bore and 5 lb shot that was principally used as an anti-personnel weapon but remained in use as quarterdeck armament until 1716.

44 Firth and Rait (eds), *Acts and Ordinances of the Interregnum 1642–1660*, vol. 2, p. 18.

45 Ibid., p. 72.

46 & 5 Will. And Mary c. 25, Robinson, *Collectanea Maritima*, p. 193.

47 Annae c. 13, s. 8.

or survived unharmed. Although there was no need for blood to be spilled, there had to be an 'engagement', i.e. combat.

Head money continued in the wars between 1793 and 1815. The Prize Act 1793[48] allowed a payment of £5 per head. It was payable where ships were captured ('taken') **or** destroyed. As before, the payment was made on each head, whether they survived the engagement or not. Where there were survivors, the number of men had to be proved by the oaths of three or more of the chief officers of the enemy ship, or of those who had survived if less than three. Head money was only payable on commissioned ships of the enemy, be they naval ships or privateers. Dutch armed transports and a Spanish armed packet were held not to qualify as they did not hold commissions as ships of war.[49] Where an enemy ship was captured while in commission as a privateer but then recaptured and sent in with a salvage crew, she was held still to be a commissioned ship of war.[50] Combat could include forcing a fleeing enemy ship onto the shore, but the destruction had to be complete so that the ship was lost to the enemy. Even where damage from the grounding and attempts to set fire to the ship meant that the French broke up the stranded vessel, a claim for head money was refused.[51]

Head money was distributed among officers and crew in accordance with the rules for prize money. Thus, it resembled prize money, but the courts took a different, and more restrictive, approach when assessing those who were entitled. It was regarded as more of a 'reward for real and active service, and for meritorious personal exertion' and thus only those ships which had brought about the destruction of the enemy were entitled.[52]

Whereas another naval ship being 'in sight' at the time would be presumed to have played a part in a capture for the purposes of prize money, the same did not apply to claims for head money from a capture or destruction. Entitlement to head money was held to apply only to those ships who were actually engaged with the captured ships in the cases of the *Superb* in 1710, the *Thoulouse* in 1715 and the *Dange* in 1761, precedents followed strictly in later cases.[53] As Sir William Scott said, 'It is not even an honest and anxious endeavour to share in the peril that shall bring the parties within the extent of the beneficial title, if the endeavour does not bring them within the capacity for actually sharing in that peril.'[54] Combat on

48 Geo. III c. 66 s. 40.
49 Several Dutch Schyts (1814) 6 Rob. 48.
50 The Matilda, 1 Dods. 367.
51 La Clorinde (1814) 1 Dods. 436; L'Elise (1814) 1 Dods. 442.
52 Ville de Varsovie (1818) 2 Dods. 301, 302.
53 Quoted in La Clorinde (1814) 1 Dods. 436, 438.
54 Ville de Varsovie (1818) 2 Dods. 301, 303.

its own did not suffice; the combat had to lead to capture or destruction. In a claim arising from the capture of the ship of war *La Clorinde, HMS Eurotas* had fought a bloody engagement with *La Clorinde* ending with both being dis-masted and incapacitated. They stood off from each other overnight, during which time *Eurotas* raised a jury rig ready to give chase in the morning. Before she could re-engage, however, *HMS Dryad*, which had come in sight at dawn, came up on the enemy and fired a few shots before accepting the surrender of *La Clorinde* and taking possession of her. *Eurotas* claimed to be entitled to the head money to the exclusion of *Dryad* on the basis that it was her combat that produced the damage that led to the surrender. She failed, however, as *La Clorinde* had survived to fight again, albeit in a severely weakened state that could not resist the fresh assault of *Dryad*. *Eurotas* was entitled to head money as a contributor to the capture, but shared with *Dryad*, which had completed the process albeit with a less costly contribution.[55]

The concept of head money was adopted when Parliament finally acted to restrain the slave trade by the Abolition Act of 1807.[56] Captors of ships condemned as slavers received the proceeds of sale of the condemned ship but also earned head money. Liberated slaves attracted head money of £20 for a man, £15 for a woman and £5 for a child of 14 or less. The rates doubled if they were on a ship seized as a prize of war.[57] The total sums paid fluctuated; £17,090 in 1810, £36,620 in 1812 and £12,269 in 1816. Despite the fact that at times the amounts awarded did not cover the costs of the legal process, in 1817 the payments were reduced to £10 per slave.[58] Even at that rate there was a drain on the Treasury, and in the 1830s under William IV the rate was reduced further to £5 per slave, in line with the head money awarded for enemy crews since Queen Anne.[59]

Head money was also used to encourage the Royal Navy to combat piracy at sea during the nineteenth century. The Piratical Ships Act 1825 provided for head money to be paid to the officers and crew of naval ships present at the 'actual taking, sinking, burning or otherwise destroying' of a pirate ship after 1 January 1820.[60] A sum of £5 was paid for every live crewman proved to be on board the pirate ship at the start of the action. The payment was increased to £20 per head for each pirate taken and secured or killed. The money was distributed as for prize money, and paid out by the Treasurer

55 La Clorinde (1814) 1 Dods. 436.
56 Geo. III c. 44.
57 Grindal, *Opposing the Slavers*, pp. 108–9.
58 Ibid., p. 203.
59 Ibid., p. 371.
60 Geo. IV c. 49.

to the navy, although it could be claimed at the out-ports. No prior adjudication by a court was required before payment could be claimed, which led to liberal local interpretations of what amounted to piracy.[61] As a result, the Piracy Act 1850 brought the determination of entitlement to head money for pirates under the jurisdiction of the Admiralty Court.[62]

Like prize law, head money continued into the twentieth century. It was expressly continued in S. 42 of the Naval Prize Act 1864, which was given effect in the First World War by an order-in-council of 2 March 1915. The rate remained at £5 per head despite 200 years of inflation. As a result, the amounts when distributed among those entitled were sometimes quite small. Nevertheless, the law reports contain a number of claims made on behalf of ships' crews involved in action. They include claims for depth-charged U-boats where there was proof of destruction.[63] Assumptions made about the destruction of U-boats allowed head money to be paid, though subsequent research has shown that the assessments of the Admiralty's Anti U-boat Division at the end of the First World War enjoyed only 48 per cent accuracy.[64] Where four German mine sweepers were destroyed by a squadron of 15 Royal Navy ships, the total award of £535 had to stretch among all the officers and crew involved. The Admiralty Court was told that the admiral in charge of the squadron would forgo his share in favour of the officers and men on whose behalf he had brought the claim.[65] In the Battle of Jutland in 1916, 151 Royal Navy ships fought the German fleet, and 11 enemy ships were recorded as destroyed. Given the difficulty in showing whose action had brought about the destruction of any particular enemy ship, the Grand Fleet agreed to treat the battle as a joint and common enterprise, an approach that was approved by the Admiralty Court in 1920 when Admirals Viscount Jellicoe and Earl Beatty applied for head money from the battle. Based on a calculation of 4,537 men on the destroyed German ships, a sum of £22,685 was awarded. Whatever the controversy surrounding the battle and public expectation of a result to rival Trafalgar, the post-war pride of the Admiralty Court was clear, with the judge, Sir Henry Duke, declaring that 'the record of these proceedings will be one of the most cherished documents in the archives of this Court.'[66]

61 Benton and Ford, *Rage for Order*, pp. 131–45.

62 & 14 Vict. C. 26.

63 'U. 61' [1921] 7 LLR 229.

64 Innes McCartney, 'The Archaeology of First World War U-Boat Losses in the English Channel and Its Impact on the Historical Record', *MM* 105 (2019), pp. 183–201.

65 [1921] 7 LLR 228.

66 In the matter of the Battle of Jutland [1920] P. 408.

Booty Distinguished

Prize money is sometimes confused with 'booty'. If ships, cargo, or any other assets of the enemy, were seized by land forces, or by conjoint expeditions of sea and land forces, they were not covered by the distribution provisions of the prize acts and proclamations. Although the Admiralty Court had jurisdiction to condemn such captures as prize to His Majesty (rather than the captor), it was reserved to the king to distribute as he saw fit by royal warrant.[67] Strictly it was such assets that were properly described as 'booty'.[68] The Admiralty Court had no jurisdiction over property captured on land by land forces exclusively until the Admiralty Court Act 1840.[69] In practice the share that the king allocated to the navy was distributed in line with the distribution of prize money, but the entitlement arose under the specific royal warrant for the expedition, rather than the prize acts and proclamations. Such warrants might be given in advance of a planned operation, but if there was no advance provision then the commanders-in-chief of the navy and the army forces involved in the captures could agree a division in writing and, if confirmed by the king, it became binding on all concerned.[70] Prizes taken during a voyage out to a joint operation against a land fortress belonged to the naval captors and no share went to the army.[71]

Britain was not alone in allowing its navy to earn prize money and freight. The next chapter considers how the United States of America adapted the British rules to its own use.

67 Prize Act 1793 s. 3.

68 Per Sir William Scott, Genoa and its Dependencies, Spezzia, Savonna, and other towns (1820) 2 Dods. 444.

69 3&4 Vic. C.65 s. 22, Banda and Kirwee Booty, 1866.

70 Prize Act 1793 s. 4.

71 Prize Act 1793 s. 5.

9.
Prize Money in the United States of America: The Birth of a Nation

Rules for the distribution of prize money from prizes captured on behalf of the United Colonies that formed the United States of America pre-dated the Declaration of Independence in 1776. They even pre-dated the resolution of the Continental Congress of 13 October 1775 that is recognised by the US navy as establishing a Continental Navy.[1] How those rules were implemented and changed sheds light on the birth of a nation.

The Continental Navy

Realising the need for a naval force, George Washington issued his first orders for a ship of the Continental Navy on 2 September 1775. Captain Nicholson Broughton was ordered to take command of the schooner *Hannah*, which has gone down in history as the first ship of the US navy.[2] News that two 'north country built brigs' had sailed from England in August loaded with arms, powder and other stores for Quebec without a convoy prompted the Continental Congress to resolve on 5 October 1775 that they should be intercepted by Washington's naval force to secure the cargo for the Continental Army. In doing so it resolved that, to encourage success in the enterprise, 'on this occasion, that the master, officers and seamen, shall be entitled to one half of the value of the prizes by them taken, the wages they receive from the respective colonies notwithstanding.' John Hancock, the President of the Continental Congress, wrote to George Washington the same day telling him of the congressional authority to send two ships to intercept the British brigs.[3] The letter expressly told Washington of the entitlement to one half of the value of prizes.

1 *Journals of the Continental Congress*, 1774–89, 13 October 1775, p. 294.
2 NDAR, vol. 1, pt 8, pp. 1287–9.
3 NDAR, vol. 2, p. 311.

Three days later, on 8 October 1775, at his headquarters at Cambridge, Massachusetts, Washington issued orders to Captain Sion Martingale to command the armed brig *Washington*.[4] *Washington*, fitted out and equipped at the Continental expense, was armed with six six-pounders, four four-pounders and ten swivel-guns and carried a crew of 74. She had originally been intended to be a schooner by the name of *Eagle*, and the orders were originally drafted with those details included. In fact, however, the vessel was rigged as a brig and named *Washington*, and the orders were amended accordingly.

Neither of the orders issued to Broughton or Martingale contained the encouragement of half the value of prizes captured, however. The instructions to both were to 'cruize against such Vessels as may be found on the High Seas or elsewhere bound inward or outward to or from Boston in the service of the Ministerial Army and to take and seize all such Vessels laden with Soldiers, Arms, Ammunition or Provisions for or from said Army or which you shall have good reason to suspect are in such service'. The 'design of this enterprize' was 'to intercept the supplies of the Enemy' and accordingly they were 'particularly charged to avoid any engagement with any armed vessel of the Enemy, tho' you may be equal in strength, or have some small advantage'. They were also 'to be extremely careful and frugal of your Ammunition; by no means to waste any of it in any salutes or for any purpose but what is absolutely necessary'.

Broughton and Martingale both held commissions in the Continental Army, but their instructions included a provision that in addition to their army pay the officers and crew of their ships were granted a one third share of any cargo on board the vessels taken and brought into port, rather than the one half that Congress had approved. Even this prize share was not as generous as might first appear. Not only were any captured vessels and their 'apparel' excluded from the grant of the one third share, but so were military and naval stores, which were expressly reserved for public use. As the authority to capture vessels at all was specifically aimed at vessels with such reserved stores, any prize share for the crew would in practice be necessarily limited. Even if there were items of cargo that were not excluded, two thirds of the value was to go to the continental authority who had fitted out and equipped the ship, and who needed funds for the fight against the

[4] NDAR, vol. 2, pt 3, pp. 354–5. The instructions were captured with the *Washington* and sent to the Admiralty by Admiral Graves, TNA, ADM1/484, and are recited in 'The Private Papers of John, Earl of Sandwich, First Lord of the Admiralty 1775–1782' (NRS) and D. Bonner Smith, 'The Capture of the Washington', *MM* 20:4 (1934), pp. 420–5.

British. Of such one third share as there might be, the distribution among the officers and crew was to be as follows:

Captain	6 shares
1st Lieutenant	5 shares
2nd Lieutenant	4 shares
Surgeon[5]	4 shares
Master	3 shares
Steward	2 shares
Mate	1½ shares
Gunner	1½ shares
Boatswain	1½ shares
Gunner's Mate and Serjeant	1½ shares
Privates	1 share each

Thus, out of a total of 94½ shares the individual sailors would get one share each and the captain would get six shares. All the officers and petty officers between them would get about one third of the available prize money and the 'privates', i.e. the ordinary sailors, would account for about two thirds of the total between them.

This was a more egalitarian distribution than in the Royal Navy. In 1775 Parliament reacted to the American rebellion by prohibiting trade with the rebellious colonies.[6] Ships found trading in breach of the prohibition were

[5] The surgeon was named in the orders for the *Washington*, but not for the *Hannah*. Otherwise, the orders were the same.

[6] The colonies of New Hampshire, Massachusetts Bay, Rhode Island, Connecticut, New York, New Jersey, Pennsylvania, the Three Lower Counties on Delaware, Maryland, Virginia, North Carolina, South Carolina and Georgia.

to be forfeit to the Crown 'as if the same were the ships and effects of Open Enemies' and subject to condemnation as prizes in the Admiralty Court. A royal proclamation of 22 December 1775 provided for the distribution of prize money from ships captured during the American rebellion.[7] In line with the pattern of distribution adopted by the British during the eighteenth century, three eighths went to the captain and flag-officers, an eighth to the other officers, an eighth to the warrant officers, an eighth to the petty officers and everyone else shared the remaining quarter.

By comparison, therefore, the senior officers in the Royal Navy received a much greater share of the spoils than their American counterparts. An American captain's share was just over 6 per cent of the prize fund, only 2 per cent of the total value of cargo eligible to be treated as a prize. That compared with a Royal Navy captain's share of a quarter of the total value of the prize ship and its cargo, even after he had accounted for the share that was taken by the flag-officers. Instead of the two thirds share that the ordinary American crewmen shared between them, their counterparts in the Royal Navy shared a mere quarter. The significant difference in the proportion of the prize proceeds that went to the ship as a whole, however, meant that the ordinary sailors in the Royal Navy were still better off. Between them they received nine thirty-sixths (9/36ths, or 25 per cent) of the proceeds, whereas their US counterparts received only eight thirty-sixths (8/36ths, or 22.5 per cent). Whilst the senior officers received more of the proceeds in the Royal Navy, they did so at the expense of the state, which granted it to them, rather than the lower decks when compared with comparable ships of the early American navy. In larger ships of the line where there was a higher ratio of ordinary sailors the comparison becomes harder, but the early US navy had no such ships.

A more egalitarian distribution of prize money as between the officers and crew was no substitute for adequate ships. On 5 December 1775 *Washington* was captured off Cape Ann, near Boston, by *HMS Fowey* under Captain George Montagu after a two-and-a-half-hour chase, the first American naval ship captured by the Royal Navy. Being short of vessels, Admiral Graves at first intended to take her into the king's service, but a survey condemned her as unseaworthy. In the words of the carpenter who inspected her, she was 'totally unserviceable … unfit for war … not fit for sea'.[8] Graves thought this an understatement, informing the Admiralty that 'she exceeds their description of her badness'.[9] The 'thin veneer of American sea power' at the start of

7 *London Gazette*, December 1775, No. 11626, p. 1.

8 NDAR, vol. 3, 112n.

9 Bonner Smith, 'The Capture of the Washington'.

the War of Independence was thus exposed to the British.[10] Seventy officers and men were sent to England as prisoners. There the destitute and nearly naked sailors were clothed and taken into the Royal Navy. The remaining four sailors, all Englishmen, stayed in America. Two were entered on the books of *Fowey* and the other two faced a court-martial as deserters from *HMS Glasgow* and *HMS Swan*.

Stung by the 'lawless manner, without even the semblance of just authority' in which the Royal Navy had seized American shipping, the Continental Congress authorised further ships to retaliate against British supplies.[11] When they came to consider the regulation of their new navy (as well as captures by privateers and colonial vessels) in debates during November 1775, they repeated the egalitarian distribution between the officers and crew that George Washington had provided for and also continued the idea of sharing the spoils where the United Colonies had paid the outlay for the voyage.[12] Privateers took the whole benefit of their prizes and distributed the proceeds according to the agreements between their owners and their crew. Where a merchant prize was captured by a vessel fitted out at the expense of any individual colony, or at the expense of the United Colonies, then two thirds of the proceeds went to the colony or the United Colonies as appropriate, and one third went to the captors. Where a ship of war was captured, however, the captors were entitled to one half of the value rather than one third. Thus was introduced the concept of graded levels of prize entitlement for the officers and crew dependent upon the supposed effort required in making a capture. This was a feature introduced by the Americans but not adopted by the British. As with the British system, the prize distribution was after deduction of the charges of condemnation.

The New Republic

The new American navy did not distinguish itself during the War of Independence and once independence was obtained, the navy was disbanded. The new republic distrusted the idea of a permanent navy. A navy did not fit easily with the military ideas of the new republic that its defence should be entrusted to the people, serving in local militias for their own defence. Privateers fitted the model, but a federal navy did not. Inland Americans

10 Willis, *The Struggle for Sea Power*, p. 101.

11 *Journals of the Continental Congress*, 1774–89, 25 November 1775, p. 372.

12 Ibid., p. 375 (as modified on 19 December 1775), affirmed 28 November 1775, p. 386.

who were not immediately dependent on sea-borne trade distrusted the idea of spending money that would largely benefit seaboard merchants. Although federalists favoured a strong central government, including a centralised navy, there were many voices who distrusted the very idea of the federal expense of a navy. Such expense might cripple the new country with its cost, and a large navy would create the risk of it providing work for itself by encouraging involvement in foreign wars.[13] It is easy to dismiss such concerns as continental isolationism and the adolescent views of an immature state. It had its origins, however, in the very causes of the American bid for independence. A century of European wars had created what Thomas Paine described in *Rights of Man* as a 'perpetual system of war and expense' that benefited monarchs and their elites but was fought and paid for by the common man.[14]

Among the more federalist-minded politicians emerging in the new republic was a young admiralty lawyer, John Adams. He was a keen navalist and took an interest in the development of a US navy from its early days in the Continental Congress through his time as second president in succession to Washington, and beyond.[15] Indeed, Adams as president kept up an active correspondence with his navy secretary, Benjamin Stoddert, about the operational deployment of the US navy, but would later complain that 'When in 1797, 8 and 9 I promoted the Fortification of our Seaports, the purchase of Navy yards, the Building a Navy etc ... I think I was more prudent than those whom opposed me: though my popularity was Sacrificed to it, and my enemies rose to power by their imprudent opposition.'[16] For all his rebellious fervour against the British in America, Adams considered that the success of British militarism was worthy of importing into the new republic. He would not have been the first or last lawyer to cast round for a precedent to copy when faced with a drafting exercise, but in his case his respect for precedent went deeper. When considering with Jefferson what their committee, formed to consider the articles of war to govern naval discipline, should report to congress in 1776 Adams noted:

13 N. R. Parrillo, *Against the Profit Motive* (Yale, 2013), pp. 316–18.

14 Colley, *The Gun, the Ship & the Pen*, p. 95.

15 Christopher McKee, *A Gentlemanly and Honorable Profession* (Annapolis, 1991), pp. 5–6.

16 Letter John Adams to Benjamin Rush, 1 September 1807, http://founders.archives/documents/Adams/99-02-5211.

> There was extant, I observed, one system of Articles of War which had carried two empires to the head of mankind. The Roman and the British; for the Articles of War are only a literal translation of the Roman. It would be vain for us to seek our own invention or the records of warlike nations [for] a more complete system of military discipline. I was, therefore, for reporting the British Articles of War totidem verbis ...[17]

Even radicals recognised the benefits that could arise from building on the language of the past. Thomas Paine, the radical espouser of the Rights of Man and their expression in the constitution of government structures, was 'not fond of quoting [the] old remains of former arrogance', but even he could see that 'we must begin somewhere ... and any rule which can be agreed on is better than none.'[18]

Although there is disagreement as to the precise sources of the eventual Articles of War submitted to the Continental Congress, it is clear that they came from various versions of the British Articles of War between 1661 and 1772 and Adams reminded his colleagues of the desperate position that they faced and that 'nothing short of Roman and British discipline can save us.'[19]

During the Continental Congress, however, there had been little time to do more than follow the lead that Washington's instructions had given on the distribution of prize money. As Adams wrote to one correspondent while the navy debates were ongoing:

> I am really engaged in constant business from seven to ten in the morning in committee, from ten to four in Congress, and from six to ten again in committee. Our assembly is scarcely numerous enough for the business; everybody is engaged, all day in Congress, and all the morning and evening in committees.[20]

The disbanding of the Continental Navy by 1785, however, gave the opportunity to re-design the navy when the need for it next arose. By then Adams was president.

17 J. E. Valle, *Rocks and Shoals* (Annapolis, 1980), pp. 40–1. Diary of John Adams, vol. 3, Monday 19 August 1776, Founding Families: Digital Editions of the Winthrops and the Adamses, ed. C. James Taylor (Boston: Massachusetts Historical Society, 2017), www.masshist.org/apde2/.

18 Thomas Paine, *Public Good* (1780), p. 24; Colley, *The Gun, the Ship & the Pen*, p. 101.

19 Valle, *Rocks and Shoals*, p. 41.

20 John Adams to Mrs Mercy Warren, 25 November 1775, *Journals of the Continental Congress*, 1774–89, p. 376 n1.

The Quasi-War: Birth of the US Navy

The United States of America had been forged in war against Britain. They had succeeded in part due to the assistance of the French and their navy. The first naval war to be fought by the US, however, would be an undeclared war against their old allies, the French. It has become known as the Quasi-War of 1798–1801. In 1794 Congress authorised the building of six frigates to protect US shipping against the depredations of the corsairs of Algiers.[21] The Algerine crisis was resolved, however, by negotiation in 1796. The authority of Congress to build six frigates expired with the coming of peace and the construction of all but three of the frigates was cancelled.[22] The US made cash payments and gifts to Algiers, including a 36-gun frigate, the *Crescent*, built for the purpose by James Hackett in Portsmouth and launched on 29 June 1797.[23] In return for a settlement of almost a million dollars and the promise of annual tribute, 85 American hostages were released and promises of the safety of US shipping in the Mediterranean were made.[24]

The outbreak of war between Britain and France in 1793 placed the young US republic in a difficult position. Trade with Britain and the Caribbean was crucial to the US. It continued after independence despite the efforts of enthusiastic young British naval captains like Nelson and Collingwood to curb the trade by enforcing the Navigation Act provisions that banned US ships from carrying trade with Britain and her remaining colonies now that the US were no longer British colonies.[25] The US tried to maintain a trading neutrality that would keep the seas open to her ships, but many in the US sympathised with the revolution against the French monarchy and some were grateful for the past support of the French navy. Like all small and militarily weak nations, US neutrality became squeezed between the might of the powerful belligerents at war with each other. The Jay Treaty between the US and Britain in 1795 resolved a number of issues left over from the Treaty of Paris in 1783, which had ended the War of Independence. It also provided for trade between the US and Britain, which pushed the increasingly violent revolutionaries in the French Directory in favour of a belligerent approach towards the US. Since 1778 a Treaty of Amity and Commerce had provided for respect for free trade between the US and the

21 Act of 27 March 1794, Homans, *Laws of the United States, in Relation to the Navy and Marine Corps*, p. 31.

22 Act of 20 April 1796, Homans, *Laws of the United States*, p. 33.

23 NDQW, vol. 1, p. 6.

24 I. W. Toll, *Six Frigates* (New York, 2008), pp. 65, 165–6.

25 Knight, *The Pursuit of Victory*, pp. 91–5.

French. A decree of the Directory of 2 July 1796, however, declared that France would treat neutrals in the same manner that they allowed Britain to treat them, which did little to ease tensions at sea. When John Adams defeated the Francophile Thomas Jefferson in the presidential election in 1796 the French responded to his inauguration with a decree of 2 March 1797 renouncing the free trade principle that goods carried in neutral ships were neutral goods. The practical effect was that US ships and cargoes were at risk of seizure by French ships of war and privateers. An undeclared commerce war had started. The US armed itself for a naval war while at the same time negotiating for peace. A three-man diplomatic mission went to Paris, but a coup in France on 4 September 1797 swept the last of those in favour of a negotiated settlement with America from power. A further French decree of 18 January 1798 proclaimed that they would consider any ship carrying British goods a valid prize. The diplomatic mission was then rebuffed in an ignominious manner that became known as the XYZ Affair, in which a bribe of $220,000 was demanded by the French negotiator before talks could even begin. US trade was at risk. In 1797, 300 US ships were lost to French prize captures, 6 per cent of its foreign trade vessels. Diplomatic moves had failed. It was time for a US navy.[26]

Until 1798 there was no separate US Navy Department. Such naval matters as there were had been overseen by the War Department. With the advent of a naval conflict the War Department struggled to cope with its burden. On 1 July 1797 Congress authorised the three frigates that had been built, the *United States*, *Constitution* and *Constellation*, to be manned and employed.[27] In the absence of any other body of rules readily available to regulate this new navy, section 8 of the Act of Congress expressly adopted the rules that had been approved by Congress back in November 1775. Further vessels were authorised on 27 April 1798.[28] As yet, however, there was no executive body up to the task of managing them. On 30 April 1798 John Adams, as president, signed an Act to establish the Department of the Navy.[29] The first Secretary of the Navy was Benjamin Stoddert, appointed by Adams in May 1798. Stoddert was a Maryland merchant who had fought, and been wounded, at the Battle of Brandywine during the War of Independence. He would prove to be an effective and conscientious administrator of the new navy.[30] He was not a lawyer, but he sat in the cabinet of a somewhat fastidious lawyer president – a president, furthermore, who had a keen

[26] M. A. Palmer, *Stoddert's War* (Annapolis, 2000), pp. 3–6.

[27] Homans, *Laws of the United States*, p. 34.

[28] Ibid., p. 37.

[29] Ibid.

[30] Palmer, *Stoddert's War*, pp. 7–11.

interest in the navy, the drafting of its regulations and issues relating to prize money. Between March and November 1777 Adams had sat as a member of the Congressional committee dealing with appeals in prize claims that styled itself along British lines as the Court of Commissioners of Appeals for the American States. As a court claiming supra-state jurisdiction it has been claimed as the forebear of the US Supreme Court, and it arose because of prize money. Indeed, Adams' involvement in prize money continued after his time on the court, when he became involved on behalf of an old client in a complicated prize dispute concerning a ship owned by an American that had been seized by a rebel privateer as an enemy British ship.[31]

The fingerprints of both Adams and Stoddert can be detected on the Navy Acts that emerged in 1799 and 1800, and which governed the regulation of the US navy for the next century and a half.[32] Although Adams favoured a permanent US navy he did so primarily as a permanent force to protect US commerce. Stoddert was a fellow navalist, but he went further and saw a navy as not just about protecting commerce but also acting as a deterrent to European naval states and increasing American prestige with the European powers.[33] It was this last function that the anti-navalists feared most, as they were concerned that it might become self-fulfilling and involve the US in European affairs they could otherwise avoid.

Whereas the British Parliament left the distribution of prize money to be determined by the executive through orders-in-council, the US treated it as a matter to be decided by Congress and incorporated expressly into an Act of Congress. Adams and Stoddert aspired to a comprehensive Act of Congress providing central, Congressional authority for the distribution of prize money. Before they could get to their first attempt in the Navy Act of 1799, however, events intervened in the form of the undeclared naval conflict with France. It was a conflict that provided an opportunity to put in place a permanent structure for a navy in response to increased support for naval action that suppressed the anti-navalist objections.

Although the US did not declare war against France, Congress authorised military action against French ships threatening US trade.[34] The provisions

31 Penhallow v The Lusanna: 1777–95, Editorial Note, Founders Online, US National Archives,https:/founders.archives.gov./documents/Adams/05-02-02-0009-0001-0001.

32 The naval Articles of War contained in the Acts remained in force with few modifications until replaced by the US Uniform Code of Military Justice in 1950. Valle, *Rocks and Shoals*, p. 44.

33 Craig L. Symonds, *Navalists and Antinavalists* (Newark, 1980), pp. 72–3.

34 The captain of a French privateer taken by a US ship in 1798 'seemed astonished when he went on board of Capt. Decatur's sloop of war, at his being taken by an American vessel, and said he knew of no war between the two republics', Report in *Columbian Centinel* newspaper, Boston, 14 July 1and 8 August 1798, NDQW, vol. III, p. 176.

dribbled out during the summer of 1798. On 28 May 1798 a Congressional resolution noted that 'armed vessels sailing under authority or pretence of authority from the Republic of France, have committed depredations of the commerce of the United States, and have recently captured the vessels and property of citizens thereof, on and near the coasts, in violation of the law of nations, and treaties between the United States and the French nation.' As a result Congress authorised the president to 'instruct and direct the commanders of the armed vessels belonging to the United States to seize, take and bring into any port of the United States, to be proceeded against according to the laws of nations, any such armed vessel which shall have committed or which shall be found hovering on the coasts of the United States, for the purpose of committing depredations on the vessels belonging to the citizens thereof.' On the same day Adams issued instructions to commanders of US armed vessels in just such terms.[35]

On 25 June 1798 Congress authorised any US merchant ships to defend themselves against, and to capture, hostile ships under French colours and the president was authorised to regulate the actions of armed US merchant ships, harnessing private enterprise to the US war effort.

On 28 June 1798 Congress turned its attention to what was to happen to French vessels brought into US ports under the provisions it had just introduced. District courts where the vessels were brought into the US were authorised to condemn the vessels as prizes, or to restore them to their US owners on payment of salvage if they had been recaptured from the French. The Act extended the differential prize distribution depending on the nature of the capture and its deemed difficulty. If a prize was of superior or equal force to the public armed vessel of the US which captured it, the captors took the whole value of the prize. If it was of inferior force, the captors received one half and the United States one half.[36] No definition of superior or inferior force was set out in the Act.

On 9 July 1798 Congress extended the area of conflict to take in 'any armed French vessel, which shall be found within the jurisdictional limits of the United States, or elsewhere on the high seas.'[37] In other words, any French vessel that was not in the territorial waters of another state was now fair game. The following day the president gave the necessary instructions to US navy commanders.[38] The scene was set for the US navy to test itself against the French navy, one of the great European naval powers. By the

[35] For the resolution and the instruction see NDQW, vol. III, pp. 87–8.

[36] Homans, *Laws of the United States*, p. 40.

[37] NDQW, vol. III, p. 181.

[38] Ibid., p. 187.

time the efforts of the US navy came to court in 1799, however, the first of the Stoddert/Adams attempts at a comprehensive Act for the regulation of the navy had been passed.

Hostilities with the French created a belated swell of patriotic naval fervour in Congress. On 25 February 1799 Congress passed three Acts which provided for the expansion of the navy. It did so despite lengthy debate about the wisdom of naval expansion and sustained objection from the anti-navalists, who still regarded a large, permanent navy as a threat to the future of the US and an expense that it could not afford and would be unwise to attempt.[39] Nevertheless, Congress passed an Act for the Augmentation of the Navy, which provided for six 74-gun ships of the line to be built, an Act authorising the establishment of two naval docks at a cost of $50,000 and an Act providing for $200,000 to be spent on acquiring timber lands to provide timber for future naval construction.[40] The sum authorised for the construction of the 74-gun ships was $1,000,000, but even that was less than the expected cost of construction. In fact, the Act did not result in the ships being built, and it would have taken years and a much larger budget to build and man them in any event.[41] Of more immediate use was a sum of $35,000 that the president was authorised to spend on acquiring smaller ships in the meantime.

Although the 74-gun ships would not be built for many a year, on 2 March 1799 Congress passed an Act for the government of the navy of the United States that would attempt to put in place a permanent structure for a fleet in being. Its provisions included regulation of prize distribution under Congressional authority. Although the process of creating a system of governance for the navy would have lasting effect, the Navy Act passed by Congress in March 1799 would itself prove to be a temporary provision, replaced by a new Act only a year later. It remains of considerable interest, however, and in 1841 when Benjamin Homans, the former chief clerk to the Navy Department, produced a compilation of the laws of the United States Navy and Marine Corps published by authority of the Navy Department, he included the Act of 1799, along with that of 1800.[42]

Section 5 of the 1799 Act attempted to introduce the idea that 'captured national ships or vessels of war shall be the property of the United States'. Property in such ships was thus vested in the United States. Where a ship was captured by the Royal Navy, by comparison, it became the property of

39 *Annals of Congress*, 5th Congress, 3rd Session, 8 February 1799, pp. 2832–54.

40 Homans, *Laws of the United States*, pp. 46–7.

41 Symonds, *Navalists and Antinavalists*, p. 74.

42 Homans, *Laws of the United States*, p. 47.

the captors following condemnation. If that ship was bought into service by the Royal Navy, it was surveyed and valued and the value thus assessed was paid over to the captors. The Royal Navy thus had an incentive to capture enemy ships of war, even though the price of doing so might be greater than capturing an unarmed merchant ship with a valuable cargo. A similar system had operated with the prize shares previously awarded to US navy ships, but the 1799 Act sought to change that. Instead of a share of the value of the prize, section 13 of the 1799 Act provided for a bounty to be paid to the US captors of any national ship of war that was taken from the enemy and brought into port. The bounty payable depended on the number and weight of cannon mounted on the captured ship and the number of officers and men taken on board:

For each cannon of 24 lbs or above	$200
For each cannon of 18 lbs	$150
For each cannon of 12 lbs	$100
For each cannon of 9 lbs	$75
For each man	$40

Any additional payment of prize money for the capture of a national ship or vessel of war over and above the bounty was left to the discretion of Congress rather than as a matter of right.

The idea of bounty paid on guns or head of enemy crew was not new. During the interregnum after the civil war in England, the Rump Parliament introduced a bounty based on the number of guns on ships destroyed in combat. Under William and Mary this was extended to captured ships. The Cruizers and Convoy Act of Queen Anne in 1708 did away with gun money in favour of head money at a rate of £5 per man. Initially this was for captured ships in addition to prize money. It was later extended to include ships destroyed in combat and head money was still payable in the Royal Navy in 1799 and would remain so into the twentieth century.

The 1799 Act did not remove prize money completely from the US navy. Where a US ship or ships captured a ship that was not a 'national ship or vessel of war', i.e. was a merchant ship or privateer, then prize money was still payable. If the captured ship was of inferior size in men *or* guns, the proceeds were to be divided equally between the United States and the officers and men of the vessel or vessels making the capture. Should they capture a ship of superior force in men or guns, however, the ship became the sole property of the captors and once it was condemned as a prize they were entitled to the entire net proceeds.

The prize share that went to the United States was intended to pay for the half-pay life pension for disabled officers, sailors and marines that was provided for by section 8 of the Act of 1799. This too had been tried before in England during the interregnum. The Acts of the Rump Parliament provided for one half of the prize share from ships of war and one third of the prize share from merchant ships to go to the Treasury 'for the relief of the sick or maimed seamen, and the widows, children and impotent parents of the slain'.[43] Though the money was not expressly hypothecated by the US Act of 1799, it was a form of self-funding of a change from payment by bounty to payment by salary and pension. This reflected a change that was underway in Britain[44] and would also be implemented in America.[45]

By the time that the Act was passed in March 1799, the first capture of a significant French naval ship of war had just occurred.[46] The issue of the prize money payable for her capture would prove an awkward one to resolve. In February 1799 the *USS Constellation* under Captain Thomas Truxton captured the French frigate *L'Insurgente* in the Caribbean. She was brought into Norfolk, Virginia, arriving in May 1799. Arrangements were already being made to bring her into the US navy and in June she was condemned as a prize by the District Court under the Act of 28 June 1798. The capture was made before the Act of 1799 was passed and there was thus no bar to a claim for prize payments for a national ship of war. If *L'Insurgente* was deemed to be of superior force, the crew would receive the entire proceeds. If inferior, they would get one half. Truxton had a rapacious reputation when it came to acquiring money and he contended that he had captured a ship of superior strength. By the time the claim came before the District Court in Norfolk in June 1799 the provisions of the Act of 1799 had been passed, although it did not apply to captures that had occurred before it came into effect. There was now, however, a Congressional provision

43 Firth and Rait (eds), *Acts and Ordinances of the Interregnum 1642–1660*, vol. II, p. 10.

44 John R. Breihan, 'William Pitt and the Commission on Fees 1785–1801', *The Historical Journal* 27:1 (1984), pp. 59–81.

45 Parrillo, *Against the Profit Motive*, pp. 183, 307–58.

46 The schooner *Croyable* that had been captured earlier on 7 July 1798 was a French privateer that had been added to the US fleet the following month as the *USS Retaliation*, Letter from US Navy Secretary Benjamin Stoddert to President John Adams, 3 August 1798, Founders Online, National Archives, http://founders.archives.gov/documents/Adams/99-02-2783.

that defined what amounted to superior force. The French ship had had 409 men on board. Even allowing for the fact that 50 of them were passengers, the number of men was superior to the American ship's 316. The French ship also carried 40 guns against the American's 38. Numerically, the French had enjoyed superiority of guns. The reality was somewhat different, however. *L'Insurgente* was 30 per cent lighter than her captor by tonnage and was armed accordingly. Whilst *L'Insurgente*'s main battery consisted of 12-pounders, *Constellation*'s consisted of 24-pounders.[47] The District Court took sworn evidence from *Constellation*'s first lieutenant, John Rogers, who recited the number of men and guns on each ship and was not questioned further by the court. On this evidence the court ruled that a superior ship had been captured and awarded the entire proceeds to the captors. It has been suggested that the court was misled by Rogers or that there was collusion between the officers and the court. Truxton's local influence was certainly considerable. A fellow captain in Norfolk at the time, Alexander Murray, wrote to Stoddert about Truxton that 'There is one thing Certain, that his Word is Law here, which may not be his fault, as Mankind will sometimes be Blinded in radiance of Glory.'[48] It has even been suggested that Rogers, a future US naval hero, had 'tried to defraud the navy, and to do so in a way that would deprive disabled veterans of their pensions.'[49] The court had, however, simply applied a test that had just been approved by Congress. When Dudley Knox, a retired captain of the US navy in charge of the US Office of Naval Records, assembled his digest of the naval documents related to the Quasi-War in 1935 under the authority of Congress in an initiative supported by President Franklin Roosevelt, he included Stoddert's letters suggesting criticism of the court ruling.[50] Stoddert, however, was in the uncomfortable position of having to deal with a ruling that was entirely consistent with a Congressional provision that had just been passed on his own watch. His frustration is understandable, but the availability of its manifestation to subsequent commentators has clouded subsequent judgements on the propriety of the court proceedings.

L'Insurgente, or *USS Insurgent* as she had now become, was assessed by a panel chaired by navy agent William Pennock and valued at $120,000. Whatever the position in Norfolk, Stoddert was not blinded by the radiance of Truxton's glory. He sought an alternative valuation from Joshua Humpheys, the builder of the US navy's frigates.[51] The 'desktop' valuation

47 Palmer, *Stoddert's War*, p. 134; Toll, *Six Frigates*, p. 123.

48 Toll, *Six Frigates*, p. 123.

49 Ibid.

50 NDQW. See below.

51 NDQW, vol. III, p. 450.

came in at $84,500. Stoddert, who was not convinced by the court ruling as to the superiority of the prize, offered Truxton the full amount of the lower valuation rather than appeal the District Court decision.[52] Truxton accepted.[53] The dispute between the Navy Department, its hero and the courts had proved an uncomfortable one. An executive discretion on prize awards for captured national ships of war would not be an easy prerogative to handle in practice. Within a year it would be gone, along with the attempt to define superiority of force.

The share of prizes and bounty awarded to the officers and crew of capturing ships under the Act of 1799 was to be distributed between them as set by section 6 of the Act:

Captain actually on board at the time	3/20ths
If under the command of a commander-in-chief or commander of a squadron having a captain on board	One of the captain's 3/20ths to such commander
Sea lieutenants and sailing master	2/20ths
Marine officers, surgeon, purser, boatswain, gunner, carpenter, master's mate and chaplain	2/20ths
Midshipmen, surgeon's mates, captain's clerk, clergyman or schoolmaster, boatswain's mates, gunner's mates, carpenter's mates, ship's steward, sailmaker, master-at-arms, armourer and coxswain	3/20ths
Gunner's yeoman, boatswain's yeoman, quartermasters, quarter-gunners, cooper, sailmaker's mates, sergeant of marines, corporal of marines, drummer and fifer, extra petty officers	3/20ths
Seamen, ordinary seamen, marines and boys	7/20ths

The captain's share of the prize money therefore rose from the 3/46ths that applied in the Continental Navy to 3/20ths; still well short of the 3/8ths

52 Ibid., p. 480.

53 Toll, *Six Frigates*, p. 124; Palmer, *Stoddert's War*, p. 134.

that applied in the Royal Navy, but a doubling of his share. For the first time the idea of a flag-officer's share was introduced. The early US navy had no admirals and early attempts to introduce them were rebuffed by Congress, which distrusted the idea of a permanent body of naval heavyweights who might want to pursue a navalist political agenda. It would be the start of the civil war before the US Congress approved the appointment of even rear-admirals, in 1861. The same fate had befallen attempts to build ships of the line, which would have required such a level of capital investment and ongoing revenue expenditure and administration that they had the potential to unbalance the finances of the new republic and distort policy so as to justify their existence and further their own power.[54] The 1799 Act recognised, however, that US ships might act in concert under the overall command of a commodore. It incorporated the same idea of a commodore with a captain under him being a flag-officer as had been applied to the Royal Navy. As with the Royal Navy, the 'flag-officer's' share was set at one third of the captain's entitlement, deducted from his share. Captains sailing under specific orders from the Navy Department were expressly (by section 12 of the 1799 Act) treated as acting separately from any superior officer. As with a Royal Navy captain under orders direct from the Admiralty, therefore, a captain under direct Navy Department orders did not have to account to a flag-officer for one third of his prize share. Section 11 of the Act of 1799 also defined the rights and privileges of 'flag-officers' that in part reflected the provisions in the royal proclamations applicable to the Royal Navy. Thus, 'flag-officers' only received a share of prize money where the capturing ships had been put under their immediate command, and they were not entitled to a share of prizes taken before the capturing ship was put under their command and had acted under their immediate orders. A 'flag-officer' returning from any station where he had command had no share of any prizes taken by ships left on the station after he was out of the limits of the station.

Section 7 of the 1799 Act also set the rates of salvage to be paid where a ship of the US or its allies was recaptured from an enemy. A recapture within 24 hours earned one eighth of the value of the vessel and cargo, within 48 hours one fifth, within 96 hours one third and after 96 hours one half. The US government claimed no part of salvage payments from recaptures. The officers and crew of US navy ships took the whole sum, distributed between them in the same proportions as prize money.[55] The

[54] Parrillo, *Against the Profit Motive*, p. 317.

[55] For this interpretation of section 7 see Benjamin Stoddert's letter to Capt. Samuel Nicholson, 12 June 1799, NDQW, vol. III, p. 330. The matter had been expressly dealt with in section 3 of the Act of 28 June 1798, Homans, *Laws of the United States*, p. 40.

commander still had to submit a full list of officers and men under section 6, article 10 of the Act, however, in order that the agents recovering the salvage payment on behalf of the captors could make the proper payments. Until this provision was made by Congress it had been thought appropriate to limit claims for salvage for the recapture of friendly English ships to the one eighth that English law allowed to English ships.[56] The more generous salvage rates payable in US courts caused complaint from English courts that joint recaptures were being taken to the US for adjudication, rather than being brought before English prize courts. Protestations that English captains should ensure that joint recaptures were brought before English courts, rather than agreeing that a joint-captor American ship could conduct the vessel to the US, stood little chance against the contrary economic argument, however.[57]

1800: A New Navy Act

The Act of 1799 was repealed and replaced by a new Act on 23 April 1800.[58] There is a frustrating lack of evidence of the discussions that led to such a rapid change. United States archivists have dedicated themselves to preserving the evidence of their founding for posterity. Even notes by John Adams about how he grew his cabbages are preserved and made available online. Neither the records of Congressional debates nor the Adams or Stoddert archives allow a glimpse into the reasons for the new Act. It seems likely that the pressures of work of which Adams had complained in 1775 were still present, and that the drafting discussions were not minuted in a form that has survived. The changes that were introduced, however, furthered Adams' agenda of creating an elitist officer corps of gentlemen for the navy.[59] They thus provide their own evidence of the reasons for change.

Adams had been thwarted in his suggestion that the US president should be called 'His Majesty the President', but his belief that titles and status should be the rewards for public service remained.[60] In addition to the requirement that commanders set a good example of 'honor and virtue', the amended Articles of War enacted by Congress required commanders to

56 Capt. Thomas Truxton to Lt Josias Speake, 3 May 1799, NDQW, vol. III, p. 129.
57 The Calypso (1828) 2 Hag. Adm. 209, 217–18.
58 Homans, *Laws of the United States*, p. 59.
59 Valle, *Rocks and Shoals*, p. 43.
60 D. G. McCullough, *John Adams* (New York, 2008), p. 406. Ironically Adams would later criticise his successors as a 'Monarchical, Antirepublican Administration' concealing information from 'Us the people': Letter, John Adams to Benjamin Rush, 1 September 1807, http://founders.archives.gov/documents/Adams/99-02-5211.

set good examples of 'patriotism and subordination.'[61] Not only was divine service to be performed on board twice a day, but it was to be performed 'in a solemn, orderly, and reverent manner' and 'all, or as many of the ship's company as can be spared from duty' were to 'attend at every performance of the worship of Almighty God.'[62] This sat somewhat uncomfortably with the requirement in the First Amendment to the US constitution adopted in 1791 that 'Congress shall make no law respecting the establishment of religion, or the free exercise thereof.'[63] The contrast between the spirit of the Articles of War and that of the First Amendment emphasises that Adams, and Congress, intended the US navy to be a separate world apart from civilian life.

Officers could not be flogged, but under Article 3 officers guilty of scandalous offences were liable to be cashiered or suffer such other punishment as a court-martial may adjudge. By a new Article 30, however, no commanding officer had the power on his own authority to discharge a commissioned or warrant officer, nor could he strike him, nor punish him otherwise than by suspension or confinement. Gone was the previous power in Article 2 for a captain to order forfeiture of two days' pay for an officer. At least in theory, therefore, the disciplining of officers was reserved to court-martial.

Even the common seaman benefited, however, from a particularly lawyerly amendment to Article 3. Sailors who misbehaved by way of profane swearing or drunkenness had been liable to be put in irons until sober *and then* flogged if the captain thought proper. This allowed for the double punishment of confinement in irons and flogging. After 1800 they could be put in irons *or* flogged at the discretion of the captain, but not exceeding 12 lashes, unless a court-martial ordered a more severe punishment.

Prize money distribution after 1800 was tweaked as follows:[64]

Captain	3/20ths
If under the command of a commander-in-chief or commander of a squadron having a captain on board	One of the captain's 3/20ths to such commander

[61] Article 1.

[62] Article 2.

[63] As Herman Melville would later point out in his polemical work *White Jacket*: Herman Melville, *White Jacket, or The World in a Man-of-War* (New York, 1850), Ch. 38.

[64] The Act of 1800, s. 6, Homans, *Laws of the United States*, p. 68.

Sea lieutenants, *captains of marines* and sailing master	2/20ths
Marine *lieutenants*, surgeons, pursers, boatswains, gunners, carpenters, master's mates and chaplains	2/20ths, save that if a ship had a captain but no lieutenant of marines then one third of a 20th was deducted from this class and added to the class above which included the captain of marines
Midshipmen, surgeon's mates, captain's clerk, clergyman or schoolmaster, boatswain's mates, gunner's mates, carpenter's mates, ship's steward, sailmaker, master-at-arms, armourer and coxswain and coopers	3½/20ths
Gunner's yeoman, boatswain's yeoman, quartermasters, quarter-gunners, sailmaker's mates, sergeants and corporals of marines, drummers and fifers, extra petty officers	2½/20ths
Seamen, ordinary seamen, marines and others doing duty on board	7/20ths

Thus, captains of marines were moved to rank with sea lieutenants and the sailing master rather than with the marine lieutenants in the class below. If there was a captain but no lieutenant of marines, however, then one third of one of the two twentieths that would have been shared with the class that would have included lieutenants of marines was deducted and added to the class that included the captain of marines. The cooper (responsible in particular for the vital job of maintaining the barrels for storage of a ships' water and beer) was moved up one class but he brought with him an additional half of a twentieth to be shared between the class of personnel into which he was moving, taken from the class below from which he had come.

The change in 1800 that had the greatest potential to increase the prize money that was received came in the definition of the property on which prize money was payable. The 1799 exclusion of national ships of war was removed and from 1800 the proceeds of all ships and vessels and the goods taken on board of those adjudged to be good prize were eligible for prize money.[65] If the captured vessel was of equal or superior force to its captors, it became the sole property of the captors. If the captured vessel was of inferior force, the proceeds were divided equally between the United States and the officers and men making the capture. The definition of superiority of force by reference to the number of men or guns that had appeared in section 5 of the Act of 1799 was not replicated in the Act of 1800. The problems with *L'Insurgente* had shown that it was more trouble than it was worth. The bounty that had previously been paid on captured ships was abolished, but a new bounty was payable of $20 for each person on board any ship of an enemy at the commencement of an engagement which was sunk or destroyed by any ship or vessel belonging to the United States of equal or inferior force. The bounty was to be distributed among the officers and men of the capturing vessel or vessels in the same manner as prize money.[66] One potential advantage of a ship being sunk or destroyed was that it made it harder to prove that the vessel was not of equal or superior force. This was especially the case in the early days of the War of 1812 where a willing public (and government) were happy to accept that US naval forces had prevailed over a superior enemy, particularly a superior British enemy of the Royal Navy.[67]

Nineteenth Century: To Empire and Abolition

US provisions for the distribution of prize money to its navy survived through the nineteenth century, but unlike the European powers they did not quite make it into the twentieth century. When the US abolition came it was endorsed by the naval establishment, but for the most particular of reasons.

An opportunity to reconsider the taking of prizes and the nature of commerce war arose in the middle of the nineteenth century during the peace process to end the Crimean War of 1853–6. The title Crimean War suggests that it principally involved the land war against the Russians over the Crimea. As Lambert has argued, however, the war involved, and was ultimately resolved by, the application of British and French naval power against Russia in the Baltic.[68] In order to ensure the goodwill of strategically

[65] The Act of 1800 s. 5, Homans, *Laws of the United States*, p. 67.

[66] The Act of 1800, s. 7, Homans, *Laws of the United States*, p. 68.

[67] Lambert, *The Challenge*, p. 78. For the ensuing later disputes, especially between William James and Theodore Roosevelt, see Lambert, *The Challenge*, p. 450, and Toll, *Six Frigates*, pp. 463–4.

[68] Andrew Lambert, *The Crimean War: British Grand Strategy against Russia, 1853–56*, 2nd edn (Farnham, 2011). See in particular the Introduction to the 1990 edition.

situated neutrals such as Sweden, Britain and France voluntarily gave up the right to use privateers against neutral shipping for the duration of the war.[69] At the end of the war the belligerent powers agreed in the Declaration of Paris in 1856 to abandon privateering for good, to recognise neutral goods, i.e. goods that were not contraband of war carried under enemy and neutral flags, and to limit seizures for breach of blockade to effective blockades imposed by naval forces sufficient to render them a reality. This proposal presented the US with a serious diplomatic dilemma. The US had positioned itself as the defender of freedom of the seas throughout its history. As early as 1776 the Continental Congress had drawn up a template for treaties to give effect to the philosophy of 'free ships, free goods.' By 1785 the US had agreed such treaties with France, Holland, Sweden and Prussia. Her neutral shipping had benefited from the wars between Britain and France after 1793 and the War of 1812 between the US and Britain had, at least in part, been brought about by a professed desire to enforce the freedom of the seas for American shipping.[70] Although attempts by the US in the 1820s to achieve international agreement for respect for freedom of the seas had failed, the desire for such agreement had remained US policy. It did so despite the fact that the defence of US commerce in times of war would rely, in the absence of a large US standing navy, on the efforts of privateers engaged in commerce war, just as the US proposed to rely on militias called up in times of war for their land defence.

The invitation to sign the Declaration of Paris presented the US with a dilemma. On the face of it the Declaration would grant the US its cherished freedom of the seas, but at the same time it would deprive the US of a key ingredient of its naval defence strategy. The US therefore renewed an earlier, unsuccessful proposal for a complete immunity for all neutral goods, whatever their nature and whatever the flag under which they were being carried. When that was, inevitably, rejected by the European powers, the US refused to sign the Declaration of Paris on the purported ground that it did not go far enough. Dismissing the European Declaration as a ploy, the US 'preserved their cherished self-image as the champions of individual rights and of commerce-based human brotherhood against the warring states' as well as their primary defence strategy.[71]

The Declaration of Paris was controversial in Britain. Some thought that Britain had surrendered its maritime power over the seas and voluntarily deprived itself of one of the most powerful weapons in its armoury for the

[69] Parrillo, *Against the Profit Motive*, p. 314.

[70] Ibid., pp. 321–2.

[71] Ibid., p. 325.

sake of goodwill amongst nations, and to soften the hardships of war on neutrals. Corbett, in 1907, still described the decision as an 'almost quixotic sacrifice'.[72] Corbett did concede, however, that by prohibiting privateering the Paris Declaration removed the 'real reason why capture at sea got a bad name'.[73] Lord Palmerston, the hard-line British prime minister with extensive experience of foreign affairs, saw the outcome differently; as a diplomatic triumph.[74] French privateers had been more effective at taking prizes than the French navy, and their navy was easier to defend against. Without privateers the main European threats of France and Russia were limited in the naval campaigns they could wage against Britain given the resources of the nineteenth-century navies. If they broke the Declaration first, then Britain would be free to revert to a commerce war using privateers and challenging neutral rights.[75] The Declaration contained no definition of 'contraband of war', so in any event there was work for lawyers in stretching the scope of cargoes that could be seized and validly condemned as prize goods. The prospect of a war between Britain and the US after the Crimean War ended was very real, and it was that prospect that coloured the approach of both nations to the Declaration.[76] In the event of war with the US, Britain was free to act as it had always done as the US had rejected the Paris Declaration. The US may have preserved their right to conduct a commerce war, but Britain still retained a superior navy that it could use to win such a war, assisted by privateers if needs be in a war with the US.

At the outbreak of civil war, however, the American decision not to sign up to the Declaration of Paris backfired.[77] The Union found itself in the unusual position of having a greater naval strength than its enemy, the Confederate rebels. A belated attempt to sign up to the Declaration of Paris to cover the dispute with the southern rebels so that European powers would treat Confederate privateers as pirates was rebuffed by the British.[78] Nevertheless the US eventually declared that it would respect the principles of the Declaration of Paris relating to neutral goods for the duration of

72 Corbett and Lambert, *21st Century Corbett*, p. 73. A. T. Mahan, Henry S. Pritchett and Sir Julian Corbett, *Some Neglected Aspects of War; Together with the Power That Makes for Peace, and the Capture of Private Property at Sea* (Boston, 1899), pp. 129–30.

73 Corbett and Lambert, *21st Century Corbett*, p. 77.

74 Lambert, *The Crimean War*, p. 341.

75 Andrew Lambert, *No More Napoleons* (London, 2025), pp. 258, 304 and 309.

76 J. M. Lemnitzer, *Power, Law and the End of Privateering* (Basingstoke, 2014), p. 60.

77 Nicholas Tracy, *Attack on Maritime Trade* (Basingstoke, 1991), p. 90.

78 Craig L. Symonds, *Lincoln and His Admirals: Abraham Lincoln, the U.S. Navy, and the Civil War* (Oxford, 2010), p. 42.

hostilities, in an effort to avoid giving neutrals any reason or excuse to support the Confederate cause.[79] When British policy permitted the Confederates to obtain the *CSS Alabama*, built in Britain, to attack Union shipping, the US sought damages from Britain and won $15,500,000 in an international arbitration that set the precedent for handling international claims.[80] At the same time, however, the Union used the lure of prize money to enforce a blockade against Confederate shipping and goods.[81] Lincoln insisted throughout the civil war that the Union remained undissolved and that the Confederate government was not a legitimate authority.[82] Nevertheless, he maintained that the blockade, traditionally open to nations at war, was also theoretically legitimate, even if he chose to ignore the idea of closing southern ports to foreign ships that had been approved by Congress.[83] In a fit of pragmatism, and by a majority, the US Supreme Court held that the Union blockade ordered by Abraham Lincoln against his fellow countrymen was constitutional and permissible.[84] Lincoln had resorted to a threat to pack the Supreme Court to get the right decision out of fear that the vote may go the wrong way,[85] but the threat did not have to be carried out and there remain only nine members of the Supreme Court.

By the Navy Act 1862 Congress provided for the distribution of prizes taken by the Union navy during the civil war. It followed a similar pattern to the early provisions, but with some adjustments.[86] Once again, the captors took the whole benefit if the captured vessel was of equal or superior force, but only half if it was of inferior force.[87] The captain of the capturing ship took a 3/20th share, with one of the twentieths going to the officer in command of the fleet where the capture was 'under the immediate command of the commanding officer of the fleet'. The remainder of the prize fund was distributed to all the others serving on board the capturing ship according to their rates of pay.[88] Whilst Congress regulated the distribution of prize

79 Lemnitzer, *Power, Law and the End of Privateering*, pp. 115–53.

80 T. H. Bingham, *Lives of the Law* (Oxford, 2011), pp. 13–40.

81 Insurgent vessels found at sea were forfeit to the United States, Act of Congress 13 July 1861, 37th Congress, Sess. 1, Ch. 3, 12 Stat 257.

82 Symonds, *Lincoln and His Admirals*, pp. 39.

83 Lemnitzer, *Power, Law and the End of Privateering*, p. 128.

84 Prize Cases (1863) 67 US 635, The Brig Amy Warwick, the Schooner Crenshaw, the Barque Hiawatha, the Schooner Brilliante.

85 Symonds, *Lincoln and His Admirals*, p. 46–7.

86 An Act for the better government of the Navy of the United States, 17 July 1862, 37th Congress, Sess. 2, Ch. 204, 12 Stat 600, 606.

87 Ibid., S. 2.

88 Ibid., S. 3.

money, the concept of prize money enjoyed widespread acceptance as a method of encouraging officers and men in the execution of their duty.[89]

Once the civil war ended US policy reverted to a small navy and reliance on defence against hostile states by commerce war. Prize money had proved popular and effective during the civil war. One estimate has suggested that prize money during the civil war amounted to an average of $300 per officer per year at a time when the pay of a midshipman was $500 a year. Four 'flag-officers' and at least ten officers of captain's rank or lower have been assessed to have received over $20,000 each at a time when the annual pay of a captain was $3,500 and of a lieutenant $1,875.[90] Despite criticisms of the system, it was accepted as a real inducement for effective compliance with orders to maintain a blockade. Even an attempt to collectivise prize funds so that they were distributed across the US navy rather than paid to the specific captors failed in Congress in 1882.[91]

Prize money was not a unique way of incentivising people to assist the pursuit of US government aims by sharing the profits. A number of provisions in the US provided for prosecutors to be paid fees from the proceeds of convictions they achieved, and were only removed when they proved impracticable as the extent of intrusive federal imposition increased.[92] During the US civil war, such were the problems with fraudulent supplies to the Union army that Lincoln introduced an Act of Congress to deal with it expressly. Anyone could bring proceedings under the Act, and they would get a half of any forfeiture and damages that were awarded for a fraud on the government.[93] Still sometimes referred to as the 'Lincoln Law', the False Claims Act remains not only on the US statute book, but in active use.[94]

By 1899, however, the US had abolished the prize money system. The case of the *MS Odenwald* is sometimes quoted as the last payment of US naval prize money, but it was in fact a payment of salvage money.[95] On 6 November 1941, a month before the US joined the Second World War, crew from *USS Omaha* and *USS Somers* on neutrality patrol in the mid-Atlantic boarded the German merchant ship *Odenwald* that was operating as a blockade runner flying false US colours and displaying the name *Willmoto* of Philadelphia. As the Americans boarded, the German crew tried to scuttle her and abandoned ship. The Americans salvaged the

89 Parrillo, *Against the Profit Motive*, p. 327.
90 Ibid., p. 326.
91 Ibid., p. 329.
92 Ibid., pp. 263ff.
93 Act of Congress of 2 March 1863, 12 Stat. 696, Ch. LXVII, S. 6.
94 USC 3729-3733.
95 Hamburg-American Line v US 168 F. 2nd 47 (1st Cir. 1948).

ship and sailed her to Puerto Rico, where she was seized by the US government. For their efforts the crew of the American ships were awarded payments by the US District Court in Puerto Rico, but as salvage payments, not prize money.

The US was amongst the first naval nations to abandon prize payments, and it did so with the endorsement of the US naval establishment. Britain would not abandon prize payments until 1945. It did so as it lost its empire and felt that a profit motive for its navy was 'inappropriate under modern conditions of war'.[96] This reflected Britain's new role in the world. It was no longer going to be the undisputed master of the seas. It had just won a world war, but it had done so with the help of the new world powers, the US and the Russians. It would make prize payments for the captures in that war, but it would not do so again.

What prompted the US to abandon prize payments when its naval power was on the rise? The US navy had begun to change during the last two decades of the nineteenth century. The intellectual drive for this change came from Alfred Thayer Mahan at the US War College, who saw the British navy as the instrument through which global market domination had been achieved and a powerful fleet navy as the way for the US to advance its own interests in a similar way. Mahan's views found favour with the Navy Secretary, Benjamin Tracy, and in 1889 Congress authorised the building of four capital ships, although disguised by their description as sea-going coastline battleships in a way that would become all too familiar to navies answerable to democratic parliaments. Then in 1898 a combination of revulsion at Spain's oppression of its Cuban civilians and the mysterious explosion of the *USS Maine* on a visit to Havana provided the impetus for a US war against Spain in the Caribbean and the Pacific. The Spanish navy proved no match for even the as yet minor league US navy, and success in the Pacific led to the acquisition of a US empire out of the blue.[97] A global empire needed a global navy, and the transition of US naval policy was properly underway. The potential maritime state that had existed in the eastern seaboard rebel colonies that joined the young USA had given way to a new continental power. The call now was for a large warfighting fleet, not to protect trade, but to challenge potential rivals.[98] The US navy welcomed its expansion and new-found status but

[96] Per A. V. (Albert Victor) Alexander, First Lord of the Admiralty, announcing the change in a brief ministerial answer at question time in the House of Commons just before Christmas 1945, Hansard, HC Debate 19 December 1945, vol. 417, col. 1313, see Preface above.

[97] Parrillo, *Against the Profit Motive*, pp. 331–2.

[98] Scott Mobley, *Progressives in Navy Blue* (Annapolis, 2018), p. 179.

recognised that in order to achieve the necessary Congressional support it should abandon the appearance of self-interest that prize money provided. Without complaint from its navy the US abandoned payment of prize money to its naval personnel in 1899.

Similar sentiments were voiced in Britain. In the build-up to the First World War many Royal Navy officers, whilst urging the retention of a right to capture at sea, thought that the prize payment system should be abolished for the good of the service.[99] Such arguments did not prevail, however. Britain abandoned prize money payments nearly half a century after the US, when it lost its empire and ceased to be the world's leading naval power. The US abandoned prize money because it gained an empire and found a new role; not as a new British-style maritime sea-state, but as a dominant continental military and naval power.[100]

US Freight Money

As in the Royal Navy, prize money was not the only way in which a ship's commander could supplement his income. He could also receive freight money for the carriage of gold, silver or jewels, referred to collectively as specie. Article 23 of the Articles of War approved by Congress in the Navy Act of 1800 made it an offence for any commander or other officer to receive or permit to be received on board his vessel any goods or merchandise except gold, silver or jewels, other than for the sole use of his vessel, without the permission of the president or the Navy Department.[101] The only exception was to save a cargo of another ship from shipwreck. An officer found to be in breach of the article at court-martial was to be cashiered and banned for life from service in the navy. The implication of the wording was that the permission of the Navy Department was not required to carry specie. As a result, US captains regarded it as their perquisite to be able to carry specie. In this they followed their Royal Navy brethren, at least until 1801.[102]

Whilst some officers sought and obtained permission from the Navy Department, the fact that it had been granted was seen as a sign that it was unnecessary to trouble the Secretary of the Navy for his permission. In 1811 James Lawrence, in command of *USS Hornet* and preparing to depart

99 Corbett and Lambert, *21st Century Corbett*, p. 89.

100 Andrew Lambert, *Seapower States* (London, 2018), pp. 289ff.

101 Homans, *Laws of the United States*, p. 62.

102 See Chapter 8.

for Europe, arranged to take on board between $180,000 and $200,000 in Spanish gold for merchants desperate to get their specie to Europe. When President Madison and Navy Secretary Paul Hamilton heard of Lawrence's arrangement, they wrote and told him that conveyance of the specie would be 'wholly inadmissible' and any application by Lawrence to convey the specie abroad would be rejected. Lawrence therefore had to return the specie to his disappointed clients.[103] By 1811 Britain was desperate for specie to fund its war in Europe, a desperation that would increase with the Peninsular campaign the following year when the US would also be at war with Britain over freedom of the seas for US ships and seamen. The desperation to get specie to Europe is confirmed by the estimate that Lawrence intended to charge 4.5 per cent by way of freight rather than the more usual 1 per cent or less.[104] A sum of over $8,000 would have been very welcome to a master commandant on $60 per month. Lawrence felt the order to land the gold deeply. Not only did he have to forgo his commission, but he felt that he had broken his word to the merchants and was at their mercy as a result. His letters of protest to the Navy Department were of no avail, however. There were strong diplomatic reasons to prevent a large shipment of specie arriving in Europe with untold consequences. *Hornet*'s mission to Europe was intended as a diplomatic attempt to persuade the French and British to repeal their measures against American shipping that had been introduced as a result of the Continental System of blockade. The mission would not succeed with either the French or the British, and war with Britain would follow in 1812.[105] Madison and his cabinet knew what Lawrence did not, that war with Britain was a real possibility. In those circumstances the US president did not want Lawrence's private ventures to further the British war effort by providing much-needed specie.[106] Being discovered by the French to be doing so would have been no better.

103 McKee, *A Gentlemanly and Honorable Profession*, p. 340.

104 Ibid., p. 341.

105 Lambert, *The Challenge*, p. 55.

106 Albert Gleaves, *James Lawrence, Captain, United States Navy, Commander of the Chesapeake* (New York, 1904), pp. 81–4.

10.
Prize Money in Context

In the fifth century St Augustine related the story of a man who, when brought before Alexander the Great for robbery, asked: 'What thou meanest by seizing the whole earth; but because I do it with a petty ship, I am called a robber, whilst thou who dost it with a great fleet art styled emperor?' What made the difference, according to St Augustine, was the application of the law.[1] And so it was in the long eighteenth century and beyond.

Pillage and Plunder?

Prize-taking in the eighteenth century was not simply 'piracy enlarged', the 'pillage and plunder' of the public imagination from the time of Drake. Nor was it some rogue activity of naval ships, or officers taking advantage of a chance to make a private profit on the side of their public duties. It was a core activity of a naval war, to bring about peace by weakening the economy of the enemy, and thus their ability to pursue hostilities. The prize money system was overseen by courts which took their responsibility to apply the rule of law seriously. It was controlled not merely by Admiralty orders, but by statute and orders-in-council making detailed provisions, including regulation of the distribution of shares. The English courts applied their own municipal law to the resolution of the prize disputes. They were not afraid to hold the government to account in its dealings with the Royal Navy where they saw fit, but the courts shared the objective of the government to win the war. The war was seen as being not just for the survival of the nation, but for the survival of world civilisation, a fight to the death where success was not as certain to those involved at the time as might appear in hindsight.

Though the courts worked with the government to achieve shared objectives, that did not mean that they were dictated to in what they did. Indeed, the ability to be independent made their work more acceptable and effective. It meant that the Admiralty could avoid having to enter into

[1] St Augustine, *The City of God Book IV*.

the bitter disputes that arose between senior officers or being drawn into overtly political decisions on matters of neutrality. It also attempted to earn the respect of neutral shipowners, merchants and governments.

The English courts looked to concepts of 'international law' as sources for English municipal law where they thought it appropriate, but that did not mean that they were subject to international law. Indeed, the English approach to international law was as much an attempt to create and influence international law as to follow it. Once the Victorian embroidery over the state of eighteenth-century prize law is removed, it is easier to see the pattern of the original in context. The so-called fathers of international law such as Grotius were no more devoid of self-interest than the municipal courts of England. Despite their reputation as 'law-givers', even the most acclaimed jurists created arguments to persuade, not laws to be bound by. The courts looked to such sources where they appeared to support the arguments that they favoured as to what the law should be, rather than as a binding guide to what the law was. In doing so they used the legal concepts of the day that the courts had been developing as part of English commercial law. Concepts of international law, or the law of nations, formed part of the creative process of the common law, but were not themselves law administered by the English courts. What operated as a restraining hand on English law and policy was not a binding system of international law, but the constant awareness that however mighty the Royal Navy might be, Britain still needed to keep allies and neutrals on side and encourage enemies to show restraint themselves. Britain, and especially William Pitt and his followers, had learned the dangers of splendid isolation during the American War of Independence. In times of crisis, friends mattered.[2]

The realisation that international law as we currently understand it is of more recent invention than sometimes pretended matters. Peeling away later concepts of international law to understand what was happening in the eighteenth century reveals the under-developed roots of international law and the need to tend its frail shoots rather than assume that it is so old and immutable that it can withstand any shocks that the world may throw at it. Further, regarding the eighteenth-century Admiralty courts as beacons of innovation in international law risks perpetuating the notion that international law is something that Britain gives, rather than receives.

2 Nathaniel Jarrett, *The Lion at Dawn: Forging British Strategy in the Age of the French Revolution 1783–1797* (Oklahoma, 2022), p. 238.

Women and the Royal Navy

The cases studied in this work reveal some less understood aspects of Georgian social life. Susanna, the widow of Admiral Lord Gardner, and Eleanor, widow of Admiral Dacres, fought to retain prize money and freight shares through the courts in their own names as executrices of their late husbands' estates, confounding the idea that in Jane Austen's time women would not take on roles of legal ownership. Austen had two beloved brothers in the Royal Navy and understood their world through their eyes. Francis and Charles Austen both saw active service in far-off places and became admirals. When Charles served on *HMS Endymion* in 1801 he received £30 in prize money from a captured privateer and bought gold chains and topaz crosses for his sisters.[3] In *Mansfield Park*, the first of Jane's works as a mature writer, published in 1814, the Royal Navy appears in the form of Fanny Price's impoverished Portsmouth family; her mother had married a lieutenant of marines 'without education, fortune, or connections'. The navy is seen as something to be admired at a distance, but ultimately to be escaped from. Mansfield Park is in Northamptonshire, as far from the sea as one can get in England. Fanny Price and her brother William, a newly appointed naval lieutenant, speculate on his gaining enough prize money to help the family and provide a little cottage for them to live in together. By the time of her last completed novel, *Persuasion*, published in 1817 after her death earlier that year, the Royal Navy appears through the amiable and wise Admiral and Mrs Croft, and the gallant Captain Wentworth. Austen's Wentworth has a fortune of £25,000 gained through his own merit and activity in the war.[4] Such a sum would be enough to marry and set himself up in a country estate in his own right. By this later work the Royal Navy comes to save genteel society from itself, despite the new-found nature of its wealth, rather than undermine it. Austen's novels do not lack spirited women, and the fictional Mrs Croft is quite capable of financial and property management, as sailors' wives had to be. Even in *Persuasion*, however, women are seen as the victims of probate disputes rather than capable protagonists. Mrs Smith is oppressed by the calculating Mr Elliot, the executor of her husband's estate. We do not know what Austen might have made of a character such as Susanna Gardner. Austen died in 1817 aged only 41, leaving a distinct image of women in the eighteenth century trapped by the expectations of society and the power of men. That image persists, even though

[3] Jane Austen, *Mansfield Park*, 1814, ed. Kathryn Sutherland (London, 2014), p. 348 n. 1; Southam, *Jane Austen and the Navy*, p. 66.

[4] Jane Austen, *Persuasion*, 1818, ed. Margaret Drabble (London, 1989), Ch. 24, p. 244.

her works can readily be construed as an expression of her critical attitudes to the society that she was portraying.[5] Behind the charming stories lies not comfortable satisfaction but biting criticism of the very image that she conjures up. Indeed, the tension between satisfaction and revulsion may be a key to why Austen's novels have achieved such a following.[6]

It is tempting to see the presence of widows as executors as some green shoot of enlightenment thinking, but that would be a mistake. In the late seventeenth century, 80–90 per cent of men appointed their widow as their executrix, and most of them were appointed as sole executor. Further, if a man died leaving assets but no will, i.e. intestate, his wife was ordinarily appointed as the administratrix of the estate.[7] By the late eighteenth century, however, the figure for widow executors had dropped to below 50 per cent, with a greater share of widows as joint rather than sole executors.[8] Traditionally widows had been entitled to a 'reasonable part' of their husband's estate, namely one third, either on intestacy or even if the husband left a will. This customary provision had been gradually eroded and was finally abolished by statute by 1725, to allow husbands to dispose of all their estate by will as they saw fit. As by marriage all a wife's property became the property of her husband, he was free to dispose of the joint property as he saw fit. This abolition was described as a procedural effort to simplify and unify the provisions for the transfer of property and thus support the notion of freedom of ownership and the rights of property. It came at a time, however, when the dynastic desires of men to ensure that their titles passing through the male line came with sufficient property to reflect the grandeur of their origin came into conflict with the desire to attend to the need to care for the wider family, including widows. It was the legal notion that within marriage a wife followed the direction of her husband that led Mr Bumble in Dickens' *Oliver Twist* famously to say that if the law supposes that then 'the law is an ass'. As Linda Colley has suggested, during the eighteenth century men and women were seen as operating in separate spheres, women in the home and men in public, but that did not stop women seeking a role in influencing public affairs.[9] Women such as Mary Wollstonecraft, the author of *The Vindication of the Rights of Women*

5 D. W. Harding, 'Regulated Hatred: An Aspect of the Work of Jane Austen', *Scrutiny* 8 (1940), pp. 346–62, at p. 351.

6 Tom Keymer, *Jane Austen: Writing, Society, Politics* (Oxford, 2020), pp. 7–11.

7 Anne Laurence, *Women in England, 1500–1760* (London, 1994), p. 235.

8 Amy Louise Erickson, 'Property and Widowhood in England 1660–1840', in Cavallo and Warner (eds), *Widowhood in Medieval and Early Modern Europe* (Abingdon, 1999), p. 156.

9 Linda Colley, *Britons* (London, 1992), pp. 237–81.

in 1792, went further and sought a role for women as citizens and not just as women, but even most men were denied the rights of citizenship through a limited franchise in elections.

The subversion of women's property rights in marriage placed greater emphasis on the private provisions, or settlements, that sought to provide for widows and siblings, especially daughters. By 1744 more than a third of the contents of the standard work of *Precedents in Conveyancing* consisted of examples of marriage settlements.[10] The provisions that were adopted led to a sophisticated system of trust law and of bonds as financial instruments that may have benefited the role of the courts in enabling industry, commerce and the rise of capitalism, but did little to protect the rights of women in marriage beyond what the men in their families chose to provide for them.[11] Whereas women's property rights were lost to their husbands on marriage in England by the law of coverture, at least once they were of age and either single or widowed they were entitled to control their own money and act in their own name rather than needing to find a man to act for them in their name, as in some European jurisdictions.

Many fields of research are rediscovering the 'lost' women of the Georgian age.[12] Naval history is part of this process, yet as Margarette Lincoln noted in 2017, 'Women's contribution to British naval supremacy in the long eighteenth century tends to be neglected or sensationalised.'[13] The reports of prize money cases provide material for a more nuanced view of the role of women. The presence of naval widow executors attests to their continuing active and public role in supervising the lives and finances of naval families on land.

Equity?

Although the Admiralty was closely involved in supervising the forces that made prize captures, it was prepared, indeed happy, to leave the resolution

10 Erickson, 'Property and Widowhood in England 1660–1840', p. 147.

11 Amy Louise Erickson, 'Coverture and Capitalism', *History Workshop Journal* 59 (2005), 1–16.

12 E.g. Bettina Baumgärtel (ed.) et al., *Angelica Kauffman* (London and Düsseldorf, 2020).

13 Margarette Lincoln, 'The Impact of Warfare on Naval Wives and Women', in Fury (ed.), *The Social History of English Seamen, 1650–1815* (Woodbridge, 2017) p. 71; despite her own work: *Naval Wives and Mistresses* (Stroud, 2011). For later contributions, see e.g. Elaine Chalus, 'Mr Dearest Tussy' about Betsy Freemantle in Colville and Davey (eds), *A New Naval History*, pp. 47–69; Ellen Gill, *Naval Families, War and Duty in Britain, 1740–1820* and *The Trafalgar Chronicle: New Series 3* (2018), a volume dedicated to women and the sea.

of disputes between officers to the courts. The Admiralty changed the law from time to time but left it to the courts to apply the law. It avoided determining prize disputes by executive order. The rules of prize distribution in Britain were promulgated through secondary legislation in the form of royal proclamations, authorised by Parliament but passed by the Privy Council. Although the US reserved such law-making to Congress, in reality there is no more evidence of public discussion within Congress than in Britain. Congress and the American public certainly argued about whether to fund a navy and if so for what purpose and to what extent, but the framing of regulatory provisions was left to members of the executive as much as in Britain, and the US provisions reflected their inheritance from the British rules.

Most of the changes to the rules governing the distribution of prize money were to clarify the rules and reflect the increasing complexity of the Royal Navy and its ships. They were mainly introduced as and when new provisions were required by virtue of a new declaration of war. The exception was the 1808 royal proclamation, which contained modernising provisions redefining the classes of petty officer and taking a one third share of prize money away from the captains and flag-officers and redistributing it in particular to the petty officers whose skills were in great demand. Although there had been calls for such a reform at the time of the mutinies in 1797, they were ignored. Various governments of differing hues came and went thereafter without addressing the issue of prize shares for the lower decks. In 1808 it was in the realisation that it was going to be a long economic conflict fought at sea by the Royal Navy that Lord Mulgrave's Admiralty finally redistributed prize shares rather than impose further on the merchants whose taxes were paying for the war. When the war ended so did the need for the redistribution, and the change was reversed.

In so far as the 1808 changes have been considered before, they have been seen in terms of effecting a greater equity between officers and men. Morriss goes so far as to assert that: '... the state promoted the principle of equity. This was evident in relations between the state and its employees. The state has had a bad press for its treatment of seamen.'[14]

A narrative based on ideas of 'equity' needs to be challenged when we see the real reason for reform. The state has had a bad press because it treated large numbers of seamen, and their families, badly. At times the law intervened. At others direct action was more effective. Inequity and bad treatment remained, however. The changes that were made to prize distribution in Britain during the eighteenth century were not an example of

[14] Morriss, *The Foundations of British Maritime Ascendancy*, p. 26.

the state wanting to make the relationship between officers and men more equitable. They were aimed at the practical task of making the conduct of the war run more smoothly and addressing practical matters such as the shortage of skilled petty officers. Where the changes coincided with a drift of liberalism, the Admiralty may have caught that breeze while it suited them, but it was not what fundamentally set the course. However long the arc of history may be, it only tended towards a more equal distribution when it suited the national interest and those in power made it happen. It was not a predestined path but took an alignment of cultural and administrative change with economic and military pressure. A tendency towards equity should not be taken for granted.

Prize money disputes had the potential to create discord and disharmony, but that discord was kept in check, and the system preserved, by the application of the rule of law in cases such as those that have been considered in this study. As a result, the system enjoyed public acceptance and the award of prize money continued in Britain through to 1945.

Bounty

Prize money was an incentive for Royal Navy officers and crew to do their duty. It was a form of bounty producing a private profit for the officers and crew involved. The sums could be enormous. Ranier and Pellew were each said to have made £300,000 out of their command of the Indian station during the Napoleonic War. Nelson bought his country estate at Merton Place for £9,000 relying on loans and prize money, and the countryside of the UK is still littered with stately piles paid for out of prize money. Prize money remained a significant financial inducement throughout the wars, providing an average annual supplement of £1.2 million to the navy.

Comparison with freight, head money and booty is instructive. Freight payments to captains for the carriage of bullion had a quite different jurisprudential basis to prize money. As payments that directly affected Britain's affairs with other states, prize money was controlled by Act of Parliament from before the eighteenth century and detailed rules were promulgated under statutory supervision. Although naval officers saw freight payments as part of the 'custom and usage' of the navy, they were actually part of the internal workings of the navy, administered as agreed between the Admiralty and the Treasury. Although abolished in 1801, they were restored in 1807 to regain control from naval officers who were taking matters into their own hands by deducting 'commission' on discharge of their cargoes of public bullion.

Head money calculated at £5 per head of the crew of enemy ships captured or destroyed in battle shared the same statutory jurisprudential basis as prize money, but by the eighteenth century prize money had far outstripped head money in significance. As seen in Chapter 8, the courts took a more restrictive approach in claims for head money than in claims for prize shares. They did so as a matter of statutory interpretation reflecting what they saw as the public policy behind the respective provisions.

Booty, i.e. enemy goods seized by or with land forces, was regulated in a more ad hoc way than prize money. Distribution was governed by specific royal warrants, rather than overarching royal proclamations. Nevertheless, some disputes still ended up before the courts. When in 1840 booty was brought within the formal jurisdiction of the courts, it was to the Admiralty Court that Parliament turned, and the rules of naval prize were adopted.

All these payments were means by which service for the Crown could provide a private profit over and above wages. In that sense prize money was not unique in providing a means to obtain private profit from public service. Such payments were widely accepted as a means of rewarding the navy in times of war, and the rule of law was used to provide some independence in resolving disputes and keeping the division of spoils within socially acceptable limits. As a result, prize money survived the reforms following the 1785 Commission on Fees and its successors at the turn of the nineteenth century, which ended a large number of sinecures and private fees for undertaking work in public office.

As can be seen from the study of US prize law, whatever the differences between the old and new nations, British prize law provided the model for the rules that the US would adopt. Early attempts at US provision sought to provide what appeared, superficially at least, to be a more egalitarian system. In doing so, the early provisions echoed those of the cash-strapped Stuarts and the leveller instincts of the Commonwealth, but practicalities brought the US back towards the proven system that had been developed by the Georgian Royal Navy. Although coming from different directions, they both abandoned prize money payments to reflect changes in their imperial status and their aspirations as world-leading naval powers. Britain abandoned prize money payments in 1945, nearly half a century after the US, when it lost its empire and ceased to be the world's leading naval power. The US had abandoned them because it gained an empire as a continental power and wanted political cover to take over a new role; not that of a maritime sea power, but that of a dominant military naval power.

Britain and Naval Power

How the British government and the courts dealt with prize claims had a significant effect on the conduct of war and international relations. Britain had the most powerful navy in the world and wanted to use that power in times of war. This was especially so in the revolutionary and Napoleonic wars that posed existential threats. As a maritime state Britain depended on trade and had a national interest in maintaining freedom of navigation and trade. This national interest was heightened, rather than reduced, in time of war, as Britain needed continued trade to fund its wars.

As a parliamentary democracy in which merchants formed a significant constituency, the merchants had to be listened to rather than merely taxed. They wanted trade to continue and be protected, but, if possible, not taken over by neutrals taking advantage of the effort that Britain was putting into maintaining war for their benefit as well as its own.

Britain's stance on these conflicting interests varied depending on whether she was a belligerent or a neutral. Even when Britain was at war, however, there were limits to what it could do to force neutrals into line. Even with the most powerful navy in the world, Britain needed allies and the goodwill of others to defeat its enemies. Upset neutrals were potential enemies. Neutrals, if treated fairly and consistently, remained friends. They were friends worth having so long as they were not picking the pockets of Britain's trade too conspicuously. Even trading 'enemies' such as Sweden when obliged by France to declare war against Britain in the Baltic after 1810, on paper at least, were kept onside by naval diplomacy. Admiral Saumarez refused to seize Swedish merchant prizes and used Britain's naval power in the Baltic to ensure vital naval supplies for the Royal Navy and to undermine Napoleon's attempted economic isolation of Britain.[15]

These balances are not matters to be struck on a permanent basis and then taken for granted. They need constant attention and adjustment by people who understand the problems, have a vision for the future and are prepared to learn from the past. The adjustments did not happen in a vacuum, but against the background of cultural changes. Naval and economic realities finally brought pressure to a head to create change in 1808 that lasted until the end of the war. The prize system both reflected and effected longer-lasting cultural change. It redistributed wealth within the naval community and society at large. It helped to win a war of national survival that became a war of national self-definition. It preserved a method

[15] Anthony Sullivan, *Man of War: The Fighting Life of Admiral James Saumarez* (Barnsley, 2017), pp. 185–6.

of reward for naval service into the twentieth century, when Britain's focus on its survival as a nation, and how it defined itself, finally changed.

The distribution of prize money to the Royal Navy in the long eighteenth century was not a form of state piracy, nor was it regulated by international law. The truth lies in between. It was part of the practical task of getting a huge naval institution to work efficiently without overburdening state finances, losing allies or embroiling Britain in more hostilities than it could cope with. It was a dynamic, flexible system and subject to the rule of law.

Appendix 1: Key Royal Prize Proclamations 1793–1815

Date	Hostile State	Notes
17 April 1793	France	
25 January 1797	Spain	Same as 1793
12 February 1800	Genoa, Papal States, Ligurian and Roman Republics	Same as before
7 July 1803	France and Batavia	End of Peace of Amiens Provided for hired armed vessels, conjoint allied captors, second masters in line of battle ships and changed flag rules
31 January 1805	Spain and Italian and Ligurian Republics	Amended provision for lieutenants of cutters
11 November 1807 23 December 1807	Denmark Russia	Omitted amendment for lieutenants of cutters
15 June 1808	All existing	Significant reforms including two classes of petty officers, and one eighth taken from captains and flag-officers and redistributed to petty officers and below.
26 October 1812	USA	
29 June 1815	France	After escape of Bonaparte from Elba

Appendix 2: Key Prize-Related Statutes

Year	Act
1708 6 Annae	**Cruizers & Convoy Act c. 13**
1776 16 Geo 3	Prize Act c. 5
1778 18 Geo 3	Prize Act c. 15
1779 19 Geo 3	Prize Act c. 5
1780 20 Geo 3	Navy Act c. 23
	Prize Act c. 9
1781 21 Geo 3	Prize Act c. 5
	Prize Act c. 44
	Navigation Act c. 19
1782 22 Geo 3	Navigation Act c. 16
	Prize Act c. 15
	Prize Act c. 25
1783 23 Geo 3	Prize Act c. 57
1786 26 Geo 3	Navy Act c. 63
1793 33 Geo 3	Prize Act c. 34 **Prize Act c. 66**
1794 34 Geo 3	Merchant Shipping Act c. 68
	Prize Act c. 42
1795 35 Geo 3	Manning of the Navy Acts, cc. 5, 9, 19, 29, 34 and 121
	Navy Pay Act c. 94, 95
1796 36 Geo 3	Manning the Navy Act c. 115
	Longitude at Sea Act c. 107
	Merchandize in Neutral Ships Act c. 76
1797 37 Geo 3	Manning of Army and Navy Act c. 4, 24, 39 (5 Scot)

	Merchandize in Neutral Ships Act c. 12
	Manning Navy Act c. 109
	Naval Courts Martial Act c. 146
	Navy Pay etc. Act c. 53
1798 38 Geo 3	Manning the Navy Act c. 46
	Prize Causes Act c. 38
1798 39 Geo 3	Annuity to Lord Nelson Act c. 1
1799 40 Geo 3	Shipping Act c. 32
1801 42 Geo 3	Merchant Shipping Act c. 19
	Prize Act c. 10
1803 43 Geo 3	Chatham Chest Act c. 119 **Prize Act c. 160**
1806 46 Geo 3	Navy Act 1806 c. 127
1807 47 Geo 3	Prize Act c. 47
1808 48 Geo 3	Sale of Prize Ship Constantia Maria Act c. 147
	Prize Goods Act c. 149
	Prize Act c. 100
1809 48 Geo 3	Prize Act c. 34
	Prize Money Act c. 123
1810 50 Geo 3	Admiralty and Prize Courts Act c. 118
1811 51 Geo 3	Prize Goods Act c. 74
1813 53 Geo 3	American Prizes Act c. 63
	Settlement of Estate of Lord Nelson Act c. 134

Bibliography

Archival Sources

All Souls Library, Oxford, England

Notebooks of Thomas Bever, MS 109 and 300

British Library, London, England

BL Add. MS 37, 877 Windham Papers, Aaron Graham correspondence 1797

BL Add. MS 34918/325 Davison canvassed opinion for Nelson

Digby family archive, Minterne House, Dorset, England

Box 22a, Accounts of Sir Henry Digby

Foyle Collection, King's College London, England

The Naval Chronicle

Sir John Knox Laughton's copy of *Memoirs and Correspondence of Admiral Lord de Saumarez*, ed. Sir John Ross

Inner Temple Library, London, England

Contemporary Law Reports, see Note on Legal Referencing and Abbreviations

Library of Congress, Washington DC

LOC GB Navy, Cont 27, Lieutenant's Logbook, *HMS Cheerly*

Lincoln's Inn Library, London, England

Parliamentary Papers Archive

National Maritime Museum, Greenwich, England (NMM)

Croker Papers

CRK/3/125 Letter Davison to Nelson 15.1.1801

CRK/3/127 Letter Davison to Nelson 27.1.1801

CRK/3/128 Letter St Vincent to Booth & Haslewood 5.1.1801

CRK/3/129 Letter Davison to Nelson 4.4.1801

CRK/6/139 Letter Haslewood to Tucker 15.3.1804

CRK/6/141 De Niza's London rep. to Tucker 1804

CRK/6/142 Draft Deed of Indemnity for Lord Nelson, Booth & Haslewood

Duncan Papers

DUN/19 Public and Private Correspondence

DUN/31 Memorandum Book

Letter Book Collection

LBK/40 Mulgrave to Collingwood 25.9.1808

Sim Comfort Collection, Wimbledon, London, England

Tucker Account Book

The National Archives, Kew, England (TNA)
ADM 1/54 Johnstone Letterbook, 1781
ADM 1/727 Admiralty Papers re 1797 Mutinies
ADM 1/398 Letters Nepean/Orde, October 1798
ADM 1/400/224 St Vincent to Admiralty 16.8.1799
ADM 1/484 Graves Papers re capture of the *Washington*
ADM 1/814 Nepean endorsement of Capt. Young letter, November 1799
ADM 1/3894 Scott to Evan Nepean, November 1799
ADM 1/5125 Seamen's Petitions 1797
ADM 1/5378 Popham Court Martial Papers
ADM 2/136/146 and 149 Admiralty Orders to Keith, August 1799
ADM 2/136/174 Admiralty Orders to St Vincent or officer commanding Mediterranean Fleet 28.8.1799
ADM 15/1 George Rose Letterbook
ADM 36/12613 Muster Book *HMS Alcmene*
ADM 37/2302 Muster Book *HMS Cheerly*
ADM 50/93 St Vincent Journal 1799
ADM 51/2170 Captain's log *HMS Cheerly*
ADM 51 Captains' Logs
ADM 52 Masters' Logs
PROB 11/1495/204 Lord Gardner will
PROB 11/1507/351 Adm. Dacres will

Printed and Online Primary Sources

Adams, John, letters of:
Founders Online, National Archives, http://founders.archives.gov/documents/Adams/99-02-02-5211
Founding Families: Digital Editions of the Winthrops and the Adamses, ed. Taylor, C. James (Boston: Massachusetts Historical Society, 2017), www.masshist.org/apde2/

Anon., *A Correct Account of The Trial at Large between Ross Donnelly, Esq. a Post Captain in His Majesty's Navy, Plaintiff and Sir Home Popham, Knt. Defendant* (London: T. Cadell and W. Davies, 1807)

— *Notifications, Orders, and Instructions, Relating to Prize Subjects during the Present War* (London, 1815)

Annual Biography and Obituary, vol. 4, 1820

Barnes, G. R. (ed.), *The Private Papers of John Earl of Sandwich, First Lord of the Admiralty 1775–1782* (Navy Records Society, 1938)

Bonner Smith, D. (ed.), *Letters of Admiral of the Fleet Earl St Vincent* (Navy Records Society, 1921)

BritishNewspaperarchive.co.uk

Clark, Gregory, *The Annual RPI and Average Earnings for Britain, 1209 to Present (New Series)*, www.MeasuringWorth.com

Clark, William Bell, William James Morgan, Willam S. Dudley and Michael J. Crawford, *Naval Documents of the American Revolution* (Washington, USA: Naval Historical Centre, 1964), NDAR

Firth, C. H. and R. S. Rait (eds), *Acts and Ordinances of the Interregnum 1642–1660*, 2 vols (London: HMSO, 1911)

Gayle Family Archive: http://gale-gaylefamilies.com/gale-gayle-families-of-the-west-indies.html

Hansard, https://hansard.parliament.uk/

Homans, Benjamin, *Laws of the United States, in Relation to the Navy and Marine Corps (1840)* (Reprinted: Gale, Sabin Americana, 2012)

Journals of the Continental Congress, 1774–89, and *Annals of Congress*, https://memory.loc.gov/

Knox, Dudley, *Naval Documents Relating to the Quasi-War between the United States and France*, 7 vols (US Office of Naval Records and Library Navy Department, 1935), NDQW

Laughton, Sir John Knox (ed.), *Letters of Lord Barham*, 3 vols (Navy Records Society, 1909)

London Gazette, https://www.thegazette.co.uk/

Marsden, Reginald Godfrey, *Documents Relating to Law and Custom of the Sea*, vol. I (Navy Records Society, 1923)

Nicolas, Nicholas Harris, *The Dispatches and Letters of Vice Admiral Lord Viscount Nelson* (London: Chatham Publishing, 1997)

Oxford National Dictionary of Biography, https://www.oxforddnb.com/

Pickering, Danby (ed.), *Statutes at Large*, from 1761

Roscoe, Edward Stanley, *Reports of Prize Cases Determined in the High Court of Admiralty, before the Lords Commissioners of Appeals in Prize Causes, and before the Judicial Committee of the Privy Council from 1745 to 1859* (London: Stevens and Sons Ltd, 1905)

Rose, George, *The Diaries and Correspondence of the Right Honourable George Rose*, vol. 2 (London: Richard Bentley, 1860)

Ross, Sir John (ed), *Memoirs and Correspondence of Admiral Lord de Saumarez*, 2 vols (London: Richard Bentley, 1838)

Wyndham, H. P. (ed.), *The Diary of the Late George Bubb Dodington, Baron of Melcombe Regis* (London, 1784)

Secondary Sources

Aaslestad, Katherine, *Revisiting Napoleon's Continental System: Local, Regional and European* (Basingstoke, Hampshire: Palgrave Macmillan, 2014)

Abbenhuis, Maartje, *An Age of Neutrals* (Cambridge, 2014)

Adams, Max, *Admiral Collingwood* (London, 2005)

Aldous, Grahame, 'Lord Nelson and Earl St Vincent: Prize Fighters', *The Mariner's Mirror* 101:2 (2015), 135–55

Aldous, Grahame, 'Mutiny: The Trial of William Muspratt of the Bounty', *Inner Temple Yearbook* (2015)

Alexander, Caroline, *The Bounty: The True Story of the Mutiny on the Bounty* (London, 2004)

Anderson, Alan, 'The Laws of War and Naval Strategy in Great Britain and the United States 1899–1909' (unpubl. PhD thesis, King's College London, 2016)

Anon., 'The Case of the Zamora', *Harvard Law Review* 30:1 (1916), 66–8

Augustine, St, *The City of God Book IV*, n.d.

Austen, Jane, *Mansfield Park*, 1814, ed. Kathryn Sutherland (London, 2014)

— *Persuasion*, 1818, ed. Margaret Drabble (London, 1989)

Baker, Casey, *Britain's War for the Mediterranean: The Fight against Revolutionary France* (Annapolis, 2024)

Baty, Thomas, 'Scottish Prize Decisions of the Seventeenth and Eighteenth Centuries', *Yale Law Review* 27:4 (1918), 453–78

Baugh, Daniel A., *The Global Seven Years' War, 1754–1763: Britain and France in a Great Power Contest* (Harlow, 2011)

Baumgärtel, Bettina (ed.), Alison Gallup (tr.), Bronwen Saunders (tr.), *Angelica Kauffman* (London: Royal Academy of Arts; Düsseldorf: Kunstpalast, 2020)

Benjamin, Daniel K., 'Golden Harvest: The British Naval Prize System, 1793–1815' (unpubl., 2009)

Benton, Lauren and Lisa Ford, *Rage for Order* (Cambridge, Mass., 2016)

Bingham, T. H., *Lives of the Law: Selected Essays and Speeches 2000–2010* (Oxford, 2011)

Black, Jeremy (ed.), *The Atlantic Slave Trade* (London, 2006)

Blackstone, Sir William, *Commentaries on the Laws of England* (Oxford, 1765–9)

Blake, Richard, *Evangelicals in the Royal Navy, 1775–1815: Blue Lights & Psalm-Singers* (Woodbridge, 2008)

Bonner Smith, D, 'The Capture of the Washington', *The Mariner's Mirror* 20:4 (1934), 420–5

Borschberg, Peter, 'The Seizure of the Sta. Catarina Revisited: The Portuguese Empire in Asia, VIC Politics and the Origins of the Dutch-Johor Alliance (1602–1616)', *Journal of Southeast Asian Studies* 33:1 (February 2002), 31–62

Bourguignon, Henry J., *Sir William Scott, Lord Stowell: Judge of the High Court of Admiralty, 1798–1828* (Cambridge, 2004)

Boxer, C. B., 'Admiral Joao Pereira Corte-Real and the Construction of Portuguese East-Indiamen in the Early Seventeenth Century', *The Mariner's Mirror* 26:4 (1940), 388–406

Breihan, John R., 'William Pitt and the Commission on Fees 1785–1801', *The Historical Journal* 27:1 (March 1984), 59–81

Brinkman, Anna, *Balancing Strategy, Sea Power, Neutrality, and Prize Law in the Seven Years' War* (Cambridge, 2024)

Brook, Timothy, *Vermeer's Hat: The Seventeenth Century and the Dawn of the Global World* (London, 2009)

Brown Scott, James, *The Armed Neutralities of 1780 and 1800* (New York, 1918)

Brunsman, Denver Alexander, *The Evil Necessity: British Naval Impressment in the Eighteenth-Century Atlantic World* (Charlottesville, 2013)

Bynkershoek, Cornelius Van, *Quaest. Juris Publici, L. i. c 3.* (1737)

Capp, Bernard, *Cromwell's Navy: The Fleet and the English Revolution 1648–1660* (Oxford, 1992)

Carrington, Dorothy, 'The Corsican Constitution of Pasquale Paoli (1755–1769)', *The English Historical Review* 88:348, 481–503

Cavallo and Warner (eds), *Widowhood in Medieval and Early Modern Europe* (Abingdon, 1999)

Colley, Linda, *Britons* (London, 1992)

— *The Gun, the Ship & the Pen* (London, 2021)

Colombos, C. John, *A Treatise on the Law of Prize* (London: The Grotius Society, 1940)

Colville, Quintin (ed.), *Nelson, Navy & Nation: The Royal Navy & the British People 1688–1815* (London. 2013)

Colville, Quintin and James Davey, *A New Naval History* (Manchester, 2019)

Corbett, Julian Stafford and Andrew D. Lambert, *21st Century Corbett: Maritime Strategy and Naval Policy for the Modern Era* (Annapolis, 2017)

Costello, Kevin, 'Habeas Corpus and Military and Naval Impressment, 1756–1816', *The Journal of Legal History* 29:2 (2008), 215–51

Cowes, William Laird, *The Royal Navy: A History from the Earliest Times to the Present* (London, 1898)

Czisnik, Marianne (ed.), *Nelson's Letters to Lady Hamilton and Related Documents*, NRS (Woodbridge, 2020)

Dancy, Jeremiah R., *The Myth of the Press Gang: Volunteers, Impressment and the Naval Manpower Problem in the Late Eighteenth Century* (Woodbridge, 2015)

Davey, Francis (ed.), *Heart of Oak: Letters from Admiral Gardner (1742–1809)* (Exeter, 2015)

Davey, James, 'Economic Warfare and the Defeat of the Continental System: The Royal Navy in the Baltic 1808–1811', *Trafalgar Chronicle* 25 (2015), p. 29

— *In Nelson's Wake: The Navy and the Napoleonic Wars* (New Haven, 2015)

— 'Mutiny and Insecurity', in Quintin Colville (ed.), *Nelson, Navy & Nation: The Royal Navy & the British People 1688–1815* (London, 2013), pp. 141–3.

Davidson, James D. G., *Admiral Lord St Vincent – Saint or Tyrant? The Life of Sir John Jervis, Nelson's Patron* (Barnsley, 2006)

Davies, J. D., *Pepys's Navy: The Ships, Men & Warfare, 1649–1689* (Barnsley, 2016)

Davis, Lance E. and Stanley L. Engerman, *Naval Blockades in Peace and War: An Economic History since 1750* (Cambridge, 2006)

Devlin, Lord, *The House of Lords and the Naval Prize Bill 1911* (Cambridge, 1968)

Downer, Martyn, *Nelson's Purse* (London, 2004)

Duffy, Michael, 'How Nick Slope became a naval historian', *The Nelson Dispatch* 12:9 (Winter 2017), 537

— *Soldiers, Sugar, and Seapower: The British Expeditions to the West Indies and the War against Revolutionary France* (Oxford, 1987)

Dull, Jonathan R., *The Age of the Ship of the Line: British and French Navies, 1650–1815* (Barnsley, 2009)

Dworkin, Ronald M., *Law's Empire* (Cambridge, Mass.: Belknap Press of Harvard Univ. Press, 1995)

Emsley, Clive, 'Repression, "terror" and the Rule of Law in England during the Decade of the French Revolution', *English Historical Review* 100:357 (1985), 801–25

Erickson, Amy Louise, 'Coverture and Capitalism', *History Workshop Journal* 59 (2005), 1–16

Feldbæk, Ole, *Denmark and the Armed Neutrality 1800–1801* (Copenhagen: Akademisk Forlag University of Copenhagen, 1980)

— *The Battle of Copenhagen 1801: Nelson and the Danes* (Barnsley: Leo Cooper, 2016)

Ferguson, Niall, *The House of Rothschild* (London: Penguin, 1998)

Fewster, J. M., 'Prize money and the British Expedition to the West Indies of 1793–4', *Journal of Imperial and Commonwealth History* 12 (1983), 1–28

Finberg, Hilda, 'Jewish Residents in Eighteenth-Century Twickenham', *Transactions of the Jewish Historical Society of England* 16, 129–35

Fox, Frank, 'The Ronas Voe Incident, 1674', *MM* 106 (2020), 408–21

Frei, Gabriela, *Great Britain, International Law, Evolution of Maritime Thought* (Oxford, 2020)

Fury, Cheryl A. (ed.), *The Social History of English Seamen, 1650–1815* (Woodbridge, 2017)

Gardiner, Robert (ed.), *Nelson against Napoleon: From the Nile to Copenhagen, 1798–1801* (London, 1997)

Garner, James Wilford, *Prize Law during the World War: A Study of the Jurisprudence of the Prize Courts 1914–1924* (New York, 1927)

Gibson Bowles, Thomas, *Sea Law and Sea Power as they Would be Affected by Recent Proposals; with Reasons Against Those Proposals* (London: John Murray, 1910)

Gill, Ellen, *Naval Families, War and Duty in Britain, 1740–1820* (Woodbridge, 2016)

Gleaves, Albert, *James Lawrence, Captain, United States Navy, Commander of the Chesapeake* (New York, 1904)

Grainger, John D., *British Campaigns in the South Atlantic, 1805–1807: Operations in the Cape and the River Plate and Their Consequences* (Barnsley, 2015)

Green, Geoffrey L., *The Royal Navy and Anglo-Jewry, 1740–1820: Traders and Those Who Served* (London, 1989)

Grewe, Wilhelm Georg and Michael Byers, *The Epochs of International Law* (Berlin; New York, 2000)

Grindal, Peter, *Opposing the Slavers* (London, 2016)

Grotius, Hugo, Richard Hakluyt, William Welwood and David Armitage, *The Free Sea* (Indianapolis, 2004)

Grotius, Hugo and Stephen C. Neff, *Hugo Grotius on the Law of War and Peace* (2012)

Gutteridge, Tony, 'Aspects of Naval Prize Agency 1793–1815', *MM* 80:1 (1994), 45–55

Hall, John A. (ed.), *The State: Critical Concepts* (London; New York, 1994)

Halliday, Paul D., *Habeas Corpus: From England to Empire* (Cambridge, Mass., 2012)

Harding, Richard, *Modern Naval History: Debates and Prospects* (London, 2016)

Hargrave, Francis, *Collectanea Juridica* (London, 1840)

Haring, C. H., 'Ledgers of the Royal Treasurers in Spanish America in the Sixteenth Century', *The Hispanic American Historical Review* 2 (1919), 173–87.

Hathaway, Oona Anne and Scott Shapiro, *The Internationalists and Their Plan to Outlaw War* (London, 2017)

Heaps, Leo, *Log of the Centurion* (Leeds, 1973)

Heckscher, Eli F., *The Continental System: An Economic Interpretation* (Oxford, 1922)

Hill, J. R., *The Prizes of War: The Naval Prize System in the Napoleonic Wars, 1793–1815* (Stroud, 1998)

Hobson, Rolf (ed.), *Navies in Northern Waters, 1721–2000*, Cass Series Naval Policy and History 26 (London: Cass, 2004)

Holdsworth, William S., *History of English Law* (London, 1903)

— 'The Relation of English Law to International Law', *Minnesota Law Review* 26:2 (January 1942), 141–52

Homans, Benjamin, *Laws of the United States, in Relation to the Navy and Marine Corps* (Reprinted: Gale, Sabin Americana, 2012)

Hore, Peter, *The Trafalgar Chronicle: Dedicated to Naval History in the Nelson Era: New Series 3: Journal of the 1805 Club* (2018)

Hore, Peter and 1805 Club, *The Trafalgar Chronicle: Journal of the 1805 Club 2* (2017)

Howarth, David, *Adventurers: The Improbable Rise of the East India Company* (Yale, 2023)

Hughes, Ben, *The British Invasion of the River Plate 1806–7: How the Redcoats Were Humbled and a Nation Was Born* (Barnsley: Pen & Sword Military, 2013)

Israel, Jonathan I., *The Dutch Republic: Its Rise, Greatness, and Fall, 1477–1806* (Oxford, 1998)

Ittersum, Martine Julia van, 'Hugo Grotius in Context: Van Heemskerk's Capture of the "Santa Caterina" and Its Justification in "De Jure Pradae" (1604–1606)', *Asian Journal of Social Science* 31:3 (2003), 511–48

James, William, *The Naval History of Great Britain During the French Revolutionary and Napoleonic Wars* (London, 1822–4)

Jarrett, Nathaniel, *The Lion at Dawn: Forging British Strategy in the Age of the French Revolution 1783–1797* (Oklahoma, 2022)

Keefer, Scott Andrew, *The Law of Nations and Britain's Quest for Naval Security: International Law and Arms Control, 1898–1914* (Basingstoke, 2016)

Kemp, Peter, *A Survey of the History and Distribution of the Naval Prize Fund* (Aldershot, 1946)

Kert, Faye, *Prize and Prejudice: Privateering and Naval Prize in Atlantic Canada in the War of 1812* (St John's, 1997)

Knight, R. J. B., *Britain against Napoleon: The Organization of Victory, 1793–1815* (London, 2013)

— *Convoys: The British Struggle against Napoleonic Europe and America* (London, 2022)

— *The Pursuit of Victory: The Life and Achievement of Horatio Nelson* (London, 2005)

Knox, William, *Helps to a Right Decision Upon the Merits of the Late Treaty of Commerce with France Addressed to the Members of Both Houses of Parliament* (London, 1787)

Koskenniemi, Martti, Walter Rech and Manuel Jiménez Fonseca (eds), *International Law and Empire: Historical Explorations* (Oxford, 2017)

Kulsrud, Carl J., *Maritime Neutrality To 1780* (Boston, 1936)

Lambert, Andrew D., *Admirals* (London, 2009)

— *No More Napoleons* (London, 2025)

— *Seapower States: Maritime Culture, Continental Empires and the Conflict That Made the Modern World* (London, 2018)

— *The Challenge: America, Britain and the War of 1812* (London, 2012)

— *The Foundations of Naval History: John Knox Laughton, the Royal Navy and the Historical Profession* (London, 1998)

Land, Isaac, 'New Scholarship on the Press Gang Part 2', *Port Towns & Urban Cultures* (2015), porttowns.port.ac.uk/press-gang2/

— 'New Scholarship on the Press Gang Part 1', *Port Towns & Urban Cultures* (2015), porttowns.port.ac.uk/press-gang-1/

Laughton, John Knox, *Studies in Naval History* (London, 1887)

Laurence, Anne, *Women in England, 1500–1760* (London, 1994)

Lauterpacht, Hersch and Elihu Lauterpacht, *International Law: Being the Collected Papers of Hersch Lauterpacht: Volume 2, The Law of Peace, Part 1: International Law in General* (London: Cambridge Univ. Press, 1975)

Lavery, Brian, *Nelson's Navy: The Ships, Men and Organisation, 1793–1815*, Repr. 1989 (London: Conway, 1992)

Le Fevre, Peter (ed.), *Precursors of Nelson: British Admirals of the Eighteenth Century* (London, 2000)

Le Fevre, Peter and Richard Harding (eds), *British Admirals of the Napoleonic Wars: The Contemporaries of Nelson* (London: Chatham Publishing, 2005)

Lemnitzer, Jan Martin, *Power, Law and the End of Privateering* (Basingstoke, 2014)

Leonard, A. B. (ed.), *Marine Insurance* (Basingstoke, 2016)

Lewis, Michael, *A Social History of the Navy 1793–1815* (London, 1960)

Lincoln, Margarette, *Naval Wives and Mistresses* (Stroud: History Press, 2011)

Loreburn, Earl, *Capture at Sea* (London, 1913)

Lovell, Mary, *A Scandalous Life* (Glasgow, 1998)

MacDougall, Philip and Ann Veronica Coats (eds), *The Naval Mutinies of 1797: Unity and Perseverance* (Woodbridge, 2011)

Mackesy, Piers, *The War for America 1775–1783* (London, 1964)

Mahan, Captain A. T., *The Life of Nelson: The Embodiment of the Sea Power of Great Britain* (London, 1897)

Marsden, Reginald Godfrey (ed.), *Documents Relating to Law and Custom of the Sea*, NRS (London, 1915)

— 'Early Prize Jurisdiction and Prize Law in England', *The English Historical Review* 24:96 (1909), 675

Mathew, Theobald, 'Law-French', *Law Quarterly Review* 54 (1938), 358–69

Maynard, John, *John Scott, Nelson's Secretary and Friend* (London, 2024)

McCartney, Innes, 'The Archaeology of First World War U-Boat Losses in the English Channel and Its Impact on the Historical Record', *MM* 105 (2019), 183–201

McCranie, Kevin D., *Admiral Lord Keith and the Naval War against Napoleon* (Gainesville, 2006)

McCullough, David G., *John Adams* (New York, 2008)

McKee, Christopher, *A Gentlemanly and Honorable Profession: The Creation of the U.S. Naval Officer Corps, 1794–1815* (Annapolis, 1991)

McLeod, A. B., *British Naval Prize Law in the Seven Years' War* (Woodbridge, 2025)

Meeks, Joshua, *France, Britain, and the Struggle for the Revolutionary Western Mediterranean* (Basingstoke, 2017)

Melville, Herman, *White Jacket, or The World in a Man-of-War* (New York and London, 1850)

Melvin, Frank Edgar, *Napoleon's Navigation System: A Study of Trade Control During the Continental Blockade* (New York, 1919)

Milton, Giles, *Nathaniel's Nutmeg, or, The True and Incredible Adventures of the Spice Trader Who Changed the Course of History* (New York, 2015)

Mobley, Scott, *Progressives in Navy Blue: Maritime Strategy, American Empire, and the Transformation of U.S. Naval Identity, 1873–1898* (Annapolis, 2018)

Monson, Sir William, Michael Oppenheim (ed.), *The Naval Tracts of Sir William Monson* (NRS, 1902)

Montesquieu, Charles de Secondat, *The Spirit of the Laws*, Cambridge Texts in the History of Political Thought (Cambridge, 1989)

Morriss, Roger, *Cockburn and the British Navy in Transition: Admiral Sir George Cockburn, 1772–1853* (Columbia, 1997)

— *Naval Power and British Culture, 1760–1850: Public Trust and Government Ideology* (Aldershot, 2004)

— *The Foundations of British Maritime Ascendancy: Resources, Logistics and the State, 1755–1815* (2014)

— *The Royal Dockyards during the Revolutionary and Napoleonic Wars* (Leicester, 1983)

Murdoch, Steve, *The Terror of the Seas? Scottish Maritime Warfare 1513–1713* (Boston, 2010)

Musteen, Jason R., *Nelson's Refuge: Gibraltar in the Age of Napoleon* (Annapolis, 2011)

Neff, Stephen C., *Justice Among Nations: A History of International Law* (Cambridge, Mass., 2014)

— (ed.), *Hugo Grotius: The Free Sea* (Cambridge, 2012)

— *The Rights and Duties of Neutrals: A General History* (Manchester, 2000)

— *War and the Law of Nations: A General History* (Cambridge, 2005)

Nicolas, Nicholas Harris, *The Dispatches and Letters of Vice Admiral Lord Viscount Nelson* (London, 1997)

Niekerk, J. P. van, 'Of Naval Courts Martial and Prize Claims: Some Legal Consequences of Commodore Johnstone's Secret Mission to the Cape of Good Hope and the "Battle" of Saldanha Bay, 1781 (Part 1)', *Fundamina, A Journal of Legal History* 21:2 (2015), 392–456

— 'The First British Occupation of the Cape of Good Hope and Two Prize Cases on Joint Capture in the High Court of Admiralty', *Fundamina, A Journal of Legal History* 11:2 (2005), 155–81

Ntovas, A. X. M. (ed.), *Halsbury's Laws of England*, 5th edn., vol. 85A, The Law of Prize (London, 2024)

Nussbaum, Arthur, *A Concise History of the Law of Nations* (New York, 1947)

O'Brian, Patrick, *HMS Surprise* (London, 1973)

Oldham, James and William Murray Mansfield, *The Mansfield Manuscripts and the Growth of English Law in the Eighteenth Century* (London, 1992)

Olson, Lynne, *Citizens of London: The Americans Who Stood with Britain in Its Darkest, Finest Hour* (London, 2015)

Oppenheim, M., *A History of the Administration of the Royal Navy 1509–1660* (London, 1896)

Padfield, Peter, *Maritime Power and the Struggle for Freedom: Naval Campaigns That Shaped the Modern World 1788–1851* (London, 2003)
Paine, Thomas, *Public Good* (1780)
Palmer, Michael A., *Stoddert's War: Naval Operations during the Quasi-War with France, 1798–1801* (Annapolis, 2000)
Pares, Richard, *Colonial Blockade and Neutral Rights 1738–1763* (Oxford, 1938)
— *War and Trade in the West Indies 1739–1763* (London, 1963)
Parrillo, Nicholas R., *Against the Profit Motive: The Salary Revolution in American Government, 1780–1940* (New Haven, 2013)
Perrin W. G., 'Pellew and the Departure of the Bantry Bay Expedition, December 1796', *MM* 6:6 (1920), 178–83
Petrie, Donald A., *The Prize Game: Lawful Looting on the High Seas in the Days of Fighting Sail* (New York, 2001)
Phillimore, Sir Augustus, *The Last of Nelson's Captains* (London, 1906)
Phillimore, Sir Robert, *Commentaries Upon International Law* (Philadelphia, 1854)
Philp, Mark, *Reforming Ideas in Britain: Politics and Language in the Shadow of the French Revolution, 1789–1815* (Cambridge, 2017)
— (ed.), *Resisting Napoleon: The British Response to the Threat of Invasion, 1797–1815* (Aldershot, 2006)
Piggott, Sir Francis, *The Free Seas in War: A Talk to the Men and Women of Great Britain on the Freedom of the Seas* (London, 1918)
— *The Freedom of the Seas Historically Treated* (London, 1919)
Pope, Dudley, *Life in Nelson's Navy* (Annapolis, 1981)
Popham, Hugh, *A Damned Cunning Fellow: The Eventful Life of Rear-Admiral Sir Home Popham, KCB, KCH, KM, FRS, 1762–1820* (Tywardreath, 1991)
Poser, Norman S., *Lord Mansfield: Justice in the Age of Reason* (Montreal, 2015)
Racine, Karen, 'This England and This Now: British Cultural and Intellectual Influence in the Spanish American Independence Era', *Hispanic American Historical Review* 90:3 (2010), 423–54
Redding, Benjamin, 'A Ship "For Which Neptune Raves": The Sovereign of the Seas, La Couronne and Seventeenth-Century International Competition over Warship Design', *MM* 104:4 (2018), 402–22
Reid, Sir Robert, 'The Capture of Private Property at Sea', *The Times*, 14 Oct. 1905
Reiter, Jacqueline, *Quicksilver Captain: The Improbable Life of Sir Home Popham* (Warwick, 2024)
Robinson, Christopher, *Collectanea Maritima; Being a Collection of Public Instruments Etc ... Tending to Illustrate the History and Practice of Prize Law* (London, 1801)
Rodger, N. A. M., 'Honour and Duty at Sea, 1660–1815', *Historical Research* 75:190 (November 2002), 425–47
— *The Command of the Ocean: A Naval History of Britain, 1649–1815* (London, 2004)

— 'The Law and Language of Private Naval Warfare', *MM* (2014), 5–13
— *The Price of Victory: A Naval History of Britain 1815–1945* (London, 2025)
— *The Wooden World: An Anatomy of the Georgian Navy* (London, 1988)
Rogers, Nicholas, 'British Impressment and Its Discontents', *The International Journal of Maritime History* 30:1 (2018), 52–73
— *The Press Gang: Naval Impressment and Its Opponents in Georgian Britain* (London, 2007)
Roscoe, Edward Stanley, *History of the English Prize Court* (London, 1924)
— *Reports of Prize Cases Determined in the High Court of Admiralty, before the Lords Commissioners of Appeals in Prize Causes, and before the Judicial Committee of the Privy Council from 1745 to 1859* (London, 1905)
— *Studies in the History of the Admiralty and Prize Courts* (London, 1932)
— *The Admiralty Jurisdiction and Practice of the High Court of Justice* (London, 1882)
Rose, George, *The Diaries and Correspondence of the Right Honourable George Rose* (London, 1860)
Ross, Sir John (ed.), *Memoirs and Correspondence of Admiral Lord de Saumarez*, 2 vols (London, 1838)
Runyan, Timothy J., 'The Rolls of Oleron and the Admiralty Court in Fourteenth-Century England', *The American Journal of Legal History* 19:2 (1975), 95–111
Rutherford, G., 'Sidelights on Commodore Johnstone's Expedition to the Cape (1942) Pt 1', *MM* 28:3, 189–212 and 'Pt 2', *MM* 28:4, 290–308
Slope, Nick, *Nelson's Navy: Recruitment, Promotion, Discipline and Death* (London, 2019)
— Review of Dancy's *Myth of the Press Gang, The Nelson Dispatch* 12:5 (2016), p. 314
Smith, Adam, *The Wealth of Nations*, ed. Andrew Skinner (London, 1999)
Smollett, T., *The Adventures of Roderick Random*, ed. P-G. Boucé (Oxford, 2008)
Southam, Brian, *Jane Austen and the Navy* (London, 2000)
Sparrow, Elizabeth, *Secret Service: British Agents in France, 1792–1815* (Woodbridge, 1999)
Spektorowski, Alberto, *Nations and Nationalism: A Global Historical Overview* (California, 2008)
Spencer, Charles, *The Spencer Family* (London, 1999)
Starkey, David J., *British Privateering Enterprise in the Eighteenth Century* (Exeter, 1990)
Stephen, James, *War in Disguise* (London, 1805)
Stirling, A. M. W., *Coke of Norfolk and His Friends* (London, 1908)
Sugden, John, *Nelson: A Dream of Glory* (London, 2005)
— *Nelson: The Sword of Albion* (London, 2013)
Sullivan, Anthony, *Man of War: The Fighting Life of Admiral James Saumarez: From the American Revolution to the Defeat of Napoleon* (Barnsley, 2017)

Sullivan, F. B., 'The Naval Schoolmaster During the Eighteenth Century and the Early Nineteenth Century', *MM* 62:4 (1976), 311–46

Symonds, Craig L., *Lincoln and His Admirals: Abraham Lincoln, the U.S. Navy, and the Civil War* (2010)

— *Navalists and Antinavalists: The Naval Policy Debate in the United States, 1785–1827* (Newark, 1980)

Taggart, Michael, 'Alexander Chaffers and the Genesis of the Vexatious Actions Act 1896', *Cambridge Law Journal* 63:3 (November 2004), 656–84

Tettenborn, A. et al. (eds), *Clerk & Lindsell on Torts*, 24th edn (London, 2023)

Thomas, Donald, *Cochrane: Britannia's Sea Wolf* (London: Cassell, 1999)

Thrasher, Peter Adam, *Pasquale Paoli: An Enlightened Hero, 1725–1807* (London, 1970)

Toll, Ian W., *Six Frigates: The Epic History of the Founding of the U.S. Navy* (New York, 2008)

Townsend, William C., *The Lives of Twelve Eminent Judges* (London, 1846)

Tracy, Nicholas, *Attack on Maritime Trade* (Basingstoke: Macmillan, 1991)

Twiss, Sir Travers (ed.), *The Black Book of the Admiralty* (London, 1871)

Valle, James E., *Rocks and Shoals: Order and Discipline in the Old Navy, 1800–1861* (Annapolis, 1980)

Vattel, Emer de, *The Law of Nations; or the Principles of the Law of Nature: Applied to the Conduct and Affairs of Nations and Sovereigns* (1758)

Vieira, Monica Brito, 'Mare Liberum v Mare Clausum: Grotius, Freitas, and Seldon's Debate on Dominion over the Seas', *Journal of the History of Ideas* 64:3 (July 2003), 361–77

Wade, Thomas Callander (ed.), *Acta Curiae Admirrallatus Scotiae, 6 Sept. 1557–11 March 1562* (Edinburgh, 1937)

Ward, Peter A., *British Naval Power in the East, 1794–1805: The Command of Admiral Peter Rainier* (Woodbridge, 2013)

Wareham, Tom, *Frigate Commander* (Barnsley, 2012)

— *The Star Captains: Frigate Command in the Napoleonic Wars* (London, 2001)

Webb, Yates and Peacock (eds), *Hampshire Studies* (Portsmouth, 1981)

White, Colin, *Nelson: The Admiral* (Stroud, 2005)

Williams, Basil, *Carteret and Newcastle: A Contrast in Contemporaries* (Cambridge, 1945)

Willis, Sam, *Fighting at Sea in the Eighteenth Century: The Art of Sailing Warfare* (Woodbridge, 2008)

— *The Struggle for Sea Power: A Naval History of American Independence* (London, 2015)

Wilson, Evan, *A Social History of British Naval Officers, 1775–1815* (Woodbridge, 2017)

Woolrych, Humphrey William, *Lives of Eminent Serjeants-at-Law of the English Bar* (London, 1869)

Index of Case Reports

Index